GOODBYE ROAD

AUSTRALIA'S BROKEN HEARTLANDS

MICHAEL GRAY GRIFFITH

Goodbye Road
Copyright Michael Gray Griffith 2025.
All rights reserved.
Print ISBN: 9781763884533
Ebook ISBN: 9781763884540
Published by The Banned Book Company 2025 in conjunction with A Sense of Place Publishing.

Reviewers and editors may use up to 1000 words of this book with attribution. Any larger extracts or other usage including video and film should be negotiated with the publisher.

Otherwise no parts of this publication may be reproduced, stored in a retrieval system, or transmitted in any form or by any means, electronic, mechanical, photocopying, recording, or otherwise, without the prior written permission of the copyright owner or the publisher.

This book is sold subject to the condition that it shall not, by way of trade or otherwise, be lent, resold, hired out, or otherwise circulated without the publisher's prior consent in any form of binding or cover other than that in which it is published and without a similar condition including this condition being imposed on the subsequent purchaser. Under no circumstances may any part of this book be photocopied for resale.

Cover design by Michael Gray Griffith. The image was taken moments before Matt Lawson was shot.
Editor John Stapleton.

 A catalogue record for this book is available from the National Library of Australia

CONTENTS

Foreword 9
Introduction 10
The Day They Shot Matt Lawson 16
A Bridge Not Too Far 21
The Siege of the Shrine 24
The Dancer 28
The New Church of the Counter Culture 35
Jesus and the Cigarettes 38
Another Dancer 40
The Joy of Outlawed Carols 44
Is a Want for Freedom Holding Us Back? 48
The Power of the Small 52
The Day the Australian Flag Became the Yellow Star . . . 56
The Deplorables Epic Road Trip 60
The Nullarbor Leper 62
The Umbrella People 65
Clarity or Insanity 68
Why We Cannot Discriminate 70
It's Time 72
Babes in the Wood 75
The Marble Bar Cook 77
Children of Epic 82
Darwin's Guardian Angels 84
HER Body, OUR Choice 88
The Pilot 90
PayPal Bans Café Locked Out 94
Boolaroo 95
The Last Leg of the Deplorables Epic Road Trip 99
An Ex-Chief Detective Speaks 101
Heading Back To Court 104
Convoy to Canberra One Year On 106
How To Unfurl Your Soul's Wings 109
Freedom's Mechanics 111
The Fragrance of Hope 115

Suspended Dr William Bay's Victory	119
The Long Drive	121
Rise, My Silent Brothers, Rise	124
Has Dazelle Been Sent Back to Us from the Light?	131
Dr Bruce Paix is an Australian Rogue Bull	133
Budgie Dreaming	136
A Vision for an Alternative Australia	138
The Hard but Necessary Path	141
We Stand With Barry and All Who Have Stood Up	143
The Silence Must End	145
Australia Day Speech	147
The Broken Bones of God	149
Café Locked Out cops 3649 Day Facebook Ban	152
The Army of Light	154
Free Speech	157
My Brother, My Brother, My Brother	161
The Persecution of Dr My Le Trinh	164
Leunig's Last Clue	167
Café Locked Out in Bendigo	169
The Persecuted Cardiac Nurse	171
The Silence of Broken Hill	172
What Rukshan Actually Captured	175
Mildura Polio	180
The Scrub Bulls of Mildura	182
The Cuckoo's Nest Blues	185
The Down Syndrome Orphan who changed my life	187
My Saviour the Junkie	189
The Long Road to a Fading Dancer	193
Australia Day in Cororooke, 2025	196
Heart of Darkness	199
Australia: The Great Silence	202
Freedom	206
The War of Manufactured Disillusionment	209
Life in the Carpark Beneath Australian Prime Minister Anthony Albanese's Clifftop Mansion	215
Welcome to the Real Battlefront	219
Ratty and the Boab Tree	223

Australia: Land of Slaves	227
So Australia, Now We Slay Our Heroes?	231
The Beautiful View from the Summit of Suffering	234
The Journey I Took To Find What I'd Lost	237
The Strategic Importance of Trolls	241
Your Greatest Gift: Freedom of Choice	244
Avalanche	247
The Cheapest Freedom	250
People B4 Profits	253
An Awoken, Broken Mother	255
Coming Home	257
Roundabout	264
Home Is Lost … Lost Is Home	268
Brussel Sprout Blues	270
Choice	276
Mainstream Media and the Return of the Australian Male	280
A Man and his Truck: The Trial of Paul Offe	283
About the Author	289

FOREWORD

I WOULD LIKE to thank everyone who shared their story, as well as everyone who has supported my journey – either through donations, by buying merchandise, or by kindly allowing us to park my bus, which is also my home, on their property.

I would also like to thank the colleagues who travelled with me for a time, with a special note to Wendy and Kret. They are a couple now, and I wish them well.

A huge thank you goes to those who helped arrange the interviews and/or produce the Café Locked Out shows – initially Rohana, and now Kelli.

I would also like to thank the mechanics who have helped keep Florence, the Freedom Bus, on the road. Then there are all the podcasters who have joined Café Locked Out and helped us build a community of podcasters, with a special call-out to Robyn and Tom.

There are also the web designers: Steve and now Kevin.

Finally, I would like to thank John Stapleton for pushing me to collate my essays into this book. Once we were ostracised we all set out not on a new journey, but an odyssey. We were forced to find new inner strengths as we began to forge new lives.

I call this path Goodbye Road.

Most of these essays are drawn from the orphans I found traveling this road.

Michael Gray Griffith, Australia, October, 2025.

INTRODUCTION

MICHAEL GRAY GRIFFITH is Australia's leading contemporary historian.

Of all the remarkably talented bloggers, vloggers, citizen journalists, musicians and artists who have emerged in Australia since the country began its tilt into totalitarianism at the beginning of 2020, Michael Gray Griffith stood out as one of the most profound, compassionate, resourceful and talented.

As the old saying about journalism goes, you don't find stories watering the garden. He attended protest after protest recording participants. And in 2022 he embarked on a journey around the country he dubbed The Epic Deplorables Road Trip. All the way, in parts of Australia most of its citizens will never see, he kept interviewing, writing and posting all the way.

Michael Gray Griffith is also the founder of the collective Café Locked Out.

His stunning work documents not just the national derangement which overtook Australia during the Covid era, when the country became notorious internationally for having the worst response to the so-called "pandemic" of anywhere on Earth, but the way a nation once renowned for its easy-going character became an authoritarian cesspit.

Thousands of Australians endured government censorship during the Covid era, many were forced to have a "vaccine" they did not want in order to keep their employment, and many thousands of others lost their jobs for refusing to go along with the government's outrageous mandates.

Michael became one of Australia's most censored writers, receiving a ten-year ban on Facebook and YouTube for daring to go against the government narrative. Facebook has a long history of collaborating with the Australian government to censor the nation's citizens on issues ranging from mass migration to multiculturalism to lockdowns. Griffith wears his Facebook ban as a badge of honour. Like other creatives during the 2020s he has established a presence on other less censored platforms, including Rumble and X.

If you were of no consequence, if, essentially, you were a fantasist without influence, nobody would bother banning you. Rather you'd just be dismissed as another blip in the wild uplands of the internet.

To this day not one Australian mainstream media outlet covers the outrageous collusion between the government and American-based big tech companies to censor the sincere, genuine, authentic voices of Australian citizens.

And to this day Australia's parasitic political class has refused to apologise or even acknowledge the damage they inflicted on their fellow countrymen, including loss of businesses, loss of employment, and numerous vaccine injuries, now a widely acknowledged international scandal.

But one voice could not be silenced, and that was Michael Gray Griffith.

In the process of recording the reality on the ground, and the protests engendered by government overreach, in speaking out so fearlessly, and by interviewing such a vast array of people as he travelled around the country, Michael became the de facto leader of Australia's Freedom Movement, a comfort and an inspiration to his thousands of followers.

With the extensive censorship which Michael Gray Griffith has endured, his controversial although subsequently vindicated stances against lockdowns, vaccines, censorship and other aspects of Australia's Covid tyranny, there is zero doubt Michael was and remains the subject of considerable interest from Australia's intelligence agencies.

In March of 2025, following a Freedom of Information request, Australia's online censor, the eSafety Commission headed by WEF-aligned Julia Inman Grant, confirmed that he was being censored by a "third party", presumably another unnamed government agency.

The relationship between the agencies and Griffith's banishment from various online platforms, along with his ceaseless persecution by online trolls, presumably government-funded operatives, is an open scandal already known to thousands of Australians. The aim of the trolls operations is to disturb, disrupt, discredit and ultimately destroy, and is perpetuated by people without honour or morals or loyalty to the truth – people driven, one can only speculate, by the same vice-like trap as almost everybody else caught in this terrible mess, the need to work to feed your family and pay your mortgage.

The same reason many people adhered to Covid tyranny in the first place.

Even now, in 2025, despite Facebook founder Mark Zuckerberg's declaration of the end of political censorship, the pages for which Michael was banned have not been reinstated. In reality, there was little that was controversial about them. They simply reflected widespread cynicism in the broader population over Australia's truly absurd pandemic measures. But in the increasingly authoritarian, if not totalitarian, drift of Australian culture, disagreeing with government policy is now enough to get you censored.

The militaristic command and control mindset which characterises figures in the upper echelons of government and which engenders these attitudes finds it impossible to understand why the Australian population simply will not comply and why their increasingly authoritarian responses simply make matters worse.

Michael built not just a dedicated following, but a team which helped him run Café Locked Out, as well as a significant number of independent podcasters which have fallen in under the same banner. It makes the Café Locked Out collective one of the most powerful players within Australia's vibrant independent media milieu.

As late as October, 2024, YouTube owned by Google, a Big Tech company closely entwined with the world's military and intelligence agencies, deleted Café Locked Out's Kulture Page, dedicated to Australian Protest Songs.

This outrageous manipulation of the Australian story, and outrageous censorship of the Australian population, attracted not a single word of protest from Australia's major political parties, including Labor, Liberal and the Greens.

Here's what the Café Locked Out team had to say about the YouTube suspension: "Café Locked Out has been online for over three tumultuous years, premiering a few weeks before the 'Siege of the Shrine', where Michael was present as a protester. Much has unfolded since, with numerous journeys, thousands of interviews and ideas explored to encourage people to join us.

"Literally from the start, we have been dealing with unprecedented levels of censorship across all our social media platforms, except Rumble.

"Regardless, we have continued to push ahead and share the discoveries from professionals, and recorded thousands of interviews, stories, and real experiences from us, the people."

Michael himself has written: "The war on truth is silent but deadly. Café Locked Out has been fighting it since 2021, and the scars are real – a 10-year Facebook ban, 23 YouTube videos deleted, our Kulture page wiped.

"Why?

"Because we dared to question vaccine mandates, share stories of the fired, the injured, the silenced. They call it misinformation, but it's censorship, plain and simple – a tool to protect the system that forced jabs on millions. Our Substack posts vanish from feeds; our X followers see shadowbans.

"Yet we persist, because truth isn't theirs to bury. Every night, we broadcast, giving voice to the nurse who lost her job, the dad who can't see his kids, the Aussie who won't bow.

"The mandates weren't just about jabs – they were about control, silencing dissent to keep us compliant. Trolls attack us, calling us anti-vaxxers, but we wear it proudly, knowing it disarms their hate. If we were irrelevant, they wouldn't bother. Café Locked Out is a beacon for the forgotten, and we'll keep shining until freedom's back.

"Join us – your voice matters."

Michael never shied away from the spiritual nature of his quest.

Indeed some might accuse him of being overly sentimental in his diatribes or evocations of a God of his understanding, but that was a part of who he was and indeed, for a significant number, a part of his appeal.

As he put it in his beautiful piece The Scrub Bulls of Mildura: "But we are not scrub bulls, for we are not livestock – unless we volunteer to act as though we are. What we are is unique slivers of the divine, each a possible hope for all of humanity. But that hope can only be seen if we allow it to shine. The best way for it to shine is to speak."

When he ended up in hospital after a heart attack in April of 2025 there was an outpouring of grief and a regalvanising of Australia's freedom movement. Griffith's voice continues to challenge, heal, and inspire, even from a hospital bed.

One of his followers wrote: "For the past four years Michael Gray Griffith has travelled across our great country, capturing the harrowing stories of a nation with a broken heart.

"Last week, his own heart gave out.

"And over the Easter weekend, he died-and was resurrected. Doctors literally stopped and then restarted his heart to perform a triple bypass.

"I don't know about you, but that sounds like an Easter miracle to me.

"Perhaps God hasn't forgotten Australia after all. Perhaps he's just telling old stories in new ways.

"And perhaps Michael, the man who gave his heart to Australia until the moment it finally broke too, has been given another chance – by God – to help finish our story."

Fanciful or not, that is the level of devotion this one man generates. There is a general view that Australia is a largely secular country, but uncannily these sentiments echo words from two millennia ago, "In the beginning was the Word, and the Word was with God, and the Word was God."

Much of what Café Locked Out and it's associated Kulture movement was about encouraging local Australian talent in the face of the overwhelming commercial onslaught of Hollywood, which has done so much to destroy Australia's native born talents, crushing them in the tsunami of high budget low intellect content, starving them of exposure, recognition, status and money.

As Michael once put it: "Art is the soul's self-healing tool, but it can only heal if it's free."

Here, collected for the first time, are the essays and short stories he penned beginning in 2020, along with extracts from interviews of him or interviews he conducted.

The extreme level of censorship which Michael has endured at the hands of the Australian authorities has made this project challenging at times.

Yet his work places him among the very finest of Australian writers working in the 2020s. In the end it took this one man to demonstrate for all to see the unconscionable malfeasance and outright fraud at the heart of the Australian story.

Not just the poet laureate and provocateur of Australia's freedom movement, Michael Gray Griffith has also been its most significant documentor.

While Facebook, YouTube, Instagram, and PayPal have on the face of it all colluded with the Australian government to silence his voice, he remains on free speech platforms such as Rumble, Substack and X. Without these platforms the Australian authorities would have largely succeeded in erasing this part of the nation's history and their own nefarious involvement in the destruction of so many lives.

Internationally Australia was widely seen as having the most authoritarian and irrational response to the Covid scare of anywhere in the world.

Many of its citizens have been severely injured physically, psychologically, financially and socially; many businesses destroyed, many dreams broken, and to this day none of the perpetrators have been held to account or had the integrity to apologise.

Indeed almost all the perpetrators of this disaster have fled into early retirement, there, one can readily assume, to fondly count their millions.

But if this really was a spiritual war, as Michael Gray Griffith and so many of the people he has celebrated in his work firmly believe, then their Day of Reckoning will come soon enough.

John Stapleton, 2025.

THE DAY THEY SHOT MATT LAWSON

We met at a quiet train station. The ten-kilometre restriction zone was still in place, and today I was choosing to challenge it. In my hands was a sign I had created myself. It read, "Australia, Land of the Free, As long as you do as you're told."

The police had made it clear that protests against the lockdowns were not allowed, so the sign was an issue. Any police officer who saw it would know exactly where I was going, but where to hide it? I had no bag to conceal it in, and it wouldn't fit under my jacket. A few times I left it on a bench seat on the empty station, strategically deciding it was too great a risk to carry, but I kept returning to retrieve it.

I had never been a lawbreaker, and I had never lived through times like these, where the police were being brutal to anyone who defied the decrees of the premier.

Then my new friends started turning up. One was a South African woman, well-to-do, demure, and yet determined. Before long I was in her brand-new Land Rover, and with this small gang we were heading to the city.

We parked in the multi-storey car park next to St Vincent's Hospital, and with my sign in nervous hands, I surveyed the city before me. There was a distinct energy to the view, a hostility that in all my time in Melbourne the city had never had.

As I lingered outside the hospital, wondering how we were going to reach the heart of the city, a big man strode past. He had the air of a leader and was surrounded by small men like me who were feeding off his courage. I joined them and began feeding off him too.

This wasn't his first protest. He spoke of how violent the police had been, of the arrests and fines, and yet here he was, the battering ram of this little band of brothers, who were now sneaking into the city via the small streets, our ears and eyes peeled for the police.

I had already lost the people I'd driven in with. Fear is a voice that is constantly trying to rationalise why retreating from danger makes logical sense. And there was no logic in proceeding. This small group of men, each stoking their courage step by doubtful step, had no chance of changing anything. It wasn't just the city we were up against, but the state, the country, the entire Western World that had already declared – but in modern speak – that they, the vaccinated, were the chosen ones, and we were the dirty Jews.

The message was so powerful that, apart from a few defiant ones, Melbourne's entire Jewish community had, without question, complied. Whatever happened today, there would be little to no sympathy for us. And yet still we moved forward, our only solace each other.

These strangers.

And then it happened. We reached Bourke Street, and before us was a river of people, all of them like us, unmasked. And as I entered the stream, people who I'd never met – men – shook my hand, patted me on the shoulders, and said, "Welcome, brother." I couldn't recall how long it had been since I first heard the word Covid, but this was the first moment I'd cried. I wasn't alone. I wasn't crazy. Here was a river of defiant humans, their faces bare to the elements, and all of them marching in the same direction.

It was also then that I met Tom Vogal. I had known of him for his short film festivals, West Side Shorts, but I had never met the man. Now we still work together, with him as the producer and host of the WTF show.

We took a few selfies together. We took pictures of the crowd and realised that our souls were singing with hope. But then we turned the corner.

The police had already been attacking the protesters. One young boy, eleven years old, had approached them with a sign that read, "Let the children play," and he had approached them alone. Then, to the horror of the crowd, some of the police officers pepper-sprayed him, smothering his face in their burning foam.

In hindsight, that was the first moment where you realised there were no rules of engagement. They had been taught to hate us and hate us they would.

In the shadow of Parliament House, there would be many scuffles with the police, but our numbers were so great that their chemical batons and gas canisters couldn't disperse us.

Suddenly we were marching, and despite the initial battle with the police, our spirits were high. I don't even know why; I guess we knew we were right. Even though few, if any, of us knew what we were up against.

Or maybe it was because we had just been tested. The police had tried everything, even brutalising our children, in order to get us to attack back, to be violent. But we hadn't. I remember these young women; they were standing in no man's land between the police and the protesters, and they were condescendingly provoking the crowd. "Where are the men?" they were asking, as the police left them alone to ask. But us men were here, now surrounded by a greater number of women, and our heads were high and our stride was confident, and I was holding my sign above my head.

And then the crowd thickened. Where Flinders Street met Swanston Street, the police had formed a line. But they were unlike any police we had seen before.

They were wearing what looked like plastic storm trooper uniforms. They had helmets with clear plastic shielding their faces, and they had circular transparent shields, and their sergeants were calling us cowards, egging us on to attack.

Even those young women, who had been in the centre before, were back and doing the same. In hindsight, we should have all sat down, a strategy we did in the protests to come. But we were Australians, and we all knew this: all we knew was that we couldn't be violent. And we knew that because it was clear that they wanted us to be.

It was now that they upped the stakes by producing weapons we'd never seen before. They were rifles that shot gel pellets, but we didn't know that. From our perspective, they looked like real rifles, and they were aimed at us, but the police officers who were clearly itching to fire, to shoot us.

"Are you going to shoot us?" I heard young men ask, with disgust. "We're your brothers," the young men around me were saying. But the crowd's disgust didn't affect the police. Still they aimed their new weapons at us. Still their sergeants called us pussies and urged us to attack.

The standoff would last for what seemed like hours but was only ten minutes or so. A standoff that was cooking to a battle until one man, who

I didn't know then, became a pressure release valve. Arms up in the air, he approached the police, calling for calm. We all watched him. This, the bravest of men.

This was Matt Lawson, and he was walking into history, for a few moments later, at point-blank range, one of the officers shot him, not with one of the new pellet guns, but with a rubber bullet. In that moment, Matthew became the first protester to be shot by the state since the Eureka Stockade.

In shock, and we were all in shock, Matthew, still with his arms up and protected from the pain by adrenaline, turned around and told them to shoot him again. They did.

It was now that the officers unleashed a deluge of pepper spray.

Fortunately, my sign prevented their foam from entering my eyes. But as I stumbled back down Flinders Street, surrounded by people covered in pepper spray, including Rukshan, another giant who as yet I didn't know, the spray worked its way up to my eyes. Until my last clear view, before it rendered me blind, was the police line following us down Flinders Street.

By this time I'd reached Elizabeth Street, but my burning eyes were blind.

Later, Rohana would pick me up in our car, and I would talk about this in my first-ever protest rant. A rant where the comments were full of artists, for I was in the arts, and other people wishing the police had used real bullets.

But back on Elizabeth Street, I had begun laughing, for I couldn't believe that this was Melbourne, my adopted and beloved city that I could no longer see. And I was utterly alone. That was until a woman asked me if I was okay.

"No, I'm blind," I said.

She then guided me to the footpath and sat me down in the gutter, where several young people, boys and girls, began caring for me. One of them poured milk onto my face, and then another young man took off his top and gave it to me, stating that I could no longer wear mine as it was thick with foam.

I don't know where the police were, but I knew where I was. I was surrounded by the Australian Spirit. And each of them, with their courage and empathy, was letting me know that we were all worth fighting for, even if the majority of us, including the police, were corrupted by a fear that was being fanned by the state.

That evening, when I had a shower, the water would reignite the pepper spray entangled in my hair, and my entire body would be on fire, including my balls, but like everyone else who was at that protest, instead of being scared off, we fired up.

Despite taking our jobs and despite the media convincing our families and friends to ostracise us, we could see that our liberty was under attack. In that time the only ones who were prepared to defend our liberty, day in and day out, were us: The founding members of the Australian Freedom Movement.

21 August, 2021.

A BRIDGE NOT TOO FAR

We didn't know where we were going. When we first turned up at the spot that was yesterday's battleground, our numbers were so small that the lines of police, including riot and mounted, matched our number. We were jittery, but we didn't move, and neither did the police. Then, as time ticked by, our numbers grew – but not by the numbers we were expecting, or rather hoping for.

At one point the police moved forward, and we were told to prepare. But they only moved forward a short distance and then they stopped again. An hour passed like this, as the tension of yesterday returned with the same chants. But then the crowd started moving, and when it did, we suddenly got to see how many of us there were.

We were no longer a pocket of defiance, or – as the media portrayed us – a load of right-wing extremists; we were a river of people whose demands were simple. We wanted choice, and no segregation. Or, in old speak, freedom. And not just for ourselves, but for our country, for our kids.

At Parliament, the police had regrouped on the steps – again with their horses and armour – as before them a sea of high-vis construction workers and other people from all walks of life started chanting again.

But before the situation could escalate, the protesters instead went for a walk down Elizabeth Street. And as they walked, their numbers grew – all of this being streamed to social media not just from the camera of the already increasingly famous podcaster Rukshan Fernando, but from thousands of cameras capturing the courage and spreading the hope.

And that was spreading like a virus that everyone wanted to catch. And the hope not only came in numbers, but muscle. Despite the periodic threat of violence, there was no point – for many of the men were so well built, and there were, well, so many of them.

This was why the marchers walked away. They weren't retreating out of fear; they were simply turning their back on the police and walking somewhere else – basically, wherever they wanted.

After two strolls around the city, they turned left.

"Where are we going?" you heard people ask. "Where else – to freedom."

For this is what this was: a march to freedom.

Then the word spread that it was the West Gate Bridge.

It was a long walk, eased by our spirits that were lifted by the gift of each other's presence, with all the truckies and cars blowing their horns in support.

I spent most of the day with Kylie, who – it turned out – was the woman who several protests before had helped me when, blinded by pepper spray, I had walked up Elizabeth Street, my arms out like flailing inadequate eyes, and laughing because I couldn't believe the tyranny that I'd seen was not only happening in my city but was being cheered on by a social media crowd.

It was Kylie and the others who helped me – people who I never saw, because despite the milk they were pouring over my face, I was still blind – who worked together to revitalise my soul with the kindness of what we used to call the Australian spirit. The spirit that could never have justified the infamous pepper-spraying of a 70-year-old woman writhing in agony on the ground – images which went worldwide, and an act of police barbarity which led to calls from members of the Republican Party in America that the USA impose sanctions against us for our government's treatment of protesters.

But this day was different. Protected by the construction workers, we walked onto the freeway and then right the way up the centre of the West Gate Bridge, below the pillars upon which the Australian flag flew in the air above another flag – their flag – the flag of the Eureka Stockade, the ultimate symbol of resistance to tyranny.

There was cheering, chanting, and dancing, and as we strode back to the city, there was something new in the air we could smell: it was the scent of victory.

This was only day two – how could tomorrow be any smaller?

When we got off the bridge, the police were back with their armour and shields, and a few of the men arced up and threw things, as the majority simply crossed the road and walked around the government's display of tyranny before yelling back at them from the other side: "Every day, every day, every day."

That done, we headed back to the city, knowing that if no one else turned up, then at least we would be back – and the reason? Ask any one of them: for our kids. For kids. For our kids. And what they mean by that is freedom for their children to choose in a country that isn't segregated.

I had already been telling people we were on the right side of history, but we were a long way from home. Well, this day we saw our home, and its name was freedom.

21 September, 2021.

THE SIEGE OF THE SHRINE

"Stop making me do this," he said, as he pounded my head into the ground with his plastic shield. "Stop making me do this."

"I'm not making you do it!" I said, though I don't know if he heard me above all the yelling and screaming.

Next to me, Giuseppe Grasso, a short and stocky Italian man, was being pounded too. On the steps of the Shrine of Remembrance, we had interlinked arms as the police, dressed like storm troopers, finally came in. But Giuseppe was strong, and he refused to let my arm go, forcing the officers to wrench us apart.

Finally, our link broken, I was thrown to the ground and cuffed – which felt like I'd always thought it would feel. As they did this, I had a knee pinned against my upper back, making it very difficult to breathe and allowing me to briefly experience what George Floyd must have. I actually wondered if this was where I would die, for there was nothing I could do as I heard them ask, "Are you happy now? Aye, are you happy?"

I was dragged up and led to a grassy area, where they sat me on the ground and took my details before eventually setting me free with the warning that if I came back, I would be jailed.

"This isn't personal," one officer kept telling me. "This isn't personal."

"Well, it feels personal," I told him, despite knowing I was not meant to speak.

"Yeah, well, think about your kids, huh," he said. "Think about your kids."

"I am – that's why I'm here. That's why we are all here." Even those of us too young to have children had been saying all day that if we didn't try to beat this tyranny now, how would we hold our heads up in the future when our children were living under it.

After that, the officer chilled out and asked me what I did, like he was actually interested. When he found out I was a playwright, he looked shocked. When he asked if I'd written anything he might know, I told him about Marooned; a suicide prevention play that the Australian Army had once toured to its barracks, for they believed it had the ability to stop men killing themselves. "Men like you," I said.

That was the last thing he asked me. After that, he uncuffed me and left me in the care of other officers. And there were lots to choose from.

This may sound dramatic and even scripted, but it's all true. The moment that saved the soul of the police for me was as we were walking away. I was now with another man, Joel, a young, well-built father who in the struggle had taken a punch to the face.

Joel wanted to ask if it was okay to wait for his brother. As we waited, I asked the officer – also a father – why the police had to be so violent. He claimed that it wasn't him. He hadn't been there. He had been here, guarding this roadblock. Then he lowered his mask and said – and was clearly frightened as he said it – "To be honest, guys, I admire what you're doing. I'm on your side."

But why did we head to the Shrine of Remembrance?

In the morning, the place we'd been told to meet was surrounded by police, and with no other protesters to be seen, it looked like it was going to be a fizzer. So, despondent, we prepared to go home. But then we came across a few construction workers and joined them in a search for the larger group.

It was then, as we crossed a park, that a black armoured vehicle known as a "bear cat" stopped suddenly, and officers dressed like a SWAT team leaped off its side and started firing rubber bullets and these other things – I'm not sure what they were.

Terrified, we ran.

Once clear, and still astonished, instead of heading home, we decided to head back to the city in search of the main group. Our rattled party was led by three young women who were determined to be heard. I'm not sure why we followed, for it was clear we didn't stand much of a chance, but then all that was waiting at home was a stifling life of compliance.

A short time later, on a city street with a slightly bigger group, the bear cat returned and again started firing indiscriminately. I was shot in the hand – a ricochet, I think – but it hurt (and still does). The man closing in leaped onto the back of the man next to me, and so I kept walking, waiting for the same thing to happen to me, but it didn't.

Once again we ran off, but this time our dispersed group met a few others, and then these numbers grew until we reached Flinders Street, where we found a major group of protesters. And that was it. Because we'd reached the centre of the city in numbers this big – and I'm not sure how many there were – they stopped firing. Instead, they blocked all the side streets as we began walking around the city, picking up numbers as we went. We displayed our injuries to each other as we walked – many people had them. One young man was bleeding from the back of his head.

Finally, even though it was on the other side of the city to where we were, someone who had a loudspeaker suggested the Shrine of Remembrance.

As they said this, it felt like a perfect idea.

Remarkably, we reached it without further incident. I was expecting the police, who had the numbers and the weapons and that armoured car, to block us. But they didn't.

Did they want us to go there? Was the person who suggested it working for the police?

Whatever the case was, we knew as we sat on the hallowed steps of the shrine that we – as powerless people – finally had a little bit of power. For as the police encircled us, it was clear to both sides that despite all their weapons and armour, they had a problem: their souls.

The mass media were on their side, effortlessly portraying us as the bad guys – rioters. We knew they couldn't find a way to shoot us here, like they'd been shooting us in the city streets all morning, all while remaining the "good guys" in black storm trooper uniforms. Despite us being heavily outnumbered, the stand-off began, with the shrine as our only protection.

It was a moment none of us saw coming, where we – looking like a group of Aussies at the cricket – belted out our chants for freedom and then sang the national anthem with the gusto of prisoners who were momentarily free, while the police pondered what to do.

Every now and again, the line of police came a few steps closer.

In all their black and behind all their shields and black face masks, it was difficult to remember that they were Australian and not an invading force. But this intimidating tactic didn't work, for we'd already been assaulted and terrorised in the streets. Instead of going home, we'd constantly regrouped until what was left had made it here.

And we were not here because we thought we were Anzacs. We were here because this place was unmistakably good – a symbol of freedom, where we hoped that the ghosts of our country's ancestors – the ones this shrine was dedicated to, the ones who sacrificed their lives fighting tyranny in other lands – would protect us.

As time passed, the police sent in undercover cops pretending to be protesters. They sat with us and suggested things like, "Look, we've made our point – let's go home and come back tomorrow." Then they had other people, who we didn't know from the battle in the streets, talking to us on loudspeakers. They offered us this deal that they had apparently negotiated with the police. If we left via St Kilda Road, we would be free to go.

But Sky News Australia was already posting the fact that those that were leaving were being arrested and even shot at with those strange weapons.

So we replied with the chant, "Stand our ground!"

The trouble the police had was our lack of a leader. We were just a group of people who were making a stand before tyranny – a group of people attracted to the one flame, the flame of freedom. This was why we stayed. We knew we would get arrested at some point.

We knew we were finished. But if we got arrested alone on the streets, or later at home, the world's media wouldn't hear about it or care. If they had to arrest us here – as we sat together peacefully demanding freedom on a monument built to celebrate freedom – then maybe, just maybe, the footage might leak out through all those black storm trooper uniforms like a bright ray of truth.

"Stop making me do this!" the officer growled, as he and others repeatedly banged the shield against my head.

"I'm not making you do it," I replied, knowing all we could hope for is that someone would hear.

22 September, 2021.

THE DANCER

These should be christened the paradoxical years, for in a time of darkness, some people found light; in a time of fear, some people found their courage; and in a time of silence, some people found their voice. I have evidence. I have recorded some of these.

That said, as I started writing this, I discovered that my memories of these last five years have fused their locations within time, and now are softening into those pieces of broken glass you find on a beach – the ones whose sharp edges have been smoothed out, and whose holy pellucidity is now and forever a cloud.

My first recollection of Covid was our tech guy talking incessantly about Wuhan and some virus that was locking that entire city down – a city few of us had heard of before – as our company's new play, Adrifting, performed to a small audience in Kew. The play was inspired by Chekhov's The Cherry Orchard, except in our time and country, the orchard was a house, the temple of the Australian Dream, and since they couldn't afford the mortgage repayments, they were about to lose it. Oh yes, and it was our first comedy.

This was a test season. I was scrutinising the audience to see if and when they looked at their phones, meaning they'd lost interest. Meanwhile, with deepening concern, the tech kept whispering about the pandemic. His wife was Chinese, so he claimed to have first-hand information, but when he whispered to me, "They're gonna shut us down too. You watch. They're gonna shut us all down."

I replied, "Watch this – they love this scene."

And as the audience laughed, it stoked my producer's smile.

Together, Rohana and I had worked hard to get the play on, so to see an engaged audience laughing was gold – especially seeing how Rohana was in it too.

"Shutting us all down?" What did that even mean?

The next afternoon, though, as we turned up to prepare for that evening's show, hand sanitisers were sitting on the bar, and sheets of paper with information about what we could do to minimise the threat of the virus. I can't recall what it said, for a part of me was thinking that it was just the government being overly cautious.

Plus, we were too busy.

Two original full-length plays on simultaneous runs, both being well received.

Another, The Magnolia Tree, only a few months away from our first fully funded regional tour, the Army preparing to tour Marooned, and several other plays waiting for their turn to try their luck on the stage.

This was the shore of our dreams. In our fifties, and thanks to lots of hard work and persistence, we had reached here on our own terms, and built a jetty. Now we were stocking our boats to see how far each play could sail.

That's why we were too busy to notice that another stage was being erected beneath our lives. One that would accommodate all of us, and this combined play was about to stop.

That said, parts of our own play had already stopped. For various reasons, none of them good, Rohana and I had been experimenting with a trial separation. So while Rohana had taken a lease on a flat above a struggling café, I was moving between house-sitting gigs and renting a room in a mate's flat.

We were trying to evaluate whether living apart would see us work better together.

Her flat was old and rundown – or, if you like, had bucket loads of character. This was the fringe of inner-city Melbourne, and her large bedroom was the front room, and her paint-peeling windows overlooked the North Balwyn shops, through which, every few minutes, the trams rattled by.

But by the time she'd allowed me to move back in – since I was always there working – Covid was here, all these shops were closed, and everyone who was on the tram, including the driver, was wearing a mask.

I remember watching these masked folk and contemplating my already forgotten place in history. It was a ghost of an entry that briefly stated, as a playwright, he'd almost made it, but then he'd died, with millions of others, in that century's plague.

It wasn't even a sad thought. To be honest, I thought it sounded cool.

Whether this was fate, or destiny, or just plain old bad luck, it was clear that it was going to be an interesting ride. Then again, if we did survive, what sort of plays would you write about and for an audience brutalised by pestilence?

This was the time when they were pushing "two weeks to stop the curve," "staying apart keeps us together," as videos from China showed citizens dropping in the streets, and videos from Italy displayed Italians singing from their balconies to celebrate the courage of their medical staff who were tirelessly working on Covid's front line.

This amount of global fear was new to us, and since medical experts were claiming that hundreds of thousands of us were going to die, and since, too, the virus was airborne, staying at home to stem the spread sounded like the best of a couple of bad ideas.

Also, since many of us were also being paid a government allowance to enable us to stay at home, Rohana and I did something we hadn't done in years… We stopped.

Initially, it wasn't bad. Up until then, life was working hard, paying bills, worrying about our children and their future, and money.

Always, there was the worry about money. But suddenly the government was giving us enough to live on, and since the theatres were closed, this was kind of like a forced holiday.

Rohana was a doer. In all our 20 years together, I'd rarely seen her do nothing for so long. Yet here, with the luxury of time, we became lovers again.

With our two teenage children haunting their rooms, where they both went to school and accessed their lost world and all their friends via the web, we'd sleep in and lay there listening to the music of the now-empty trams, before, out of boredom, Rohana signed up for an online flamenco class, and I decided to have a crack at writing novels.

I gave myself a goal of writing a thousand words a day for each novel. In the morning, I wrote one, and then in the afternoon I'd write a thousand words of another, while downstairs, in the living room we rarely used, Rohana filled the flat with her petite stomps before, in the afternoon, we'd edit the work together, before spending time consuming something neither of us had consumed before… Podcasts.

We weren't awake then. Like many, we had suspicions about many things, but rarely discussed them, because they didn't directly affect our lives, plus we had a passion for our work.

I had already taken it for granted that the virus had been engineered in a lab, but rather than believing in depopulation, I thought the virus had escaped, and now the authorities were scrambling to control the damage and hide the truth of their incompetence, and I was on the phone to my father, who lived in Perth, suggesting that he keep mum inside, for with her compromised immune system, she was definitely in danger from the virus. At that point in time, living deep within the worlds of my emerging novels, I still hadn't sensed anything nefarious. Instead, I, like Rohana, was just secretly praying that all this would pass quickly, so we could get back to the boards.

And then our prayers were answered.

As soon as the first lockdown was over, we commenced a pre-planned, city and regional tour of our play, The Magnolia Tree.

Once again, we were a small theatre company on the road: setting up our set on various stages, watching the audiences arrive, then pulling the stage down and packing up the van with it, before heading to the next gig.

There were masks everywhere, elbow handshakes, but bottom line, I just kept working and enjoying the tour.

My son was with me. He was our roadie, and I knew, as it was happening, that this time was precious. Not only did we work hard and well together, but driving between gigs, he'd be the DJ, playing me music I'd never heard, and generally, without even knowing it, gifting me with his presence.

But then, on the morning of our last gig in Sale, the government claimed they had recorded one or two cases of Covid, and they had decided that from midnight, the entire state would be locked down again.

After that performance, where we played to a theatre that was only a third full because a lot of the audience had cancelled due to fear, we packed up and raced back to the city and our children, hoping we could make it before midnight, in case the police or the army locked us out of the city.

But there were no border patrols. There were just the lights of Melbourne, glittering as though nothing had changed, and a sense that things were beginning to spiral out of control.

Thanks to social media, we were now receiving information from two sources: mainstream media and online, and the jigsaw pieces that were being delivered to us via the web did not match the picture being fed to us by the government. Worse than that, a lot of our government claims didn't make sense.

Daily, they kept spruiking fear, fanned by mainstream media, and the more claims they made, the more holes appeared in their story.

Plus, unlike those videos from China, we began noticing that people weren't dropping dead in the streets; instead, the media and the government were just acting as though they were.

Were they just making mistakes under pressure? Or was it truly possible that something else was happening – something darker and on a global scale?

Yet if you brought up your concerns with people, they didn't see it.

They just trusted the government, which they saw as benevolent. It was around about then, during a phone call with my father, just as they were just starting to sell these new vaccines, developed in an impossibly short amount of time, that I asked him what he thought was going on.

"I think they've decided to cull us," he said.

"Me too," I replied, and that belief must have been lingering under my skin, looking for a way to break through the part of me that wanted to hold on to what was already being lost, and not wanting to believe that what I suspected to be true was true.

Suddenly, I changed my tune, and suggested that in order to keep mum safe, they should avoid the vaccine. Just give it some time.

They did. Three times they cancelled their appointment, before on the fourth attempt, they went and took it.

It was now that I also noticed that the public's blindness was becoming darker. While we could see what we believed were glaringly obvious holes in the unfolding narrative, fewer and fewer people around us could. And the more holes we found, the more we wanted to point them out, only to find even less people wanted to know. Instead, they started putting this ring around their online profiles: "I just got vaccinated, you're welcome."

And as few people questioned that, from our evening window, it felt like we could see lights going out. One by one, as the encroaching darkness began to lay siege to our little flat.

To keep our own lights burning, I used the fuel of common sense to create and post rants. Short ones asking simple questions, and while some people agreed, others began attacking. But they weren't debating the substance of my rants, but rather me personally for having the audacity to challenge their government.

I just had questions that no one else seemed to be asking. But instead of receiving answers, people in the theatre world – supporters who liked our work – were contacting me secretly and urging me to stay silent. Warning that by speaking out, I was endangering my theatrical career.

At this point, the theatres were all closed again, and it appeared that they would be for a long time.

At this point, the novels were both written and posted on Amazon, where no one was reading them.

Also at this point, I'd started remaining indoors – not because I was scared of the virus, but because I couldn't understand why so many people were silent. Whenever I was in the supermarket, I searched their eyes for a connection, but most people avoided this, and or quickly looked away.

At this point, the government had already upped the stakes once again by bringing in the first curfew.

A curfew? What? Now the virus can tell the time?

But if their goal was to up the fear, it was working.

It was now winter, and below our window, after nine, the street was always empty – apart from the trams. Even if they pulled up at the stop across from our window, the masked people who emerged would quickly scurry away, as though they knew that something was hunting the streets for them.

At this point, Café Locked Out was weeks away from being born, and still unaware of any marches, locked up in our own flat, we watched the government singing the praises of the jabs, as MSM and the public sang along like a choir.

I do recall one man, on an ABC radio talkback show, stating proudly that he'd already downloaded his vaccine passport, and that anyone who refused to get vaccinated should be forced to and jailed, and instead of challenging him, the host agreed. What made it worse was that all the people calling in were on the government's side.

And to make sure we understood that there were now sides, they began talking of segregation and job losses.

Then one night, around midnight, as Rohana tried to sleep, I sat at the window searching the street again for who knew what.

I could not see then that our theatre careers would soon be gone, or that our marriage would also finally fail, or that from the ashes of both, I would become a podcaster.

All I could feel then, in my silent soul, was the persistent approach of an encroaching dark.

A darkness from which suddenly a young man emerged, and alone he stood under a streetlight.

My first instinct was to call the police. It was my duty as a citizen to dob in this dangerous non-conformist. Then, with my next thought, I began reining myself in.

What are you doing? He's not hurting anything.

This was the momentary battle to defend who I was from who their fear was trying to make me become. It felt like I was trying to extract poison.

And then I stopped fighting, for despite seeing that he was unaware that anyone was watching him, upon his tiny stage and below his streetlight spot, this young man began to dance. It was a slow-moving breakdance, and even though he quickly turned around and vanished back into the dark from whence he came, sitting here now, I can still see him dance – because in the dark of those memories, this young man was and still is a light.

And despite the fact that I will never know his name, or where he came from, nor will he ever know that I wrote this about him, if this story moves you enough to like or share it, or even retell it, then the light of his artistic moment of courage could continue to spread, like an elixir of hope for us all.

15 October, 2021.

THE NEW CHURCH OF THE COUNTER CULTURE

She finally took her daughter to get the jab.

Why?

Her daughter loved dancing, but she wouldn't be able to attend her classes unless she was vaccinated. Her daughter hated needles. Her mother held her hand as the vaccinator did their thing. When it was over, her daughter looked up at her mother and said, "Okay, now I can dance."

A few days later, her mother was near St Paul's Cathedral. Feeling as though she were falling, she went inside, only to be met by two black-uniformed security guards at the door.

They wanted to know if she was double-jabbed.

She told them how she had lost her job, had no future, and just wanted to speak with her God for guidance. But it made no difference. If she couldn't provide her status – she wasn't getting in.

"Are you even Christians?" she asked.

"We work for a security firm," one of them replied.

Still feeling as though she were falling, but burning now, she asked, "What am I supposed to do?"

They didn't answer at first, but as she walked away, one of them called after her, "Follow your path."

Unsure whether he was mocking her, she turned around and charged at the gap between them.

They stopped her.

"What are you doing?" one asked.

"What does it look like? I'm following the path back to my God."

Still refused entry, but hurting, she wandered off and found us in the new church – the one we were building on the stone steps of Parliament House. We had no priests; the priests were too scared to come. Anyone could pick up the loudspeaker and offer the rest of us a sermon. Our walls were constructed from homemade banners calling for freedom, and as the line of police looked down from the higher steps, we – who owned no ceiling other than the heavens – welcomed all those seeking shelter from tyranny.

You could sit quietly, talk, or make a speech. We had food and water supplied by the public. And while the government and media called us all manner of names to try to get the rest of Victoria to hate us, we knew this place was sacred, beautiful. These were the Steps of Solace, the foundation of our forming church, and this mother – now a parishioner – had just joined us.

For several weeks, the protesters had been turning up daily and sitting on the steps. But after the bill passed the lower house and moved to the upper house, the protesters set up camp. For two weeks, they slept there, kettled between two parallel rows of orange bollards installed by the council to try to move them on.

Instead, the protesters used them as seats and the walls of their church. The only church in Victoria where no vaccination status was required. A church whose forming dogma was interwoven with decency. A church that celebrated mass each Saturday with a march through the city, where the vaccinated – disgruntled with the government – walk alongside those who have chosen not to get vaccinated. It is a church being built by the people. A church called by and calling for freedom.

It's true that, after a great fight, we lost the battle over the bill.

It's also true that, as the police moved us on, a thunderstorm washed all of our chalk writing off these steps. But this isn't the end. This is just the latest test of our resolve. It's as if life is asking us two questions:

What do you want?

Freedom.

When do you want it?

That Saturday, we met at the Steps of Parliament at 12 p.m., then marched from there. Make a sign and come on down, hold it up high like a prayer, we urged.

Unite with us again, or for the first time, and help us show those installing this authoritarian regime that we can not only take a good punch, but that rather than being dismantled, the church is now within us all – and is building, forever building. The battle to take back and defend not only our freedoms, but those of our children and grandchildren – well, that war has just begun.

20 October, 2021.

JESUS AND THE CIGARETTES

THE OTHER EVENING, on the stone steps of Parliament, a protester – out of rollie papers – went to smoke a cigarette's worth of tobacco out of a bong.

But then a police officer came over and gave her the money to buy not a packet of papers, but a packet of cigarettes.

But why tell you this?

Well, in a war, isn't sharing stories that can heal the divide the other side is installing... justified?

I used to think that the truth was fixed. But now I know it's not. Now I know that all my truths are also the foundation of my freedom – which is the ability to make a conscious choice. And when it comes to right and wrong, I have chosen to make the same choice people have made for thousands of years. A choice that, in my case, stretches all the way back to the teachings I learned as a boy.

The teachings of Jesus.

These are simple quotes, such as: "Do unto others as you would have them do unto you."

Teachings – like lights in the distance – for those souls that choose to steer by them.

And I have, in my time, strayed from them. But even so, they were always there.

They are teachings I now understand have been – and are still being – attacked and defended constantly, in a battle that has been raging even before the man, or his myth, died.

The extreme of one side, I call evil.

The extreme of the other is love.

It's that simple.

Interestingly, I'm also learning that neither side can destroy the other.

That, I believe, was the lesson of his Resurrection:

Love can't ever be destroyed – not even by death. But then, neither can hate.

It's like the two draw a deep line in the sands of our souls. And we are left with one weapon to choose which side we want to live our lives on.

And that weapon is choice.

Right now, across the world – in my eyes – evil is on the move. And as always, it is trying to masquerade as good.

And people, wanting all this strife to go away, people who long for tranquil lives, are deciding – since they feel small – that the best strategy is to ignore their moral compass and steer toward power, in the hope that those wielding the power will be benevolent. Or at least ignore them.

Others are not so sure.

This is why people are calling this time – especially in Victoria – a spiritual war.

We are being told that segregation is not only good for us, but the moral path.

We are being asked to redefine integrity as compliance and silence.

And while I agree that integrity can include compliance, if it's done in collective silence, then that is subjugation.

That is people hoping to avoid conflict.

Sadly, though, it is becoming clear that at certain times in life, if you want to be faithful to the beauty of your own conscience, then you simply can't escape conflict.

For me, this is one of those times. Because segregation is wrong.

But there is real hope now. I see it every day.

Although hate's dark lights are glimmering, it appears more of us are finding the courage to listen to our souls – and are now steering our way towards them.

And each time we find our true course, our own soul ignites and glows – and in doing so becomes a light for another.

That's what I saw in my mind when that young man on the steps of Parliament told me about the police officer who crossed the orange bollards – installed there to divide us – and bought that protester, that warrior for freedom, a packet of cigarettes.

30 October, 2021.

ANOTHER DANCER

AGAINST HER OWN instincts, she finally took her daughter to get the jab.

Why?

Her daughter loved dancing, but she wouldn't be able to attend her classes unless she was vaccinated.

Her daughter hated needles, so her mother held her hand while the vaccinator did their thing. When it was over, the girl looked up and said, "Okay, now I can dance."

A few days later, the mother stood before St Paul's Cathedral. Feeling as though she were falling, she moved to enter, only to be met at the door by two black-uniformed security guards.

They wanted to know if she was fully vaccinated.

She told them she had lost her job, had no future, and only wanted to speak with her God for guidance.

It made no difference. No vaccine status – no entry. "Are you even Christians?" she asked.

"We work for a security firm," one replied.

The fact that they were Muslims – and it was a fact – stung. Would Muslims stand for Christians barring them from a mosque over a man-made concoction?

Still falling, now burning, she asked, "Then what am I supposed to do?"

They said nothing at first. As she walked away, one called after her, "Follow your path."

Unsure whether he mocked her, she spun and charged at the gap between them. They closed ranks. "What are you doing?" one asked.

"What does it look like? I'm following the path back to my God." Refused again, hurting, she wandered from the State's largest house of God and found us building a new church on the cold steps of Parliament House.

We had no priests – ours were too scared to come – so anyone could take the megaphone and preach.

Our walls were bedsheets and cardboard scrawled with FREEDOM. Police frowned from the higher steps; we – who owned no ceiling but the sky – welcomed every lost lamb.

You could sit, talk, sing, play, or speak. Food and water arrived from strangers. While the government and media called us every name they had, we knew this place was sacred.

These were the Steps of Solace, the possible foundation of our forming church. The lost mother had just joined the parish.

For weeks, protesters came daily. After the Pandemic Bill cleared the Victorian Lower House, they set up camp. Two weeks they slept there, kettled between orange bollards the council hoped would move them on. Instead, the bollards became pews and walls.

The only church in Victoria that did not ask for vaccination status. A church where anyone could hear confession.

She was in her early twenties, dressed like a scientist – plain, functional op-shop clothes that looked old when she bought them.

Elbows on knees, she stared down Bourke Street without seeing it. "I'm studying chemistry," she told me. "Next year I was planning to start my PhD, but they won't let me sit exams unless I'm vaccinated.

"I told them I have questions. My lecturers said, 'In this circumstance you don't ask questions, you just do.' My family says the same."

"But you're studying to be a scientist," I said. "Another word for science is questions."

She nodded, still staring at the masked. She wasn't masked. Later, she was gone. I never saw her again.

Then a man appeared, mid-forties, agitated.

"Is this the Steps of Solace?"

Before I could move, others led him to the stone pews so he could spill whatever burden made him cry in the street.

Our dogma was simple: decency. Every Saturday we celebrated mass with a march through the city, the unmasked and mostly unvaccinated walking between those who had chosen to comply.

A church built by the people.

Unofficially named Freedom.

I wonder if Romans sneered "Christian" the way our public sneered "anti-vaxxer," then "cooker."

I wonder if the first hymns sounded as defiant as Bradley Marshall and Paul Kasper singing their new protest song "Rise" while we crowded around Bradley's keyboard.

For a time, Billy Aum became our reluctant leader: a charismatic yet reluctant organiser and co-founder of Melbourne's Australian Unified Movement (AUM), a pro-freedom, anti-mandate activist group that rallied against lockdowns and vaccine policies through vigils and protests in 2022.

Despite the scorn raining down upon us from the government, their media allies, and the gullible within our own families and communities, there were some supporters arriving in Ferraris stuffed with pizzas.

After a long fight, one independent politician flipped – $600,000 government "investment" for his pet project – and the Pandemic Bill passed.

Lawyers had warned us. One QC read the draft in bed, was so horrified she got up, moved to the bathroom, and vomited while her husband slept.

Among the new powers: Incarcerate anyone deemed a danger during a pandemic – no trial.

Hold them for up to two years in the new Wellness Centre at Mickleham, a flat-pack concentration camp.

Once a week you could write the warden begging release; if he approved, the letter went to the Health Minister. Even if they freed you by mistake, you paid for your own imprisonment.

End of habeas corpus.

Despite 400,000 marching down Burke Road, the bill passed.

Next morning, police cleared the last of us as a thunderstorm washed away our chalk writing, the crucifixes we'd drawn to fortify our church.

But it wasn't the end – only the latest test. Life kept asking two questions:

What do you want?

Freedom.

When do you want it?

Every Saturday we met at Parliament Steps, flags and banners and megaphones. At noon we marched, signs aloft like prayers, chanting those two questions like hymns.

Similar temporary churches rose across Australia. Together we answered a spiritual call to Canberra and, for a few days, built a cathedral called Epic.

Now, for reasons not all clear, the megaphones are quiet, the flags rolled. The black-sheep flock disperses, leaving the most stubborn.

Edward – born in Sri Lanka, carpenter – finishes his shift, parks, and letter-drops a thousand leaflets warning about Australia signing sovereignty to the WHO.

Every weekend around Sydney, Rosemary Marshall and George Kesic planted Forests of the Fallen, the moving details of those who had died from the vaccine, their stories attached to sticks and planted in parks. They filmed the stories of those still dazed by what the government did. Each person giving their testimony sounded like someone looking for a church, a shelter from the storm.

I only wish that, the night before our eviction, instead of chalk I'd chiselled one last message into Parliament's steps – something hard to wash away, simple, powerful: God help us.

1 November, 2021.

THE JOY OF OUTLAWED CAROLS

It was twilight when I reached her. She was sitting on a blanket with her two young boys as the choir sang carols from the Cenotaph. Myself and a helper were distributing programs and candy canes, carrying a tub full of donations. There were around four hundred people here, mostly families, but not all. The vaccinated and the unvaccinated coming together to celebrate, as Australians always do at this time of year, Carols by Candlelight.

As I handed her a program so she could sing along, she knew my name, and I could see she was upset.

"Do you want a hug?" I asked. "They're free." So she stood up, and in my arms, she broke.

But, before we go on, why were we here?

I think it was Saturday morning. We were in front of Parliament House, hugging and smiling at each other as we arrived, with our flags and our signs and our megaphones hanging off our shoulders like well-fired weapons. Before us and on the steps, the police were lined up, their masks on and their hands covered in blue gloves – all theatre to show the world that we were the diseased.

In response, we had set up our own army: the Free Hug Army. A small brigade, constituted mainly of grandmothers, who would walk down the edges of the Saturday marches offering hugs to the masked-up people. Often, these grandmothers would receive almost a hundred hugs per march. Sometimes I saw men towering and trembling over these little grandmothers, before they'd launch forward and not hug, but clutch them, as though this senior lady was saving them – but from what?

One man who is seared into my memory took so long to hug Tracey – our greatest hugger – that I felt I could hear his soul wrestling with itself. His girlfriend was holding his hand and trying to hold him back. You could almost hear her say, "You have to do the right thing." But before him, this tiny older lady was holding out her arms. "But my grandmother is offering me a hug." Tracey won.

Tracey won a lot.

I was in a park, resting with all the other marchers, when I was approached by an emissary from an underground Catholic group.

They were after our help. Dan Andrews had declared that this Christmas, unvaccinated children wouldn't be allowed to attend this year's Carols by Candlelight.

Their plan was to set up a renegade event to which everyone was welcome to attend, and they not only wanted us to help organise it, but they wanted Damien Richardson and me to MC it.

We agreed.

The park was in Clarinda, a family-friendly suburb in Melbourne's southeast.

Bradley Marshall, who looked and sang like an angel, was setting up the speakers with his father and his uncle on a concrete gazebo. He would be joined later by Paul Kasper. Together they had composed the song "Rise," which they had sung on the steps of Parliament and on the stages of some of the largest marches.

They were beloved.
We watch the world through mired eyes
Fixed on the altars of hypocrisy
The blue church serves its holy wine
The poison of this new theocracy
Pre-Chorus
We stood by and watched the free world die
Not this time, We'll Rise
Chorus
We will rise
To set the world on fire
Some souls are not for hire
No you won't take me!
We will rise.

Rise by Paul Kasper and Bradley Marshall

They would also be joined by a choir of young hardcore Christians, who each had a book full of old hymns. Tonight we were going back to basics.

It was odd to be walking through the crowd, welcoming people, hugging and smiling and revving everyone up, while also keeping an eye on those passing. Would the police really turn up and arrest us? If they did, what would we do? For there were children everywhere.

Only moments before we began, the choir left.

The word from the Catholic group behind all this was that one of them had been called by the Archbishop, and they had been warned off. And so they left.

Suddenly we had a crowd, candles, children – but no choir.

So I decided to tell the crowd what had happened and asked if any of them could sing.

I could have cried with joy as here and there people stood up and came forward.

And so, with a new choir formed, and thanks to the previous choir leaving their hymn books behind, we began the festivities.

Previous to Covid, I'd never had much of a relationship with God, but if God was anywhere that night, he was here listening to Bradley lead the choir as we all sang along.

After all the songs were sung, Damien and I were hugging people before the stage. It was easy for me, for I was holding up one of our Free Hugs signs, but Damien didn't like holding the sign, so I used to secretly hold it above his head.

This series of moments was fun because I believe we all knew we had all worked together to create something precious. Something perhaps even the angels would speak about.

But then, before Damien and me, were all these little children.

They looked puzzled because I don't think they'd seen adults hugging before. These were the children who were growing up under the rules of social distancing.

So I bent down to them and asked, "Would you like a hug?" And not only did they smile and nod, but they raised their hands, and so Damien and I spent some time hugging them all.

But early in the evening, as Damien MC'd and the singers sang, I was walking around the crowd with a bucket full of Christmas candy canes and a soul that was singing. It was then that I came across a single mum with two young boys.

After allowing me to give her boys some lollies, she stood and gave me a hug, then said she was going crazy.

She'd had to take two jobs to keep a roof over the heads of these two boys, but that wasn't why she started to cry.

She told me she felt like everyone at work had gone crazy, and she couldn't talk. She couldn't share her thoughts with anyone, not even her family. And so the loneliness was driving her here, where in my arms, under these ancient hymns, she cried like someone who knew there was nothing else to do but cry.

Christmas, 2021.

IS A WANT FOR FREEDOM HOLDING US BACK?

Freedom is the right to put your family home on the line, in order to fund a business that all your friends are telling you is a mad risk, but you know that if you don't try, you'll end up feeling like a coward.

How could freedom ever hold anyone back when freedom is what drives us?

The human spirit's hunger for freedom is why, despite all those years we've forced them to waste, those asylum seekers we imprisoned on Manus Island won't give in and go home.

We celebrated freedom when we spent millions sending out a patrol boat to see if Tony Bullimore, a man attempting to sail solo around the world, had survived after his yacht had capsized in one of the loneliest parts of the ocean. And he had.

And we rejoiced, for this little man had sailed right up to the border of his freedom, which was his death, and survived.

Freedom is a Cambodian woman known as Sony, who used to sing all the easy listening classics while working in a laundry in a nursing home in Murrumbeena, a Melbourne suburb renowned for its leafy streets.

A woman who had managed to not only survive the killing fields of her home, Cambodia, where several times she was marched away from her children and made to kneel before her countrymen's corpses, as other armed children pondered whether to kill her. A woman who, while walking to Vietnam with her five children, adopted another child on the way and brought him here too, to freedom, where I believe he became a lawyer.

And while her job here entailed cleaning soiled sheets and clothes and those expensive cloth nappy wraps, still she sang, every day, her sweet out-of-tune voice rising above the mechanical sound of the industrial washing machines and dryers. Songs sung to celebrate freedom.

Freedom is a cyclist riding across the Nullarbor Plains who is wondering one minute why they are doing it because it's such a long way, and the next moment they are in awe of all the space, the freedom, that they are slowly pedalling through.

Freedom is the right to meet a stranger in a café, and then twenty minutes later be in a bed somewhere getting it on.

Freedom is the right to choose not to take chemotherapy and instead tackle the great test of cancer in the way that your soul feels is best for you.

Freedom is the right to put your family home on the line, in order to fund a business that all your friends are telling you is a mad risk, but you know that if you don't try, you'll end up feeling like while you were here, you never had the courage to chase dreams and live.

Freedom is the right to accept that you've been born into the wrong gender, and in order to free the real you, you can decide to have yourself medically reassigned.

Freedom is the right to know how precious life is, and then smoke and drink and take drugs, or ride motorbikes, or sky dive or swim with sharks, regardless.

It's the right to know you are going to die yet live like you are immortal.

Freedom is the reason we have prisons; for to most of us the thought of losing our freedom is horrendous. Then again, it's also the right to risk breaking the law.

Freedom is the right to be good, quiet, opinionated, noble or selfish. To be a saint or an arsehole.

The other day, on the steps of the Shrine of Remembrance, built to celebrate freedom, a load of Australians defending freedom sang the national anthem with gusto, especially the words "We are young and free". We were here to remind the storm troopers that despite being a part of the Western World, which was built on democracy and freedom, that they were no longer free.

And that our so-called leaders would now order these troops to use violence and tear gas and rubber bullets and outrageous fines to make sure the Australians standing before them got the memo.

But the one who hasn't received the memo is you. You don't want to be lectured about freedom by people who are holding everyone back. Holding everyone back from where?

An apartheid country ruled by tyranny? A country where freedom is a status that to attain, they will have to constantly update this status through the needle of another booster shot?

A country where the freedom to critically debate, to think, to question the official narrative is censored? A country where freedom is a lie. A lie you will force us to teach our children.

Now I admit, it has been and is a tough time, a time where defending individual freedom is more expensive than usual. And the cost is death.

Yet in the past we sacrificed more than one hundred thousand soldiers to it, to foreign wars, even though in virtually all cases our freedom wasn't under a direct threat.

And so if people have to die now, it is an unfortunate and terrible price to pay, but the cost of losing freedom is to our society in general, and our children's future, simply unaffordable.

I found the voices in my head talking directly to our political overlords: I don't know how you justify what you are doing now. The millions you are spending on your personal media teams and on your storm troopers – money that you could have spent on hospitals.

And apart from the emotional and spiritual damage, your plan of a segregated community, where unvaccinated people could be jailed for entering a vaccinated-only establishment, will make it economically impossible for businesses to thrive and start paying back the enormous bill we have all racked up with these endless lockdowns.

Now you are making it socially acceptable to brutalise those who disagree with you. You have divided work colleagues, friends and – worst of all – families. You have threatened to jail doctors and nurses who dare to question the narrative, and you have had your troops open fire on unarmed protesters.

And now you are about to take a sledgehammer to our already broken economy, as you force those who wish to hang onto their freedom to walk away from their jobs, their livelihoods. Australians who know something you've forgotten, or don't care about.

And that is what the core of our freedom is. It isn't about being able to go to a pub or a concert or to travel or any of the other things I have mentioned – they are the privileges of our country's deeper and most fundamental freedom, the freedom of choice, which, for whatever your reason, good or bad, you want to steal and replace with the freedom to be a part of an obedient herd.

Trouble is, for you and us, and this is why we protest, the bedrock of our free society is the individual's freedom to choose.

Especially the individual's right to say no, and this includes the choice to decide for ourselves, without retribution, what does and does not go into our body.

So Mister I don't want to debate, you have a decision to make: either you can back off and let our free society heal and deal with this virus with decency, tolerance and common sense, or you can become ever more violent as you try to crush our freedom of choice.

And to anyone else out there, please try and remember: this is not our leaders' country – it is our country. Despite all the lockdowns, we are architects and the custodians. So perhaps it's time for us to discuss what that means.

27 December, 2021.

THE POWER OF THE SMALL

WE MET HER in Ballarat. She was wearing a specially designed backpack with a solid transparent back, wide air holes at the top, and an odd flat base upon which a kitten sat. She told me the kitten had been abandoned, then went on to share how she had been a wildlife rescuer specialising in injured kangaroos – a volunteer job she could no longer do because of the mandates.

While interviewing her, she teared up with frustration, wanting to know who, when she searched a paddock – often at night, and usually alone – for a kangaroo that had been hit by a vehicle, she could possibly spread Covid to. But since the mandates trumped reason, she'd been told her services were no longer required.

Frustrated, she had come here to be interviewed by us.

She knew the wildlife organisation was already severely short on volunteers, and that out there, somewhere, injured animals were dying instead of being healed in her care. All of this for the sake of "health".

She was a gentle woman, a mother who you might mistake for being too soft for this world, but that assumption would be a mistake. Now she came to all the marches. She took photos and chanted for freedom. The previous week, her youngest son joined her. He wanted to come and arrived dressed in a Spiderman suit, bulging with polyester muscles, holding a "Free Hugs" sign.

At this march, he and his mother teamed up with me as we escorted the "Free Hug Army" down the sides of the protest. My job was to use my megaphone to encourage the masked people to hug and to congratulate those who did.

"Here comes the Free Hug Army, healing our country's divide one hug at a time. Masks are slavery; hugs are bravery." And the like.

As Spiderman tired, I lifted him onto my shoulders, and together we carried on.

There is a great joy in watching people conquer communal fear by simply opening their arms and accepting a hug.

What's really interesting is how passionately they do hug. They close their eyes, their faces melting into smiles – like lost people who have been found. Often, they immediately move on to hug another one of our huggers, or even three. It's a celebration. Many tear up. Whenever I put Spiderman down, he would hold up his sign, and protesters would line up to hug him. They'd buzz around him. As we moved along, they started offering him high-fives as he rode perched on my shoulders.

But today, as we marched, keeping to the wings of the great herd of Victorians moving – hopefully – toward freedom, I realised Spiderman was bridging our divide all on his own.

Whether it was because he was a little boy, or because Spiderman is a beloved hero to many, he was also attracting the police like moths to a flame. And this metaphor is apt, because it's been clear to us all that the police have been advised to avoid interacting with us.

To do so could risk them getting reported and having their wings singed – especially if photographed doing so. Because our side is always hunting for evidence of their humanity, we are attuned to these photographic opportunities.

On one street, the police stood with their backs to the empty stores. As we passed each one, Spiderman offered them his open hand. Most of them, despite their blue gloves, high-fived him. I watched them in the store glass reflection. Often, they hesitated initially, but he kept his hand extended. He insisted. More often than not, they broke from protocol and connected.

Later, as we amassed outside police headquarters, the officers stood lined up before their multistorey building like an army guarding their keep from orcs. They even had a long row of mounted police.

Cavalry. Did they really think we Victorians were going to storm their castle? To do what?

Or were they setting up photo opportunities for the mainstream media to misrepresent us – a large, peaceful group of concerned citizens – as a threat? Something those glued to their wide-screen TVs should fear, disdain, and hate to the point of demanding we be taken away?

Regardless of the palpable tension, Spidey and I moved along the line near the police. I knew there would be no problems. Then, one large sergeant – all muscles, body armour, and mask – headed straight toward me.

At first, we were confused. Then he began motioning to my rider, and his intentions became clear. The sergeant wanted to know if Spiderman, who had his hand extended to the officers now ignoring him, was thirsty.

My ward nodded, and the sergeant went off, returning with a cool plastic bottle. He reached his arm across no man's land – like half a bridge – until Spiderman's little arm completed the bridge, taking the bottle and saying, "Thank you."

It was only a brief connection, but that bridge was ancient.

Inside the Spiderman suit was an innocent little boy enjoying the attention. Most of us – police and protesters alike – had a natural inclination to protect him.

If something awful had happened, a fight between the police and us, none of us, I wager, would have expected this child to save us.

He would have been spirited away to safety, even if the people who removed him had to risk their own. Because this is what people – and many living things – do. They protect the young.

I have seen small birds risking their lives to attack a hawk flying too near their nest. I have seen parents sacrifice their dreams, working long hours in soul-crushing jobs, so their children can have what they need. And throughout history, most parents have done this without acknowledgment or any reward greater than knowing that they are doing what must be done.

Protecting the young is a pragmatic law of nature, a decree by the gods of love that we have obeyed since we lived in caves. Yet now, we are being sold a law, for the sake of our health, that states this young boy must risk his own health with a trial vaccine, to protect old people – us. And since he is too young to understand this, we are forcing him to do it.

Perhaps we should teach him to shoot a rifle so that, if invaded, we can send these five-year-olds to the front lines. For he wants to help. That's why he wore the suit of his favourite superhero.

Sometimes it feels like we have collided with a parallel universe whose values are consuming ours – a reality where their morality is opposite to ours, where apathy outweighs empathy, and compliance is integrity.

But today, this one little boy, a soldier of our besieged morality, wore his red polyester armour. Without realising it, he allowed both sides of our conflict to come together in communal love for our children. In doing so, he achieved more to heal our country's growing divide than all our politicians combined.

Which begs the question: if one little boy can accomplish this in an afternoon – and have fun doing it – what can you do to change things?

26 January, 2022.

THE DAY THE AUSTRALIAN FLAG BECAME THE YELLOW STAR

We set up the image of a father and his young daughter facing a policeman on the empty forecourt of Australia's Parliament House. The daughter was holding an ensign national flag, with its bright red background. The ensign flag was flown by Australian registered ships to indicate Australian nationality and was widely adopted by the Freedom movement.

The day before, we had stood before the doors of Parliament with all our flags and banners and T-shirts with messages that all read Freedom. But today we weren't allowed any closer than the bollards.

We had been told too that the only flag allowed past this point was the blue flag, and that it had to be flown the right way up, and we weren't allowed to have any flag poles. We didn't know what law they were using, and our tribe felt sadly bereft as a result of such rumours.

We decided that since the police were there, we'd send a little girl forward, with her father, to see what this police officer would do. The rumour was true.

A few days later, on the Sunday after the great march, a major radio station in Canberra was asking the locals to dob in any vehicle or person displaying our flag to the police, so that they could come and move them on or arrest them. It was on this day, in our nation's capital, that our national flag became the yellow star.

But why do the protesters love the flag when their country has cast them out?

Initially, we called the new system apartheid and segregation, but with segregation there is, as a rule, somewhere for the oppressed to go. We protesters had nowhere. We were the unwanted, the untouchables, the fully or partially unvaccinated, and yet so many of us proudly carried the flag, both the blue and the red versions.

Why? Many walk around wearing the flag as a cape. Not that it protects you, for Mary, a grandmother, was wearing it that way the day two police officers shoved her to the ground then pepper-sprayed her fallen face, twice.

Mary was in her seventies. Despite being born in communist Croatia, she wore the flag of her adopted nation – our flag – like a cape. She had come to the protest in Richmond to see what was going on. What she didn't know was that, by defending freedom in her own way, she was seen by the State, and its police force, as a scrub bull – a spreader of hope that had to be dealt with.

She became famous when a Victorian police officer shoved her to the ground and pepper-sprayed her straight in her face. His colleague, another officer, sprayed her too.

As I write this, I wonder: Do the officers who committed this blatantly irresponsible cruelty have pets? Maybe a dog? Did they pat them or take them for a run that evening as we all waited to hear if she had survived?

The State would go on to lie, claiming Mary was a man dressed in disguise. To our knowledge, neither police officer ever faced charges. Why should they? They had completed their mission: to scare all the other cows back into their Victorian abodes and keep them locked down.

Here, in the Australian Capital Territory, they had new weapons trained upon us as we sang the national anthem and listened to more speeches, as our flags flew high over the grass before Parliament House.

Some want a new flag. They want the Union Jack removed. But I feel, from my observations, that our tribe doesn't see the Union Jack, or even the stars. The flag instead represents the country we have lost, the one we are here fighting for. To us, it is no longer the national flag, for those in power have continued to betray all of its values. This flag, both the red and the blue, is our flag. The red ensign being the more revolutionary of the two. And they aren't just flying from our vehicles and our poles, but from the hill we are rigorously defending. The moral high ground.

They know that they can never take this ground, for to hold it you have to live in the truth, and their world is constructed of endless layers of lies.

But they want us off, for they know that our courage is infectious.

This is why they were not allowing us to work. They were trying to starve us into submission. All over Australia we had been besieged.

This was why the week-long gathering at the Epic Showgrounds in Canberra, including the largest demonstrations in the nation's history, was indeed so Epic. It was a union of isolated groups and individuals who came together from all over the land to celebrate and, in the great march, display to the world their resilience, their commitment, and their power.

This is also why, on the following Monday, after the majority of protesters had gone home, the police invaded Epic Camp in force. They brought their new sonic weapons, they brought dogs and rubber bullets, and they marched through the camp in a long line, arresting anyone who refused to move. They wanted to try to reclaim the high ground. To show the world who was really in charge. For the rest of the day they did the same in other camps all over the ACT, and then, for the rest of the week, they kept trying to move those who had remained on.

What they didn't understand was that their actions were empty. It was a lesson they didn't learn when they evicted us from the grass before the National Library.

The moral high ground wasn't below our feet. It was in our souls and our hearts. It was in our DNA.

It was in the ideas we bounced off each other as our fired-up entrepreneurial spirits searched for new ways to add pressure. To hold the line. It was in the donations for food and camping gear and money as, around the world, people reached out to support our cause.

It was in our promise to come back. And we will be back.

Whenever I see a flag now, I know that the person flying it is on our side. The side fighting for the right to choose what goes into our body. The one fighting for the freedom to travel, to work, to build a life and pursue happiness. To protect our children.

And it was from this defiance that we drew our hope. For we were fighting from a source of passion, whereas all their side had left to defend their totalitarian narrative was a thinning line of unhappy-looking police officers who were fighting for a pay packet – and defending what?

A system determined to starve any Australian who chooses to defend freedom into compliance. A system determined to inoculate their children with a poorly tested vaccine that was injuring people – and worse. Already the horror stories of adverse reactions were easy to find.

Sadly now their blue gloves, and ear plugs to protect them from the sonic weapons, their bullet-proof vests, and pepper sprays, and their revolvers were all empty symbols. A gutted truth. A plastic shadow of a real uniform once worn by past heroes, but now worn by those betraying everything that was great about our country. A betrayal never so acute as when, with all their toys of oppression, they hunted the nation's capital for anyone flying our nation's flag.

Fortunately for them, their new masters had given them all something to hide their growing and irremovable shame behind: a face mask.

25 February, 2022.

THE DEPLORABLES EPIC ROAD TRIP

When I headed off, I thought I might be driving into a war zone. By the fourth day, I know I'm too late. The war has passed. My country had been invaded, occupied, its people subdued.

But the soldiers didn't patrol the streets; they patrolled the soul. Their unit patch is a single word: Fear.

The truly conquered wear their masks like medals – noses sealed, smiles erased, eyes timid as rabbits at the mouth of a burrow. Others let the mask dangle under the chin, ready to yank it up or rip it off the instant common sense was miraculously declared.

The first group scared me. They're often young, heads high, parading obedience in designer masks worn like swastikas. Inside they may waver; outside they look delighted by the new authoritarian chic, the endless swelling of the State. Police and politicians reward them by dancing maskless at their marches – no gloves, no guns, just applause.

The last group gathers around our little truck, Charlotte. Some clutch the flag – upside down, country in distress. Others are simply relieved to stand in a circle Fear hasn't yet conquered. We are no longer only the unjabbed; we are also the double-jabbed who refuse the booster. They are our hope. We need hope.

While the media bang on about Ukraine, they ignore the vaccine injured lying on this battlefield at home.

People are forbidden to die in truth. If you're famous, maybe your sudden collapse is blamed on a juice cleanse.

Mr and Mrs No One simply vanish, kept alive only by hushed whispers in safe kitchens.

The wounded fare no better. Tell a white-coat your chest pain started after the jab and you're sent home with a Valium and a suggestion to "work on your anxiety."

Myocarditis used to be so rare that the hospital wired you to a monitor for days. My brother got it over a decade ago; it took a visiting cardiologist to name it.

Now the specialists are booked solid. Cardiac units are adding myocarditis wings.

And still the conquered, under orders from the Fear inside them, polish the silence instead of burning the hubs.

But we are not all defeated.

Joe knows we'll win. Seventy-plus, he's been here before. In Portugal his father was jailed as a dissident; Joe stayed and joined him inside. Then the whole entrenched regime simply fell.

No mass hangings – just exile, a handful of martyrs, and a people who took their freedom back.

Until Joe spoke, I'd never heard of that war. The old freedom fighter laughed when he recalled how he gets referred to as a Nazi.

"The Nazis were the ones we died fighting," he said, as his hand rubbed the back of his neck, the campfire flickering in his glasses.

"Trust me, Michael – we will win."

And this wasn't some party eavesdropping. It was another gathering of guardians: every age, every background, most disowned by their own kin. We defend the country's spirit without guns – only passion, only integrity.

Find these people. Join them.

In the years ahead you will either tell your children, "I stood with them," or lie and say you did, while the last black-uniformed soldier squatting in your soul caws laughter like the crows in the paddocks around this, yet another resistance farm.

18 March, 2022.

THE NULLARBOR LEPER

The people mover was new, and the afternoon sun was deepening its maroon paint as the mother of five filled its boot with bags of shopping.

Around the RV her young children, still in their school uniforms, were playing in this tiny wheat town's empty street, each one wearing their own personalised mask, and each mask firmly secured.

As I entered the store I saw, amongst the other masked shoppers and staff, the ghost of the young man who approached us at the Nullarbor roadhouse.

Out there, in the middle of nowhere, the great plains only support a handful of small, distant anorexic trees – that's what Nullarbor means, no trees – and there this man, who was wearing a worn black overcoat with its collar up to shield his skinny neck and his chin with its three days of stubble from the desert's chilling wind, was shyly asking us what the banners on our truck were about.

We told him we were touring the country, capturing the stories of Australians who had the courage to speak, and that the mainstream media ignored. We wanted to add their voices to the narrative, for we believed that presently our greatest weapons were our voices.

We were interested to hear how they had been affected by the restrictions of the last two years, and what their thoughts were of the current state of the country and where it was heading. We were also wanting to challenge the West Australian border. That's where we were heading now.

"That's where I came from. I'm from Perth," he said. "I'm trying to reach Brisbane. Do you think I'll get into South Australia? I tried to reach there a few months ago, but they turned me back at Ceduna. I had to drive all the way back to Perth." And his tone stated that he still couldn't believe this.

After checking that no one else could hear, he said, low, "I'm unvaccinated".

"Same," we replied.

But this didn't warm his spirit.

"It's the New World Order," he said. "I've always known it was coming. I've been telling people for ages, but I just… I just never thought it would arrive."

He was heading to Brisbane. That's where his elderly parents, Hungarian migrants, lived. Both in their eighties, they were also unvaccinated and were calling what was happening in our country now – for how they saw it – communism.

Together they had fled tyranny to offer their children a life where they could enjoy personal freedoms, and now here their son was: a medical leper, a disenfranchised citizen on the run from what he called a tyrannical state. Unemployed due to noncompliance, unsure if he could even reach them.

We talked some more, but he never relaxed. He was like a rabbit, keeping all his senses primed for a fox or a hunter.

We gave him our fruit and vegetables, and then I was back – over two thousand kilometres away – in this store, at the till, watching these masked children play, their eyes smiling above their masks as their mother routinely loaded her car with their weekly shopping.

It made me realise what I already knew. Society is a load of people agreeing to a set of rules and laws, but now the rules that I grew up with have changed. And these changes included altering the meanings of words and phrases that I thought were incorruptible. Like "integrity," which now meant silent compliance.

"My Body My Choice" now meant "My Body Their Choice"; apartheid was no longer segregation – it was just the righteous punishment of the selfish – and bullying these selfish people was the decent thing to do, even if they were children.

The new rules also were clear: if you were injured by the vaccine, the expected course of action was that you would keep that to yourself. Even if it killed a loved one, it was not socially acceptable for you to allow them to die in that truth.

Incredibly, critical thinking – our pragmatic go-to tool, so vital it could almost be called a survival instinct – had now been changed to groupthink, which you could not question, and freedom – our once glorious and abundant freedom – was now only available via subscription. These new rules had no space for empathy. For the sake of the community's health, cold cruelty was now morally preferred.

And if for some reason you decided you couldn't abide by these new rules, then you were travelling with this dispossessed man, crossing an ancient land – this barren plain whose culture was now difficult to recognise – and heading towards a future you didn't want to reach, while out of your windows these masked children ran around their mother and continued to laugh as they played.

6 April, 2022.

THE UMBRELLA PEOPLE

At the western rim of the great reset, where the compliant – who are the majority – peer at us over their masks like baffled and beaten prisoners leading themselves, without prompting, to somewhere it appears they don't want to go, we heard about, and then sought out, the Umbrella People.

Most mature late thirties plus to people late in their seventies, they came from both sides and collated outside the entrance to Western Australia's Governor's House.

They carried no banners, no megaphones, and they all unpacked smiles as they approached each other, and there were handshakes and shoulder pats and hugs. And most of them were carrying umbrellas.

The sidewalk was narrow, and they lined both sides, leaving a corridor in the middle for the masked tribe to pass through.

Their leader, Leigh, was a tall man. An ex-firefighter, and despite his years, he had the abundant confidence in his swagger as he carried the big PA speaker towards the gate to explain why so many people were here and following him.

You could see the fires burn and him there before the flames, leading his team with that Larkin grin clearly built on empathy, into the burning front line, determined to save the lives and property of the people who never imagined that this much reality would be hunting for them.

And this diverse platoon – volunteers from suburbs, many cast out by the masked tribe, including their families and friends, exiled from their jobs and dreams – flocked to him, for his courage was so infectious he left them all smiling.

For days, come rain and hail and despite often brutal Western Australian sun, he came here to defend the freedoms won by his ancestors. An abundant liberty the masked had already handed over, so that they could try and retain their mounds of dirt that they hadn't yet realised would never be worth the price of theirs and their children's souls.

Even if we won, there would be no statues built to honour this man, except perhaps in the stories old people would somewhere in the future tell people who wouldn't listen, about the defiance of the Umbrella People.

It was Leigh who came up with the idea of the umbrellas. The plan was firstly to shield them from the sun, who in the summer would beat those willing to stand under it here as though this pavement was an anvil. And secondly, to make this group look larger than it was.

Every day they met at 8 a.m. and then they stayed until 10, but Leigh told me, once they had – through their persistence – drawn thousands here, then they would never leave. Then we'll stay, he told me, until the Governor relented and dissolved this oppressive government and allowed Western Australians everywhere to vote in new leaders.

Inside the Governor's mansion, protected by its walls and iron gates, its cameras and lush gardens, Kim Beazley – another big man, a former leader of the Australian Labor Party and former Ambassador to the US, a Rhodes Scholar who had clearly benefited from his life in politics – ignored the Umbrella People.

And soon he would be gone, replaced by the ex-Police Commissioner Chris Dawson, who had rolled out the vaccine mandates which had destroyed the culture he was born into. A man who would take possession of this mansion at the behest of the Premier who was the architect of all this change.

For a state blessed with so much sun, and crowned with an often immense blue sky, it felt strange to feel as though we were all standing below thick grey clouds that would still gather above the umbrellas of this little outpost.

And so we set out capturing their stories. Recording the experiences and thoughts of any of these soldiers who were willing to use their voices as weapons of recruitment – for anyone out there who no longer wanted to be led to a future they didn't want to reach. One man, originally from Holland, told me how his grandfather had been a part of the resistance group who had tried to make it harder for the Nazis to locate the Jews. A man who had spent the rest of the war in hiding as the Nazis imprisoned his wife and brother in order to try to flush him out.

His grandfather was present here, he said, with his now ageing grandson, because defiance was in his DNA and because he too wouldn't conform, and had become the equivalent of a Jew.

One man had framed a stained-glass tribute to celebrate them all and their leader Leigh. In the top of the frame was a digger's slouch hat, and below it a sea of crowded and brightly coloured umbrellas. And as I write this now, I'm wondering if this presence I can feel in my soul is God, and if there is a place that we used to know as heaven, and if, on its cloudy walls, the angels have hung copies of this framed gift, so that their endless sun – this force for good – is decorating their white wings with the colour spectrum of this platoon's courage.

15 April, 2022.

CLARITY OR INSANITY

Despite all that I don't understand – and there is so much that I don't understand – the great gift the Movement has given me is that thanks to this global event, my tribe has risen and distilled itself from the many, and since accepting me into its ranks, I have never felt alone.

Also, once I had chosen the position of defending my concept of freedom – not that I had much choice – I also found what I had been looking for all my life: purpose. And an ever-deepening resolve that in return for my full commitment, Fear has been banished from my soul. The Movement has filled my tanks, day after day, with the energy I require to keep pushing forward.

Last night I slept by the side of the road. There was a weeping tree caressing my swag, and an owl asking the universe – on repeat – the question I hear so many people ask.

The question that ironically might be the answer. Who.

And I slept.

We are on the move again, as we have been for more than 45 days.

Here we are driving through a forest returning to green after a great fire scarred all of its trunks black, and as we travel, I know I am not a tourist, but a soldier on a mission for an army without a headquarters and without a leader – or at least not one that is made of flesh.

My orders come not like military or written orders, but in the form of an instinctual pull, as though up ahead, in my destiny, there is a force – like a magnet – calling me forth.

I can understand a language now that has no words, no sounds. Instead, we speak it using a deep tongue I never needed before now. We sing the songs of this language when we hug each other, or warmly shake hands.

And we celebrate its poetry in the tears that flow when a recruit, fresh to the line, breaks once they realise they are not alone. That they are not mad.

And if I am mad, then I am not alone in my insanity. Instead, in a world that is relentlessly selling cruelty as a necessary morality, I am blessed with a soul that can't be bought, and a heart that aches as it waits for those who are buying – the ones who believe they are sane.

21 April, 2022.

WHY WE CANNOT DISCRIMINATE

Gandhi once said, "An eye for an eye leaves the whole world blind." Currently our side is facing the same discrimination that the indigenous faced for decades, though over time they faced far worse.

That said, in many states we can't work without complying, and we haven't been able to use many facilities from pools to pubs to cafés – even hospitals. We are also constantly vilified in the mainstream media and by politicians, using terms like anti-vaxxers and the like.

Basically the entire upper echelon of society and those who support this change to a society governed by fear, instead of courage, are selling us to the world as the problem. This is a divide and conquer strategy that we fight by not complying to it. Instead we use love.

For in order to successfully navigate ourselves through this moral fog, to win, we will need the vaccinated – who will become more and more disgruntled with the callousness of the new system – to turn around and join our ranks. Which many are currently doing.

Therefore, to continue to encourage this exodus from their tyranny, we have to welcome those brothers and sisters back with open arms and let them know that they can return. This means we cannot use terms like Pure Blood, or even sheep.

Regardless of why people made their decisions, or how cold they have been, all of that has to be left in the past; the only thing that matters now is the future, and not so much our immediate future but the future of our children and their children.

We can't leave them this world – at least not without a rigorous fight – and across the country people are fighting. They are getting organised; they are trialling new ideas and trying not only to hold the line but regain it.

I suggest we lead by action, by simply continuing to do what we are doing, which is building a community on a foundation of inclusion and empathy and now unconditional forgiveness. And I understand that this can be difficult. This is also happening wherever I go.

In all this crap the moral high ground is and will continue to be held by us, simply through the spiritually organic qualities of our growing tribe.

Make no mistake, this is a war, and it's a spiritual war, but it won't be won by waiting for God to turn up, but by using God as an advisor and adhering to our values, and steering ourselves, in everything we do, via the compass in our souls.

24 April, 2022.

IT'S TIME

First they came for the communists. Then they came for the trade unionists. Then they came for the Jews. And then they came for me – and there was no one left to speak out.

First they came for the nursing home workers, but I wasn't one, so I said nothing.

Then they came for the registered nurses who, after heroically working through the initial days of the pandemic, have now been dismissed for gross misconduct for refusing to be vaccinated.

And even though I felt this wasn't fair and saw the posts of these nurses calling for us to join them on the protest lines, because I wasn't a nurse, I didn't join them, or like or share their posts, and in my work's staffroom, when a colleague asked me – quietly – what I thought about it, I just shrugged and said nothing.

Then they came for everyone else, but whilst I secretly watched all the protest videos – which left me full of tears – and whilst I could also see that the mainstream media was blatantly lying by underreporting the numbers of protesters and calling them names that were hateful and wrong, and despite also now hearing about all these people who were getting Covid despite being fully vaccinated, and or having severe adverse reactions to the jab, I decided that to keep my house and stay out of trouble I would take the jab, and since I didn't have an adverse reaction and because I didn't get sick – despite wanting to, and I really did – I decided in the end to play it safe and say nothing.

For the same reasons, I took the second. Then, a few nights later, my heart woke me up. It was beating like I had been sprinting, and it wouldn't stop. So I called an ambulance, and one of the first things the paramedics asked me was, "Have you been vaccinated?"

"Yes," I said. "Why?" But they just shook their heads and said nothing.

Then, in the emergency ward of a hospital, with my heart still trying to run out of my chest, a nurse came over and told me that it was time to take my booster.

Are you kidding me? I've just taken the second shot and now I'm having a heart attack.

But instead of listening, they sent a doctor in who gave me a lecture on why I must be fully vaccinated, while condescendingly blaming my struggling heart on anxiety. Anxiety! Of course I have anxiety. "Then stay off the internet," he said.

A few hours later they told me to go see a cardiologist and sent me home. But every cardiologist I called was booked up for months. Then, with my heart still sick and feeling like going to hospital was a waste of time, my boss sent me an email which informed me that, unless I took the booster, they would have to let me go.

What? You can't do that. I've worked for you for over twenty years, and I'm injured. The vaccine has injured me. "It's not us," they said. "We hate doing this; it's the government mandates."

I was so enraged I made a sign: Australia, Land of the Free, just as long as you do as you're told, and I stormed down to the steps of Parliament to join in the protests, but the steps were empty, and a homeless man told me that protesters don't come here anymore.

Determined to fight and be heard, I joined all the protesting Telegram groups I could find, but I found that no one had posted on them for a while. It seemed like every freedom fighter that I had been secretly following was gone.

Undeterred, I put out the call on Facebook for others to help me restart the battle, to fight against their relentless coercion, the blatant injustice – for we are, and always will be, a free country, where "my body my choice" is gold. But then Facebook took my post down and banned me for a week with a note that said if I kept posting misinformation they would ban me for ninety days, or longer.

So with nobody left to listen to me roar, and with no lines of people to stand shoulder to shoulder with in this great fight, and with the mainstream media talking about other things, I'm here, in a pop-up clinic.

Before me, a young technician is preparing my booster, and with my broken heart feeling like it's falling, I'm trying to focus on the face of a kind young person who is looking down at me from a poster on the wall, and next to their lovely smile their blurb states that in order to remain safe, I should book in now to get my fourth booster.

26 April, 2022.

BABES IN THE WOOD

Her hands – that have worked in shearing sheds all across the land; a roustabout and then a wool classer until she left the shearers to use these hands to work on the docks up north, learning to drive cranes and tie up the cargo ships to the docks after they had ridden the high tide into port to fill their hulls full of iron ore – and this is only a snippet of her history of manual work.

And yet tonight, in this cheaply rented donger, her hands were gently caressing me. In her early forties, she'd spent her life following the heart of her gypsy soul, job-drifting through a man's world, a true disciple of Germaine Greer – and yet she's never heard of the revolutionary woman, nor is she that interested in feminist ideology, despite being, by simply having the courage to be herself, one of its poster children.

And while her smile is a woman's, and her body's grace is a woman's, and she twists and groans like only a woman can, she then arches her back and grabs the rear of my feeding head with the iron grip of a working-class man.

Thoroughly independent, she's left her secret hold, and is now using her soul to redecorate this tiny room, but as the air conditioner softly whirs, she pulls me closer and deeply buries her head in my neck, like I was some sort of human cave offering her shelter from this storm.

Isn't it amazing, she whispers, with her eyes closed, how good it feels to have another body next to yours.

For all her skills and despite her work ethic, she was now an economic refugee, cast out because her veins are free of their mRNA vaccine. She's already lost her job at the ports, and while she's picked up another job – forklift organising a yard – the job was well below her skill set, as was the wage, which wasn't enough for her to keep living in this mining and predominantly three-jabbed town.

But it's harder to move now, as she's had family move here, and she has friends, roots – even though many of them can't understand why she refuses to give in.

Maybe that's why she's holding onto me. We are like babes lost in the woods, taking a break from searching for the country we've lost, to try and get some sleep.

Even when she kisses me, it's like a drowning person desperate to breathe, but by inhaling deeply, she fills me with her precious air.

In the morning she rose and made us a cup of coffee, and as I sat in the bed watching all of this woman, her gypsy soul offered me the rare delight of seeing her like this.

And I wondered as I watched the downlights shading the curve of her scrumptious bum how many of the male workers she has worked with craved to reach this view, or because they knew she was unvaxxed was she now seen as less, as something unclean, untouchable. If so, then I pray that in your new world I remain forever blind, for to me I felt blessed to be privy to her rare and secret sunrise.

This woman, whose freedom to be herself was now being curtailed by a government that needed to steal it from her – for suddenly they were obsessed with culturally and economically destroying her world because they were so concerned for her health.

Then, cups in hand, she comes back to the bed – this woman whose body and story I have been exploring all night – and as she hands me my cup of instant coffee, which is all this motel room offered, I say, "I'm really loving watching you," and then, after she sits and kisses me deeply and says, "Good," without her smile, "because I want you to watch me too."

5 May, 2022.

THE MARBLE BAR COOK

Once she'd lost her job for not taking the jab – and she'd worked in a nursing home – she'd sat in her rented apartment and watched her world fall apart via the periscope of her phone. The job had taken a while to get. At her age, it was almost impossible to get an interview. But she'd loved it. After her marriage had finally fallen apart, and since her two kids both lived interstate where they were constructing their own lives, the residents and the staff had become her new family.

The staff especially had helped her survive the toil, for despite all the standing machines and hoists, the work was hard on her body, which was now in its early sixties.

She'd often thought, when younger, when her offspring were still children, that by this age she'd be retired, maybe even travelling around the country she'd been born in but had never seen. Or at least not much of it.

The Gold Coast, where they'd taken their children several times so they could play in the adventure parks or watch the sun setting out of the high-rise apartment they'd hired, which for a few days gave them all a sense of what the view would be like if they were rich.

She'd been born to Catholic parents and had a Catholic upbringing, including school, but in her teens she'd drifted away from the Church. She didn't even know why – despite everything inside the Church looking the same – she felt disconnected from those in the pews until finally she never returned.

That said, she still wore a crucifix and often talked to God as she tried to understand why so few things unfolded the way that she thought they would. Like her marriage. She'd felt his heart move away from her like a ship slowly sailing towards the horizon ever since the birth of their second child. And while she'd tried hard to stop this drift, the reason her efforts had failed was that her heart had started drifting in the opposite direction.

In the end, the only time they seemed to connect was in the storms of their arguments. But those storms were long gone, as was he.

Though when he left, the world she'd built around them – the one she'd used conversations with God to try to plug the leaks and repair – the floor collapsed.

It didn't help that her ex, without her knowing, had taken out a second mortgage. One he couldn't service. She'd always left the finances to him. She didn't care about money because the bills were always paid and there was always food on the table. Even in the colder times, there was always enough until one day there wasn't. A short time later, the business she worked for, as a cleaner, also closed down. They didn't even have the money to pay any of the employees what they were owed. Suddenly, life moved on without her. That's how it felt.

But then one day, something inside her kicked her up, and she started constructing a new life. A rented flat, a new job, and as the years passed, she started having fun again.

There was even a man, far younger than her, who would come over sporadically for a bit of fun, and though he would never stay – and she knew that – the hunger he always brought with him used to give her back her beauty.

She adopted a cat that appeared out of nowhere, and as her kids built their lives in other cities, and her ex became someone she rarely thought of, she and the cat started to live. She took art lessons, tai chi lessons; she would get her tarot done, and once a fortnight, if she had the spare cash, she'd go to the pokies and try her luck – and always with one eye open for a man.

He didn't have to be that handsome, though she wouldn't have said no, and he didn't have to be a doctor or famous; he could even be damaged, for she loved healing. She was good at it. To date, he hadn't turned up. Instead, her cat died – which she found more painful than her husband leaving – and then, a short time later, while still grieving, she learned a new word: Covid.

At first, she believed all the TV was telling her. But then, since she was also observing the world via her phone, a few things started not to make sense. Finally, as the TV informed everyone that they would need to be jabbed to work, instead of her reaching out to God, God spoke to her via a clarity in her soul.

He didn't want her to take it. He wasn't telling, but urging her to say no. So she did. Suddenly, once again, she was nowhere. She was dismissed by a short email. Her children called her crazy and told her that she wouldn't be able to see their children until she was fully vaccinated, and her friends cut her loose. Even her young lover stopped coming.

Yet still, her soul told her she was on the right path – not that she could see a path from her flat where she was locked down. By the end of the third lockdown, she knew she was in trouble. The mandates were not lifting and her savings were almost gone. She had taken out some of her superannuation, as the government had suggested, but this wad of cash was it.

With no jobs on offer for the non-compliant, she began looking further afield. But where? Then providence saw a Facebook group appear on her feed. Because Covid had seen the amount of international travellers sink, farms and cattle stations were reaching out to Australians to fill their vacancies.

And there it was. A cattle station near Marble Bar, which was as large as Singapore, was looking for a cook. She searched Google Earth and found that Marble Bar was not only remote but was famous in Australia for having some of the hottest temperatures. It well earned its moniker, the hottest town Down Under.

After calling the number, the rancher offered her the job and said if she turned up, he would reimburse her the money for the fuel.

Then the fourth lockdown ended. Outside, everyone was still masked up, and she knew that another one was coming. You could sense it in the air. Victorian Premier Daniel Andrews was drunk on power.

And so she packed up her Honda Jazz with everything she could fit, leaving just enough space for her to recline the driving seat back so she could sleep, and using Google Maps as a guide, she placed what she couldn't fit in her car but could bear to dump in the cheapest storage container she could find, and left the ruins of what she'd thought life would be and went searching for new views. This was the longest drive of her life, and as soon as she'd escaped the city, she fell in love with the road.

In one hotel, in a tiny town, she bought some vodka mixes and had her own party to celebrate this new woman who was emerging from within. She'd never known she was strong. But there was no fear. Instead, she was waking up either in these cheap hotels or in her car, excited by what she might find in this new unfolding day.

Finally, she reached Ceduna, the last town before the Nullarbor. Almost a thousand kilometres away was the West Australian border, which was currently locked to people like her. The unvaccinated.

She spent two days there, hoping and praying that the border would open. Two days chatting with God, and then calling the station owner, telling him – or explaining – that she was on her way but might just be a little late.

She even looked at alternative routes, but all of them came with warnings that they were suitable for four-wheel drives only. At night, she'd walk to the edge of town and stare off into the direction she was heading. Despite being thousands of kilometres away, it felt so close. Like all that stood between her and the kitchen where she would be working was a thin sheet of glass she just couldn't get through.

Then, if she looked behind her, there was nothing there at all.

When I met her, she'd just cooked breakfast for three young jackaroos preparing for a day of mustering. The cattle needed to be tagged and the bulls castrated. Later that day, they would pack up one of the four-wheel-drive buggies for her, which came with a roof to protect her from the sun, and alone she would drive around the perimeter, checking to see if the camels had broken the fence.

Never had she envisioned that she would be capable of doing something like this, and yet here she was, passing snakes that raced to get out of her way, and watching wedge-tailed eagles gliding from one thermal to another. This land looked like it had been originally hewn by God using only a chisel, then he'd left it to the bush to try and soften the edges.

There was even a creek that ran through the property in which she would lay naked, the sun warming her as the water cooled what skin she had offered its fast-paced current. No one had ever met this woman. This was a woman she'd unwrapped herself with the tools of courage.

She wasn't even scared of the fact that the job wasn't permanent. For this woman was confident to find another station or a roadhouse that would hire her. As she let the sun dry her and as the buggy waited for her to return to the fence, she looked around and realised she was the only life she could see in any direction.

If it wasn't freedom, then it was close. The only weight pulling down her smile was the pains in her kidneys. Stubborn pains that woke her up at night and wouldn't let her sleep. Pains she could feel now, as well as those other strange sensations she'd also never experienced, made their presence known.

The station owner had been so upset and apologetic. Unvaccinated, as was his whole family, he wished he'd brought this up with her when she called saying she might be a bit late. But it wasn't something that people were comfortable talking about. Silence was the norm. Even in the clinic, no one had spoken – apart from the nurse, who, once she had finished, had offered her a sticker that congratulated her for getting vaccinated.

The first one had not affected her at all, physically. And since God, no matter how hard she asked him, could offer her no way through the border, she had decided to take the second.

Now she was here. But look at where she was. This part of the fence wove through country that continually took her breath away.

It had an ancient majesty that left you feeling both humbled and oddly at home.

Out of all the views she had viewed in this length of time that had decorated her life, none compared to this.

If whatever was wrong with her decided to end her story here, she had already decided she was OK with that.

In fact, after all the old people she'd watched die in the nursing home, their cooling bodies waiting to be collected as the busy staff continued caring for the others, and the Director of Nursing called the next family on the list and told them that there was a bed free, dying out here in all this beauty would feel, she thought, like an answered prayer.

8 May, 2022.

CHILDREN OF EPIC

She is sitting in an open-air bath
That she got given and set up next to her tent,
Which is decorated by this string of bulbs,
Illuminating softly all the material that she has left. But she glows like
There's a sun inside her soul,
Soothing anyone brave enough to see.
She's a blend of a painting and a poem
Written in a language that I am out here trying to learn.
For above her, our universe is dark
And stretches past our stars to who the hell knows where,
But she supports all of its silent weight by looking up, from her bath,
And gently smiling as she converses with the birds.
There's a horse nearby who dances with her
Like a young lover desperate to impress.
And every morning she walks along Cable Beach naked,
In what she calls her church.
And the sun is painting her ageing body
On the altar
Where she's been trying to lay her pain,
But those prayers are still waiting to be answered
In those lines time's carving into her face.
She's a refugee from her own people.
She's a leper and I think she might be Jesus too,
For around her the other lepers are dancing
Despite us stripping all their dreams away.
To you they are selfish and deplorable,
But to me inside their dignity and grace,

Inside that kindness that they simply won't discard,
Is all we have left to show our gods
That despite the cold darkness our cowardice is creating,
This woman and her outcast friends are tonight
As beautiful as I can imagine any flower that ever bloomed
In the Garden of Eden.

10 May, 2022.

DARWIN'S GUARDIAN ANGELS

You never hear much of guardian angels anymore. They were like a passing fad of those who needed to believe that the universe was so interested in them that they were designated a secret friend who, through intuition – that voice in your gut – tried to keep you to your allotted path.

To me, the job used to sound so boring I would joke that the only direction my guardian angel kept trying to direct me to was under a bus. Now though, I think the job would be so taxing that her angel would need their own angel – not to lead but rather to console them.

I'm in Darwin. We have four days here to collect stories and prepare ourselves for the next leg of this journey into the darkness between here and home. A darkness that many of our brothers and sisters are determined to hold over us. A darkness under which we find shelter with the candles held by those in our tribe.

I see the painters of darkness on posters. They are smiling as they warn us of Covid, as they continue to sell us their truth that "up is down," that "left is right," that the lack of empathy which has infected the land is actually the work of God.

Maybe this deep sense that something is deeply awry in the broader realm – Australia – leads us to the point where, even though we can't see the destination, we know we are on the right path. Maybe this sense is the work of guardian angels. Silent illuminated beings, fighting side by side with all the members of our besieged tribe.

It's 5 a.m. and still dark. The flying foxes are yet to fly home. I can hear them squabbling – over what? I don't know – as other birds sing and chatter as if to celebrate the fact that they have survived another night. And this night was warm.

It's winter here, the dry season they call it, but the air is a warm soup.

In Melbourne, they are waking up under their doonas, wondering whether it's better to stay there, whereas here I'm topless and pausing only to look at the dark that is still full of so many human qualities that I no longer understand.

Meg is young, and in order to finish her first year in university where she is trying to become a primary school teacher, she had to take the juice – twice – like so many other Victorians. But Meg, in her early twenties, is only the size of an average seven-year-old, a little person, and after doing lots of her own online research she asked her doctor, "Why do I have to take an adult's dose? Don't you think there is a chance it could affect me, considering my size?" And her doctor replied – and I quote – "I don't know."

After the first dose she spent a week and a half in bed. Now, still suffering from extreme fatigue, she has deferred her study for a year out of fear of the booster and become a hermit. Her words.

In a former world I once took for granted, the medical establishment – and society in general – would have said, "Of course you don't have to take it. Your body, your choice."

But in this new human-scape, where the darkness remains even after the sun rises – where so many hearts appear to beat unaffected by another's pain – the state politician her mum approached, pleading for sense, for mercy, told her it was a federal issue, before her federal minister went on to inform her that no, they are wrong; this is an issue for the state.

As I finished writing that paragraph, some strange bird – the likes of which I have never heard – just cried out like it was wailing. Its notes are still hanging in the air as this darkness silently smothers them.

I was told yesterday too, in another WTF moment, about a woman. A pro-jab new mother who now has a new job. Helping her one-year-old baby, who was born sick, recover from the fact that it has had to have one of its kidneys removed. The mother, who is naturally devastated, is still pushing for the rest of the family to get jabbed.

Was it the jab?

Who knows?

You?

We heard about this baby on this balcony as we – a small group of unvaccinated people in Darwin – prepared to head out for dinner.

We were all deeply affected, but as I watched my colleagues shake their heads with their eyes full of disbelief, I wondered again: are we the hope for the future, or a flock of soft-hearted dodos that our culture's relentless social evolution has yet to eradicate?

I hear the calls of our replacements in the comments – maybe by the trolls whose indifferent malice I don't reply to – for they are sung using notes that I don't want to sing.

Northern Territory Premier Michael Gunner is gone. Perhaps because he did it, our generous host – who is already preparing to leave Darwin – suggested. The cost of living is so high here that if you don't have work, you can't survive, and since Gunner mandated all businesses, most of the unvaxxed must have left. Darwin, she said, is a vaxxed city.

She doesn't know for certain though, because like all endangered and hunted species, our tribe has learned to hide themselves well.

We learned this on the Nullarbor Plains. Near the then-closed Western Australian border, we sat on the side of the road watching the roadtrains pass and wondered if we were the only unvaxxed people out here, but at the Nullarbor roadhouse we met another leper on the run. The Nullarbor Leper.

I'm sick of lies. I find myself now craving the truth no matter how unbelievable and cruel it is.

Oh look, here comes the sun. The sky in front of me is being stained red as if some great battle over the horizon is aflame.

Today we are going to the rally here. Our battle.

Why? What's the point if this city is all vaxxed?

Well, perhaps "the point" has nothing to do with it.

I have to go. I just know it, and deep inside me my gut instinct is at peace with this decision.

No. No, this was and is my choice.

A while ago, I decided that despite the consequences, I would rather die fighting on this hill once and on my feet than die every day on my knees in their new, reset world. And what I write next may sound like delusions of grandeur, but while I do believe – or rather I have an unfathomably deep faith – that I have been chosen and accepted to be a soldier for God, I also know that if I am delusional, then that is fine too, for in this spreading silent darkness, their definition of insanity is the only illuminated path.

13 May, 2022.

HER BODY, OUR CHOICE

IF I HAVE to take it, I'll take it, but they are not touching my daughter.

Before the mandates she had been working in retail. Now she hasn't worked since December. It's mid-May.

Darwin is expensive and the dole is nowhere near enough. With few jobs on offer for the unvaccinated, she has only a few options. Move interstate, despite Darwin being her home; start her own business, without money, for her savings are almost gone; or give in and take the jab.

It was a TED Talk with Bill Gates that saw her become suspicious. He was talking about population control and vaccines. It saw her wander off down our crowded rabbit holes until she reached here, where she was talking to me about working her way up to complying.

She doesn't want to do it.

"It's rape," she said. "That's what it is. It's rape."

And as she said this I wondered what had happened to all those who had passionately pushed "My Body My Choice" for decades. It used to be a poster on the sides of buses. It used to be woven into our vernacular, and we liked it being there because from a sovereignty perspective it made sacred sense.

Now it is like a gutted nursery rhyme from a forgotten war, sung only by those people – especially women – who do not want to be vaccinated.

These women are now called selfish. Outcast, not just from employment but from friends and families.

Their pride and integrity, their determination to hold onto their freedom to choose what goes into their bodies, economically besieged until we – as a society now ruled by fear – coerce and insult them, until once we have broken them into conceding, we silently rape them.

We are all rapists now. And you know it.

And for all of our good intentions, for all the accolades we give ourselves and our democracy, we have devolved into a choir of condescending crows, watching from the sidelines as we wait for this young mum to give up her principles and do what we tell her to do. Even though we all now know that the products don't work as they are supposed to, and instead they could hurt her or worse. Then, to finish the job, we slap her in the face by telling her it was her choice.

Then, astoundingly, because of political desperation in the midterm elections in the USA, they are challenging Roe v. Wade and — oh look what they've dragged out and brushed off. Your body, your choice. But look at me, trying to make people in authority care. If she was a nurse or a doctor, you wouldn't lift a finger to help, so why would I even bother to hope that you would care for a young unjabbed mum who used to work in retail?

15 May, 2022.

THE PILOT

Somewhere close but forever unreachable, a curlew is wailing like a soul lost in the night, and as I lay in my swag, I understand that thanks to Covid – and all its bullshit – this bird is now singing my song.

Today I'll be tagging along with Luke and other ringers as they muster cattle on remote and rugged property lost somewhere behind Mt Isa.

It's 5.30 a.m., and today my day starts now.

After taking a piss, the dawn reveals these gum tree-covered iron ore hills that I couldn't see when we arrived last night. They are the fossilised remnants of a taller range; broken vertebrae that time keeps cracking, but as yet has failed to remove them from the view. Near the donga – a demountable shed with the camp kitchen inside – the ringers are yawning as they haunt the rekindled fire.

Thinner than bones, they have camp coffees in their hands, red dirt in their skin, and with rollies in their lips they watch the fire with a reverent silence, their private eyes full of their unanswered questions, as their jacket collars stand erect to shield their necks from the morning chill.

One of them is a helicopter pilot, and today I will watch – in awe – as he flies over this range like a dragonfly with a death wish.

Luke told me that these flyers operate in what other helicopter pilots call the death curve. If anything goes wrong up there, they will be so close to the ground when it does that there will be no time to do anything but leave us.

Yet despite a life of constant risk this pilot is a quiet man; even his reactions seem too slow and considered for his line of work. Although he's friendly and laughs at the wit of these other men – and even graciously accepts the few jibes aimed at him, jibes he does not return – the flames reveal that there is a curlew in his eyes, but whatever he's searching for isn't hiding in these flames.

Last night I approached him for an interview, but he didn't want to share his story.

This morning though, he tells me how he can spend upwards of six months living in his tiny flying machine that doesn't even have doors. Alone he'll travel all over the upper half of this hard vastness, flying over landscapes that perhaps only he will get to see, for the sun and the rains are constantly repainting it.

His helicopter has no heater, and there is no altimeter or speedo.

There is just a stick, a few switches, two plastic seats, himself and a .22 rifle holstered between the seats. That's for the cattle that falter as they flee from his blades – and or the wild dogs.

He's licensed to fly several helicopters, including the six-seaters they use to fly riggers out to the offshore oil rigs, but he prefers the mustering. Out here he has no one looking over his shoulder, and when I ask him, he tells me that he never gets sick of the view. That's one of the main reasons he's out here, he said; just another lonesome spectator to the glory of God's more isolated work.

He started flying when he was nineteen. Now in his mid-fifties he talks about his business partner, who is also his wife, with respect and fondness. She's out there somewhere, looking after their finances as he stands here huddled in his jacket, half-lit by the fire – a silhouette against the dawn as he waits for the station owner to arrive with the plans for the day.

Soon I will watch him vanishing over the remnants of mountains, flying through the trees so close to the ground and at a speed that even though I'll be watching it, I won't believe it.

There is a border between life and death and this man spends his working hours tearing across it – backwards, forwards and up and down. He is a cowboy in the sky, herding more cattle into the pens than all these ringers in their scratched and dented four-wheel-drive buggies put together.

It's also his job to chase down the cows that manage to evade these ringers and, using fear, coerce these cattle back to the compliant, even defeated, herd.

The only man-made thing I've seen fly with greater dexterity is a drone, and that's what's coming to replace him.

The cost of his services is steep, as is the cost of petrol – and that is still rising. By comparison, drones are a dime a dozen, and if they fall out of the sky no one dies, and for the cost of one helicopter they could replace him with hundreds.

Luke told me later that they were already trialling them on other stations, and a few days later on the road to Normanton, even our little drone – the Australian Security Intelligence Organisation, the domestic spy agency more commonly known as ASIO – will manage to scare an entire herd of cows.

If that evolution happens, most of Australia will never hear about it. Those that do will marvel at the cleverness of the drones and even agree that it's far safer and cheaper, leaving only these ringers – and others like them on other homesteads – to periodically bring up the helicopter pilot's name and celebrate his exploits around campfires as they battle to offset the darkness and the cold.

It makes you wonder why life goes to all this trouble of giving us not only life, but this stage, only to have history racing up from behind, hungry to devour us all. Even these mountains, gilded with the morning sun, can't sate its appetite.

On a break though the pilot takes one of the ringers' sons up for a quick joy flight, zooming him over the trees and the broken hills in a series of moments that will become for the boy a defining memory. On the ground, dust-covered ringers laugh at their own envy. In their holding pen the cattle – who have barely if ever seen humans – huddle together and study, through the fence, these men huddled around their buggies, hunting the sky for the returning chopper. The ringers are unaware, as they roll their cigarettes, how rare they are in this age of compliance: these descendants of unknown heroes, these apostles of the gum trees, these hard-working, free-loving cattle-mustering men.

In the late afternoon the pilot will fly off to his next job, and come evening – for he is not allowed to fly at night – he'll either land near the closest homestead, where country hospitality will see them offer him a bed, or, if he is too far out, he'll land out in the remote bush. Then after pulling out his swag from the passenger seat, he'll build his own fire under the dark emu and her pale wash. According to indigenous legend, the dark emu is the space between the stars. The pale wash is the Milky Way.

I can see him there now, in a mind-image stolen from history. Alone, and with no want to move, he's studying the flames with longer eyes as inch by inch they come so close that if he turned around he'd see them dancing in the eyes of the black men that history already – and forevermore – devoured.

30 May, 2022.

PAYPAL BANS CAFÉ LOCKED OUT

Under a banner with the PayPal logo and the heading "We need some information from you" came the following note.

Dear Michael Gray Griffith,

We have recently reviewed your usage of PayPal's services, as reflected in our records and on your website.

Due to the nature of your activities, we have chosen to discontinue service to you in accordance with PayPal's User Agreement.

As a result, we have placed a permanent limitation on your account. We ask that you please remove all references to PayPal from your website.

This includes removing PayPal as a payment option, as well as the PayPal logo and/or shopping cart.

If you have a remaining balance, you may withdraw the money to your bank account. Information on how to withdraw money from your PayPal account can be found via our Help Center.

We thank you in advance for your cooperation.

Sincerely,

PayPal

Responses to this email address are not monitored.

31 May, 2022.

BOOLAROO

On a shy dirt road, thin and overgrown, below the towering and humming forest of turbines, I came across the old house, constructed out of bricks moulded from the hard earth now reclaiming its walls. There was graffiti on some of the last remaining plaster. The ceiling and roof had become the floor, allowing you to look up at the sky, which seemed to be using its weight to help the earth erase this house.

After World War One, the government gave parcels of this land to soldiers returning from the trenches. I even came across the ruins of a school with a fading plaque called the "School of the Future." They must have come out here in their Model T-Fords or carts, thinking that the war was behind them, but these ruins speak of another war, and the ruins are all that remain.

I tried to capture this with my phone; however, that part of the view that left you reverently quiet as you explored the few rooms was beyond the lens to capture. But my soul could capture it. This was why I'd asked to take our little truck to the next town alone. I was missing my kids, even though they were young adults now. And I missed my past life – the theatre, the thrill of watching the audience turning up as the actors in the change rooms were psyching themselves up.

On nothing but pure determination, Rohana and I had not only set up The Wolves Theatre Company, but in more recent times we'd been doing so well that we were living off it. Touring our plays town to town, we'd even been invited to perform for the Australian Army, whose head psychologist had declared that our play Marooned was a revolution in suicide prevention.

They told me they'd tried every program the government had offered, and none of them worked. Now they were going to try theatre – a new

Australian play. We even got invited to Canberra, where our actors performed for the Chief of Army and a host of other VIPs. We wowed them.

Afterwards, we were standing there before the most powerful soldier, and he told us the only decision they had to make now was whether watching the play for their enlisted personnel would be voluntary or mandatory. Mandatory – the first time that word had really reached me. I remember thinking, if they decide on mandatory, then we could become millionaires.

Back in Melbourne, our newest play, the comedy Adrifting, was wowing audiences, and other great things were happening too. Our dream of living as contemporary artists had been realised, and better still, our plays were helping people. To us, this was theatre heaven. And then Covid arrived and they closed all the theatres. Our hopes that it was only a speed bump were dashed when the first lockdown ended and we commenced our first funded tour of our play The Magnolia Tree.

Around this time, yet another play, The Shadows and The Hues, was earmarked for serious funding. Suddenly, despite Covid, we were in serious talks with the acclaimed director Bruce Beresford, who was quoted as saying he read scripts all the time, and that this was the best thing he'd read in years. He went on to say the play was the equivalent of a Pinter play, except it was a brand-new voice.

I remember resting my hand on his wrist, which confused him, to which I added, "You're Bruce Beresford." I said this because I was not used to this much good luck. But then a moment later, a voice in my head said, "Enjoy the view, Michael. This is as high as you'll go."

A short time later, the government decreed that theatres would be segregated. Only the vaccinated would be allowed in. On all the theatre pages, everyone was celebrating this. I remember a major theatre director posting how relieved he was because he could think of nothing worse than sitting next to a filthy anti-vaxxer.

Meanwhile, those who liked my work were urging me to stay silent.

"Don't throw it all away," I was told. "You could be heading to New York."

But instead, with Rohana's blessing, I posted a live video in which I declared that segregation was a cancer on the culture's soul, and our theatre company, the Wolves, would not participate.

And so we were cancelled. And so now I was here, standing in the ruins of someone's dream house. Someone who was long gone.

Back in the truck, with Wendy and Kret following in Wendy's Winnebago, I wound my way through the gorge to a town called Boolaroo. Port Augusta was next, and then after a few more side roads, we'd be on the Nullarbor heading to the Western Australia border, which we were not allowed to cross because we were unvaccinated. Which was also the reason we were going. Us – three members of the Freedom Movement that had popped up organically all over the country. And most of us with this strange sensation that we knew we were on the right path, even though we didn't know where we were going.

And then I was here.

At first glance, Boolaroo was a quiet, wide, and empty street, with a few shops and government buildings lining each side. The only building with any character was the bakery. We'd heard that the owners had refused to participate in the Covid mandates. There had been no pushing of QR codes, and mask-wearing hadn't been and wasn't being enforced.

Taking in its isolation, you'd wonder why the authorities would bother pushing their mandates out here, but they had. One of the owners told us that they'd repeatedly sent police up from Adelaide to try and intimidate them into compliance. It hadn't worked, which was why we were here.

We'd decided to try to shoot a short documentary, and in the bakery we were setting up the cameras when the shop filled with people. So I whispered to the owner that I'd wait until she'd served her customers, when she laughed and said, "They aren't here for me. They're here for you."

Most towns we stopped at, we let them know we were coming, but because this town was so remote we hadn't bothered. Apart from a few, these people weren't locals. They were medical refugees fleeing the mandates of Melbourne and Adelaide. They were out here trying to find places to hide or a job they could apply for as an unvaccinated person. There were few places to hide, and even fewer jobs.

That said, I wasn't an entertainer; I was an apprentice recorder of stories. It had started in Melbourne, in the great marches, and then crystallised in Canberra at the Epic gathering. All these people arriving from all over Australia, their vehicles packed with camping gear, and their faces flush with hope. With no mainstream media asking them who they were and why they'd come, I started asking them, for it was clear that each of them had chosen to play a passionate, active part in history.

That passion was not infectious, at least in terms of mainstream Australia, but it was healing. Since most of us were losing our careers, our friends, our families, and some of us our houses, and what many of us thought were our dreams, this passion was a mercy. And since my amputation from theatre, this passion to tell the stories of my country had been healing me. So I knew I had to keep going. To return true to myself and ultimately true to my country, there was no choice in the matter.

That's what all these people crowding into this remote bakery were here to do; they'd driven from all around the country to have their stories recorded. So that's what we did. We set up our cameras, our microphones, and allowed as many of these people to speak as possible. I was compelled to, for they were all from my new tribe. These beautifully brave Australians who had risked or sacrificed everything they held dear to defend something that, pre-Covid, we had all taken for granted. The idea that as Australians common decency dictated we care for and respect each other.

1 June, 2022.

THE LAST LEG OF THE DEPLORABLES EPIC ROAD TRIP

"We have all become historians – capturing a history they are already trying to erase."

It is the 1st of July, 2022. We have been on the road over 100 days, and we are due back in Melbourne on July 4th.

The journey has changed us all, yet the tide of tyranny is continuing to come in.

"You're a protester; you're not a citizen," the Australian Federal Police officer said to one of the women I interviewed, Pauline. The interview – and what Pauline had seen and suffered – rams home to my soul the fact that our police have lost their way.

On a positive note, the goal of this journey – born from experiences at the Epic Camp in February – was to replant the joy, hope, and sense of new community all around Australia, like your grandmother reseeding a neighbour's plant.

But this was arrogant, for Epic is seeding itself everywhere from Portland to Boolaroo to Darwin. We have proved that by going there physically and meeting these seedlings. These warriors.

I now believe that the Shrine was where the Resistance was officially conceived, and Epic was the womb where our glorious and growing resistance was born.

And even though we are making mistakes, that's just because we are learning to use our limbs, to speak with our new voice, to discern what we are seeing with our liberated eyes, coloured in the hue and the hunger of freedom.

Before returning to Melbourne, we will continue to record these people's stories. It is an honour to do so, and all three of us feel humbled and warmed to be a part of this growing tribe – this rising counter-culture that will one day be the king tide that will wash away all their perversions.

Now we have to philosophise, decide what we need from a culture – not just for us but for the future generations – for this defined need will allow us to see our destination, the new country we will help build, and once we can see it, we will reach it, create it, for as a people that's what we have the skills, passion, and responsibility to do.

And whilst we may never reach there – for this will be a long struggle – we will have the privilege of being its foundation. That's why we are, if we have the courage and the love to be so, the architects of the new Australia. Our Australia, built on a foundation of inclusion, empathy, and freedom.

Our Last Days on Tour: People are asking how we feel and what's next. We have been all around the country interviewing people everywhere, most of whom are very concerned about the future of our culture, despite many people claiming everything has gone back to normal.

So to return to Canberra and find the Australian Federal Police assaulting a mature woman – grandmothers who are here fighting for the liberty of their grandchildren – reignites the lingering fire in our souls.

There is a large section of our community who we no longer understand. They stay quiet as unconscionable things happen. They seem to have no lines in the sand called "enough is enough," and are content to be spectators as everything good about our country burns.

So today and tomorrow we are heading home with quiet hearts and are wondering if we are returning to a home or to a trench.

Out there somewhere – or inside, or both – there is a God of Good, and he is our backer and our guide, and the reason we know this is because the strength and beauty and nobility of the Australian people we have met have both restored and cemented our faith.

They are all beacons of hope, each defending what is under siege – our culture's spirit – and not only is that worth fighting for, it's worth dying for, which is why in the end we will win, and why for us coming home is not our journey's end.

6 July, 2022.

AN EX-CHIEF DETECTIVE SPEAKS

In the Café Locked Out podcast An Ex-Chief Detective Speaks, published on July 19, 2022, I interviewed Andrew, a former Victorian Chief Detective with 30 years of service, who resigned in 2021 over police enforcement of Covid-19 mandates.

Recorded during Griffith's 115-day Australian road trip, the 17-minute episode exposes the Victorian Police's transformation into a "political enforcement wing," aligning with the frequent critique of Australia falling headlong into a totalitarian future.

Andrew's revelations about internal police pressure, unethical practices, and cultural shifts resonate with the themes of mandate-driven authoritarianism.

Andrew begins by outlining his career, emphasising his investigative expertise: "I was a Chief Detective for over a decade, handling serious crime – murders, fraud, corruption.

"Thirty years in, I knew the system inside out."

He resigned after Victoria's 2021 lockdowns, unable to reconcile his oath with the enforcement of mandates.

"The police became a political tool," he states. "We were told to enforce health orders – fines, arrests, rubber bullets – against Aussies who just wanted to work or protest. It wasn't policing; it was control."

I interjected, connecting this to Café Locked Out's mission: "That's why we're here, Andrew – to capture stories like yours. When did you see the shift?"

Andrew pinpoints 2020–2021, when Chief Commissioner Shane Patton prioritised mandate compliance over community trust: "Patton's directives were clear – no dissent, no exemptions. We were briefed to treat protesters as threats, not citizens.

"I saw officers – good blokes – pressured to bash people at rallies like the Shrine."

I replied: "You mean the September 2021 protest? I was there, cuffed, shot at. What were you told about us?"

Andrew reveals internal bias: "You were labelled 'anti-vaxxers,' 'rioters.' Briefings painted you as dangerous, but I knew better – you were families, tradies, nurses. It was propaganda to justify force."

The detective detailed ethical breaches, including falsified reports: "Officers were encouraged to exaggerate protest violence in logs to secure convictions. I refused to sign off on those – it cost me promotions."

I responded, linking his experience to censorship: "That's like our Facebook ban – they silence truth to protect the system. Did you face pushback for resisting?"

Andrew confirms: "Constantly. Superiors warned me to 'fall in line' or retire. The culture shifted – loyalty to the state, not the public. Young recruits were trained to obey, not question."

Andrew reflects on public trust's collapse: "People used to respect us – now they fear us. Mandates turned cops into the enemy. I'd see kids scared at checkpoints, parents fined for no masks. It broke my heart."

I asked: "What about vaccine injuries? Did you hear anything?"

Andrew nods: "Off the record, officers talked – heart issues, clots, in colleagues and families. But we were gagged, told to report 'misinformation.' AHPRA's rules bled into policing."

AHPRA – Australian Health Practitioner Regulation Agency, the national body responsible for registering and regulating health professionals (like doctors, nurses, and pharmacists) across Australia, allegedly to protect public safety. It works alongside 15 National Boards to implement the National Registration and Accreditation Scheme. To its many critics, AHPRA lost all credibility during the Covid era.

I challenged Andrew on solutions: "You've left, but what now? How do we fix this?"

Andrew advocated reform: "We need independent oversight, not political commissioners. Police must serve people, not premiers. And whistleblowers – like me – need protection, not punishment."

He added a personal note: "I'm speaking here because I owe it to Aussies – I failed them by staying silent too long."

I closed, affirming Café Locked Out's role: "That's why we're recording, Andrew – your voice is Australia's truth. Thanks for your courage."

19 July, 2022.

HEADING BACK TO COURT

Next week, I'm back in court, and this time it feels different. After three adjournments, the police are still claiming they can't find the bodycam footage from the day they arrested me.

It's a curious thing – technology that's supposed to be infallible, yet somehow, when it's convenient, it goes missing. I know what happened that day. They know what happened. But without that footage, it's my word against theirs, and in a system that seems to favour the state, that's a steep hill to climb.

This all started because I refused to stay silent.

Café Locked Out began as a way to give voice to those who were being crushed by mandates, locked out of their lives for daring to question. We were artists, workers, parents – ordinary Australians who saw the erosion of our freedoms and decided to speak. That choice put a target on my back. The arrest wasn't just about me; it was a message to anyone who dares to challenge the narrative.

But here's the thing: I'm not afraid. Every time they drag me into court, it's a reminder of why we fight. Café Locked Out isn't just a podcast or a platform; it's a community of people who believe in truth, in freedom, in the Australia we grew up in.

We've documented stories of nurses fired for refusing the jab, of families torn apart, of businesses destroyed. Those stories matter, and they're worth defending.

The legal battles are exhausting, and the system is designed to wear you down. But every time I think about giving up, I remember the people we've met through Café Locked Out – the ones who've lost everything but still stand tall. They're the reason I'll walk into that courtroom next week, head high, ready to fight again.

If you're reading this, you're part of this fight too. Whether you're sharing our podcasts, talking to your mates, or just refusing to comply with the madness, you're keeping the spirit of resistance alive. So, thank you. Keep speaking, keep questioning, and keep pushing back. They can't silence us all.

30 October, 2022.

CONVOY TO CANBERRA ONE YEAR ON

Are we the Last Fort? Reflections on the first Convoy Camp Site, outside Parliament House in Canberra.

Day three was cooler, but only weather-wise. Every hour, on the hour, the police entered the camp and did a walk-through. Masked up and initially polite, they strode through the growing camp, surrounded by protesters who were trying to convince the officers to come over to our side.

Lots of us were angry. We'd driven here from all over the land in a search for simple things. The right to work, the right to socialise, the right to choose what went into their bodies.

It was initially agreed upon that these walk-throughs would happen every hour, but since we had no designated leader, there were several schools of thought regarding this. Some wanted the police to stay out, others wanted them to be allowed to do their walk-through only twice a day, while others – who felt we had nothing to hide, and needed to find a way to convince the police to join us – were happy for them to wander through.

Matt Lawson, the Melbourne man who was shot in the stomach at close range by a rubber bullet, was filmed having a calm yet persuasive conversation with a policeman. A young policeman admitted that he agreed with all of Matt's points, which covered everything from the erosion of freedoms to questioning the efficacy of the vaccines. Yet even though he agreed, he did not join us. Not that one sympathetic young cop would be enough to stop the escalation of tension.

Within a few hours the police had changed their tactics. Now they were not only going to walk through whenever they wanted to, but they blocked the main entrance, and whilst they let our cars out, they were not letting these people back in.

They also began telling us that we were illegally camping, or trespassing. But many in the camp believed that legally this wasn't a police issue; this was a council issue – not that anyone from the council had come to talk to us yet.

Then two women, who appeared to be from Canberra, called us all in a huddle to inform us that this land we were on was indigenous land, and that the local elders had given us their blessing, so we were safe.

Suddenly, at the rear of the camp, four unmarked four-wheel drives with darkened glass pulled up in a line, and with their engines running. They were in a line – a modern-day cavalry – waiting for their orders to charge.

I live-streamed this as my good friend, the photographer Daniel – a Māori in his late sixties – sat on the grass before them. I joined him, then soon after other freedom seekers – for the words "freedom fighters" felt wrong – sat next to us.

We believed that despite the police strategy of intimidation they wouldn't run us over. Not here. Not in Australia.

But then two of these four-wheel drives reversed, then drove at speed into the camp, passing a group of young children who were playing cricket, and just as they did several officers from a tactical branch burst out of the remaining four-wheel drives and ran into the camp.

We stood up and followed these men.

By the time we reached the centre of the camp it was a mess. The police were kettling themselves, and as their colleagues arrested someone, we freedom seekers surrounded the officers. With our hands in the air – to show the world that we were unarmed – we all started chanting, "You serve us. You serve us."

The rest was a shit-fest. You could argue that the police were just doing their job, but you could argue too that since we were peaceful, someone up high had ordered them to enter the camp and use a show of force to frighten us off.

But instead of spreading fear, these officers were met by old people who had come here from all over the country because they were over the fear. One of these was a 73-year-old man called Les, who was thrown to the ground, then – with several police holding him down – another officer brought his pepper-spray can up to his face until Les could see the nozzle, and then they sprayed him in the face.

For our side, this was a victory. All of us had our phones out and were live-streaming everything. And whilst some people at home would try to find a way to exonerate the tactics of the police, the visuals of how these police officers were now passionately brutalising our old people told another story.

This is Australia? People were asking, and their voices were the voices of the broken-hearted. This is Australia?

One man hugged me because I was crying. He was crying too. Lots of people were. And not from the pepper spray or the fear, but from disbelief that these police officers – who should have been our heroes, these grandchildren of the Anzacs – were now our oppressors.

But they were oppressed too. For it was clear that their masters knew that lots more people were coming. Lots more. And so they wanted the head of the forming snake cut off.

They wanted us gone.

I have been saying for a while that we were all surfing an incoming wave of tyranny. Well, what we were now was the first ripples of another wave: a gathering tsunami of people – Australians wanting to defend what people all over the world crave – freedom.

Even as I wrote my original impressions, people kept coming up to me and introducing themselves. They had come from everywhere. Two women had just arrived from Townsville. Two days of solid driving.

This park was now the front line. You could feel it. We all could. Would we be the agents of change? Would our wave wash away their tyranny? Or would we be the last stand of everything that was beloved about our country? A fort crushed by officers trying to pay their mortgages; officers who, if that happened, would have to try to live in a house built upon – and haunted by – our ghosts.

22 February, 2023.

HOW TO UNFURL YOUR SOUL'S WINGS

Café Locked Out travels the country looking for Australians brave enough to take on the invading and consuming silence with nothing other than their voice. We are also welcomed by hosts who are all passionate and brave defenders of free speech.

Freedom of speech is a hard-earned gift from our past generations. A holy tool from which you can fix problems, and construct not only your dreams, but a world where your children can realise theirs. It is the liberating weapon you need to tackle all those who wish to conceal you under the cage of who they think you should be, and how they think you should think and feel.

Did you really fight your way out of the nothingness to reach this miraculous light, just to be a quiet slave?

To give birth to new slaves?

I know you know the answer. And I also know that you have everything you need inside you to become a beacon of hope for the ones here who are lost and those who are yet to come.

And all you need to do to activate that version of you – which "fear" fears the most – is to find your own courage.

And once you do, with ears you didn't know you possessed, you will hear angels cheer, and feel God – who is always waiting within you – nod and smile, for he will know that you have just begun the inner journey to find what he wanted you to find: his greatest gift, the Holy Grail, which is the noblest and strongest version of you.

That version of you – who will allow a piece of heaven to reach and bless this earth.

For now, no matter what they do, they will never be able to enslave you, for your heart will beat to the drum of liberty, and your soul, fuelled by your own courage and God's good light, will have finally broken their chains of fear binding the wings we were all born with – the wings they have always tried, and they are trying now, to conceal, for they fear them.

Those human wings; your wings, that freedom of speech can unfurl.

10 April, 2023.

FREEDOM'S MECHANICS

Bill's front yard is a movie set for a great novel as yet unwritten. The middle-aged forest borders the undulating paddock, overlooked by Bill's dogs, who sleep on the veranda and watch the winding dirt road for visitors to bark at.

Hidden in the low rolling hills behind Port Macquarie, the floor of the trees that circle the great shed is populated with cars waiting to be restored, sold, or wrecked. While they wait, the forest, in its own time, decorates their rusting bodies with lush creepers.

One decaying bus is now a platform for a staghorn that offers its hands of leaves to the sun. The quiet trees are dappled with light. Imagine foxes giving birth in the back seat of a Corolla, or rats stealing insulation from under bonnets to make warm nests for their offspring, who will grow among the engines – fading dreams that drivers once imbued them with. Even now, as I travel far away, I can see these cars in my mind's eye and hear them yearning to be rescued by other drivers' dreams.

Inside the cathedral of a shed, with its hoists and dirt bikes waiting to be repaired, all manner of tools and parts from forgotten vehicles have found a place to call their own. High above, fat spiders wait quietly in dusty webs for the never-ending supply of bugs drawn to the suspended LED lights.

At night, while waiting for sleep in Florence, the music of these insects was so loud I could almost see their waves rolling above me. Each instrument calling for love. Was this music an endless ballad of loneliness, or were they making love above and all around me, praising their luck with a symphony – just a brief piece of their joyous prayer?

Florence is up on stands, her front wheels removed. Phil, Rosco, and Bill are around her, bringing all their expertise to the many problems she has.

Phil has busied himself fixing her dents, while Bill started on the injectors. Since the parts for them wouldn't be ready for days, this shed, this farm, became my home once again – if only briefly.

I doubt the New World Order will ever know that these men and this shed exist, yet if it wasn't for Klaus Schwab, I would never have found this property – this haven of mechanical and spiritual solace. The forest is deep and hungry, conjuring monsters from the crackling movement of kangaroos and bush turkeys – creatures who somehow escaped our desire to farm birds like them for food. Down at the fence line, a deep creek ebbs toward the ocean, its tributaries feeding the unspoken wisdom of its flow, including the soft, deepening lines in Bill's face. If there are fish in there, no doubt their wet scales in the sunlight would gleam like the flashes of humour in Bill's eyes.

We call them the resistance mechanics. I'm only one of a stream of travelling freedom fighters who come seeking shelter, to talk about life and the challenges of our unfolding world, while laughing at anything that tickles our funny bone. And so often, we are laughing.

Bill is jabbed – so he thought he would be safe. He took two doses just to travel to Vietnam, where he could finally join friends for those wild motorbike rides, crisscrossing the country in a blur of jungle haze and freedom. The first shot passed without a ripple, but the second hit like a thunderclap: during a routine training ride near home, he was climbing off his trail bike, ripping off his gear, and collapsing to the ground as his heart hammered at an impossible speed. Would those slow-passing clouds be the last thing he'd see? Yet, despite submitting to the jabs, he, like so many others, was barred from travel for months.

Those pains have now passed, but he monitors himself as if a timebomb ticks in his veins. The anger from this is discernible but never used against us.

Rosco never took it. As Florence is dented from my driving, Rosco's heart and soul are dented from life. There are unrepaired cracks from his youth that I won't share here. His long-time, on-and-off girlfriend was killed by the jab after obediently listening to her doctor instead of Rosco.

Despite the damage, there is deep kindness in his eyes, and I could always feel his empathy with these new nerve endings I've come to trust as much as my critical thinking.

In the shed lives an old cat. Rosco found it in a past backyard, dumped, starving, and cold. He took it in and has cared for it ever since. When he leaves, it cries out for him as Phil and Bill, with good humour and gentle tones, try to soothe the cat's concerns, repeatedly informing it that Rosco will be back soon.

Rosco almost died recently. He began to feel ill but, not wanting to go to hospital because he is unjabbed, tried to tough it out. When Bill asked me to check on him, it was clear he had had or was having a stroke. For a second opinion, I called a doctor, suspended for questioning the narrative. Over a video call, he agreed, and Rosco went to hospital. While he has made a remarkable recovery, he is slower now as he works as Bill's assistant.

Both he and Phil live in buses that will never drive again.

Phil, also unjabbed, makes a living buying cars cheaply, fixing them up, and selling them. His record is 42 cars in one year. Every car is a problem, and he fixes them with bush mechanic ingenuity and patience.

I won't share his backstory, but I will share his kindness and energy. He worked on Florence tirelessly, and she now has a heater for the colder nights.

Each evening there, I went live on Café Locked Out from the shed.

Afterward, Bill and I shared organic Brussels sprouts while he, Rosco, and I talked about the maelstrom – the world racing around the calm eye of this shed.

When it comes to leaving, a part of me always wants to stay, to learn the tools and live at their pace – the pace of trees, the pace of eagles gliding over the land, the pace of men who find kinship and purpose.

But leave I must, bouncing over the long dirt road that winds to this shed, with Florence below and around me, feeling and sounding like a refreshed warrior bear.

If our country were an ageing bus, these three men – freedom fighters in the mechanical ranks – could not only have fixed her but, because of their skill, kindness, and love for their country, we would be a different people as we drove into whatever future others, whom we'll never meet, are attempting to build for us.

I can see some of the people I've met on my travels now, transformed into cars. Their dents are rusting, and under spreading creepers, animals make love and create families in their bowels as they wait for the men in the shed – souls hewn from the cloth once called what it takes to be an Australian man – to come down and begin their repair.

Like they repaired me.

19 May, 2023.

THE FRAGRANCE OF HOPE

Australia has plants that need something brutal to happen in order for them to germinate: fire.

Drive through a burnt forest a few months after the flames have passed, and below the blackened trees standing as hopeless as gravestones, you will find around their base a new dawn of bright green leaves.

Come back in a year, and these shoots will have become the architects of their new forest.

Covid was our culture's great fire, and you – the Freedom Movement, in all its forms – have been busily establishing yourselves. Thanks to all the members for your ever-growing ingenuity, resilience, and determination, our future could be yours to create.

You, I believe, are the architects of the new Australia.

I can see a country built upon the integrity of your souls.

Whilst this is an enormous challenge and a life-changing blessing that can offer you deep purpose, it also comes with great responsibility – a responsibility you have already proven you are worthy of.

The councils are already reacting to your growth and persistence, trying their best to lock out your voice. But it won't work for long. Come the elections, you will win seats; I know because this is already happening. I've seen it.

All over the country, networks are being created, and as some fall over for various reasons, stronger ones are established on their collapse as you learn from your mistakes. You are all living proof that failure is the essential and inescapable path to success. When you are not frightened of failing, you are unstoppable.

Our ideas, our actions, will become the legends of our new country: Stand in the Park, live-streamed reporting, The Forest of the Fallen, My

Place, and others, and of course, the birthplace of the Australian Freedom Movement, Camp Epic.

And new ideas, like 8:32, will keep coming, because we will harvest them from the forest where all our ideas are created – the Wild Forest of Free Speech.

A freedom that, despite their censorship, we have stoically defended.

Always, I hear you bouncing ideas off each other – vigorous, explorative conversations where fresh ideas are inspected and challenged, yet the owner of the idea isn't judged.

This is because the owner is a free-thinking individual, and our tribe not only values free thinkers but offers another precious freedom: the ability to be yourself, to choose for yourself, to think for yourself, to speak for yourself. Those freedoms will be the engine of our victory.

I don't know when, but we will win.

But before we reach that victory, there are some things we must do. First, we must forgive the others – not our leaders, but their followers, our brothers and sisters. One reason we must do this is strategy.

We have significant challenges heading our way, and our best chance of overcoming them is with greater numbers – their numbers.

So, how do we attract them back to freedom? What should our marketing campaign look like?

We don't need to create a marketing campaign because we already have one: you.

We need you to continue to be you.

Every time you are out there being yourself, it is like taking a lap of victory. Bit by bit, one by one, the rest will see it, get it, want it, need it.

And if they don't, forgiving helps too. We have important, essential work to do, and since we are proceeding regardless, we need to journey forward with clean souls – as clean as the leaves of fresh shoots growing after a bushfire.

We don't have time to waste on resentment and bitterness – that is a power they will hold over you. Free yourself from their judgment, which we know was flawed. I know it's hard, but let it go.

You don't need their acknowledgment, and what they need is guidance, love, and you.

One by one, they will come to realise that.

The third thing we need is a destination – an idea of what our new Australia will look like.

Or so I thought. But I was wrong. We can already see it – not with our eyes, but with our needs, with our actions.

The Covid fire might be passing, but what it has done has been good for us. We have now reached a point where our dead wood and the weeds that entangled us from decades of easy living have been burned off by segregation, by how you bravely did what was right, not what was popular, by your willingness to accept and endure pain – even when the end to this pain wasn't in sight – by the courage you had to defend your freedom.

You are now the foundation of the Australian Freedom Movement, a brand-new tribe that, despite all its persecution, loves to give and help others.

We may not have articulated it, but together we have learned the profoundly deep power of empathy.

To a coward, empathy looks like weakness, but to us we know it is stronger than fear.

They can't build a sustainable culture that anyone would want to live in on fear, whereas we can build a warm country, a free country, a lucky country, upon empathy.

That is our destination. That is where all our compasses are pointing. Can you see it?

I can, and I don't even have to dream. There it is – an Australia we are building upon the greatest foundation block in the universe: love.

When they cast you out, they expected you to fold, to come back begging on your knees, or – if you refused – to die out there, alone.

But you didn't do any of those things. Instead, you have become our beautiful plumb line in the sand, the blueprint upon which we will build a better country for our children and those yet to be born.

And finally, there is one more discovery I have made.

Thanks to you, I have learned that the hope we've created emits a fragrance – a fragrance I first smelled in the marches in Melbourne, a fragrance reaching out to us from the future that has imbued itself into my soul.

So, what does it smell like, this fragrant hope you are all creating?

At first, I thought it smelled like the promise of victory. But then I realised it was more than a promise. Now I know that this fragrance of hope is the scent of our new Australia, reaching out to us like a beacon from the future.

A fragrance that smells to me like home.

20 May, 2023.

SUSPENDED DR WILLIAM BAY'S VICTORY

ONE FORM OF true history doesn't rely on natural catastrophes but on the way individuals face fear.

If they comply without a rigorous challenge, then within history they will be a statistic; but if they rise to meet fear face-to-face, their spines rigid with belief and the determination of purpose, their souls — those liberated souls — overflowing with freedom, then come what may, these people can become pauses in history, moments of clarity that ripple through the following pages in warm currents of hope.

Without them, risking everything to drag us out of the ever-hungry clutches of fear, we could be lost forever inside our heavily surveilled, materialistic desert.

They are the guardians of our humanity; and to date — despite all the fear, the death, the wars, the despots — humanity has survived.

Now it is under attack again, and once more the guardians are rising.

There were faeces on the concrete floor of the holding cell: shit mixed with dried blood, stale urine, and William's cold bare feet. He had no contact with the outside world — no knowledge that people were ringing the Brisbane Watch House continually, asking how he was and demanding his release.

Seven times they came back to him with bail conditions, every one designed to make him agree he would not return to the city and protest outside the high-rise that housed his enemy: AHPRA, the Australian Health Practitioner Regulation Agency.

When I first saw him in court, locked inside a glass witness box, he wore no fear. All their bullying had slipped from his skin like water. The magistrate – who could plainly see no law had been broken – released him "at large" (his words). A little later, in blue scrubs, Billy walked out of the watch-house smiling the smile of a new man. He knew he had been tested, and he had passed.

Any last doubt inside him had been answered. Instead of using fear to destroy him, their bullying had made him grow; and with news of his victory going viral on the social platforms, he was now an even greater force to reckon with.

Alone – although he believes God helped him, and he could be right – his courage and conviction had beaten the system. Now, if AHPRA wants to stop him and his High Court challenge to their validity, they're out of soft options.

"Are you really a doctor?" one remand prisoner asked as Billy sat there in his blue scrubs.

"Suspended," said Billy.

"Then why are you in here?"

"I was defending free speech."

"Are you kidding?" said another prisoner. "What happened to our democracy?"

Outside, as William strode through the city workers with us all around and behind him, his head was up, his eyes bright; it was almost possible to believe he was glowing – a human lion striding back to the base of AHPRA.

Most passers-by had no knowledge – and less interest – yet Billy kept going, forging against their indifferent current.

If we survive – if we win, and by winning I mean dragging Australia back, or forward, to something better than this – then this man will be etched into our historical record, a landmark cemented on the road to liberty.

He will be there in his scrubs, head back, megaphone to his lips, one hand pointing forward – forever pointing toward the country he may never reach – but you might, thanks to the immense courage of people like suspended Doctor William Bay.

27 May, 2023.

THE LONG DRIVE

There is so much space out here – it's as if the gods left before they could bother with mountains, valleys, or grand forests. You could misplace an entire civilisation inside it.

We did, and they are still lost. On the beaches near Eucla – cliffs you have to climb down to reach – lie mounds of broken shellfish and the hand-chipped stones the indigenous used to prise them open thousands of years ago. Mounds that took generations to build, now replaced by nothing. No resorts overlook the serene ocean, which wave by wave keeps carving the cliffs of the Great Australian Bight.

You could scream until your lungs burst; no one would hear except the odd crow flapping over to see if you might end up on its menu. Even the earth-shaking roar of a road train is swallowed whole by the space, then forgotten in the silence.

How did she not simply veer off this straight, endless road, her grief and rage combing the plain for anywhere to escape the loss? This woman we encountered.

A few weeks earlier, half-protected by shock, she and her husband had driven this same highway toward Kalgoorlie. They were from Adelaide; they had just been told their eldest son was dead. He'd driven off the road in Kalgoorlie itself, but witnesses said he was already slumped over the wheel. He'd been vaccinated – no choice. He loved the mines, and the mines had given him the ultimatum. Now his body would join those minerals, or at least it would once they finally got it back.

Allegation: the coroner was holding the body in Perth because Premier Mark McGowan was also in Kalgoorlie, coaxing a reluctant town to get jabbed, and the last thing the government needed was local evidence the jabs could kill. Allegations, like we said.

In town she still had another son. Police had asked him to identify his brother's body. He believed the jab had killed him – had seen his brother black out at the wheel before the car left the road. Yet, mad for karate, he took the shot so he could return to class. It paralysed him. Now the grieving parents had two boys to care for: one in a coffin, one in a wheelchair.

At last she arranged for the eldest to be freighted to Adelaide.

All she had to do was get herself home. But times had changed.

State borders were welded shut. Days on the phone to the South Australian government made no promise that when she reached Ceduna – the South Australian edge of the vast Nullarbor Plains – anyone would let her in. She might have to swing round and drive 1800 kilometres back, alone – if Western Australia even let her back. The nearest checkpoint lay 480 kilometres behind her.

In Ceduna a caravan park bulged with West Australians waiting for their own border to reopen – refugees in their country, punished for refusing the needle. Crazy, yet this was the arithmetic she faced: alone, leaving her husband to nurse their now-paralysed son, she started the long drive home to bury the other.

These were the stories Australia's mainstream media never told the public – and by their negligence and deceit, they failed in their duty of care.

The Nullarbor is never busy. In ordinary times there might be a car or truck every ten minutes; in that season, almost none. The Nullarbor became not just one of the longest straight roads on Earth but the loneliest.

Even at a thousand kilometres a day she would still have miles to go, slabs of it without internet except near the roadhouses, sometimes 300 kilometres apart. A tourist in simpler times might call the flat view boring; might call it spiritual. How often do you travel through country where, standing on your car's roof, you become the tallest feature? Where the clouds have room to tell entire stories – dark storms to the right promising to chase you, caravans of cumulus migrating to a horizon you will never kiss.

But with your heart torn open, the only thread holding her together was the stubborn need to cross a border so she could bury her boy, and for her, so totally grief-stricken, the road must have stretched forever.

Unvaccinated, she would sleep in the car – roadhouses refused her a bed and made her mask up to buy a sandwich. Did she find God out there? If she was the only soul from horizon to horizon, He wouldn't have trouble spotting her; no queue would block her from His throne where she could ask what was the point of knitting this miracle inside me, letting him grow into my young man bristling with dreams, only to leave him broken in a wreck.

His name will never be etched on a shrine celebrating the sacrifice he – and so many others – made for the community. No day will mark their loss, no apology will come. Only silence, the same silence buffering the car while she tried to sleep under the immensity.

Then, finally, the border. By now every defence was armed; no one would stop her entering. She had decided, and the closer she came to Ceduna, the fiercer the resolve. She was a grizzly bear mother separated from her cub – good luck to any official who stepped between them.

But no one tried. The border station was shuttered, lights off. She lost it then, she told me – after all that tension she wanted to ram the barrier. Instead she drove on to Adelaide, still nine hours away.

She isn't rich, isn't famous; no government note will ever acknowledge her loss. She is simply a middle-aged woman you could pass in a mall without noticing – an Australian suburbanite who reached the funeral her husband could not attend.

There, masked mourners – limited in number by government mandate – gathered in silence, none allowed to mention why they were there, that being the rule of the greater hush smothering the country. She completed her duties and said goodbye to the boy whose face and story, every weekend, now drift back and forth in the breezes that move through the people's unofficial shrine: the Forest of the Fallen.

1 June 2023.

RISE, MY SILENT BROTHERS, RISE

When I was three, my Uncle David – who was a living superhero to me – pulled me onto his lap and let me steer his delivery van through the streets of our small town in Wales. And as I giggled, I pissed my pants while he laughed. This is my clearest, earliest memory – and I'm amazed I can still find it.

Fortunately, even though I was only a little boy, I'd cleverly filed it under the category called "a man". A while later, when I was about ten, my family was picnicking near a waterfall in South Australia. The waterfall had a natural slide, and teenage boys were sliding down it. Then, as we all watched, an excited toddler staggered out onto the rocks and slipped.

Chances are he would have slid right over the edge and we would have lost him. But death never got a chance to retrieve him, because as soon as he fell, several fathers leapt from their picnic blankets and ran over the rocks to grab him.

This memory I stored under the category called "men".

Any of these fathers could also have slipped and been hurt – or worse. And that injury, or their own death, could have put their families in deep distress. But did they think about that? No. They were so motivated to save a child who wasn't theirs that they all ran into the same category in my memory called "the protectors".

I have loads of these categories and subcategories, but the only man who has his own category is my father. My father is a philosopher and a poet. Yet you would never know it, because he was born into a generation of silent men who were taught to keep all their poetry in their heads.

Every day he walks up a hill near his home in Western Australia, and once he reaches the summit, he sits on a log I call the Altar of Red Church Hill, from where he watches Perth wake up. "I wrote a poem once, in which I hoped that one day the Fremantle Doctor – a famous cooling wind that annually relieves the summer heat in the far southwest – would blow all his poetry out of his head and transport it across the country into mine."

He is to me a foundation I can never live up to, a mountain I can never climb, an ocean I can never swim across nor reach the floor of.

Now he is spending the last days of his life caring for my mother as she deteriorates first. And he does so with the humility, humour, and dependability of a stone – a stone that has a heart full of love.

Before Covid, I was talking to my dad about society's current view of men, and he said, "Now I'm the enemy."

We live in a time where our questions are many and unanswered, and our souls are constantly flabbergasted. It's like some weird reality show slipped out of our TVs and conquered us.

Yesterday, I was watching a man complain that although his baby had latched onto his nipple, he wasn't yet producing milk.

But I've been wondering if the reason the Covid fog found it so easy to smother us was because the powers that be had already disempowered our men.

When I was growing up, women's toilets were off-limits, or as we used to call it in kindergarten and grade one when we were all playing Kiss Chasey – "bar-less", which meant out of bounds. Kiss Chasey was a part of my generation's childhood – where the boys chased the girls and if they caught one were allowed a peck on the cheek. But no boys were allowed near the girls' toilets. Not ever.

Now, I often have women complaining to me that they no longer have a toilet in the city for themselves. To me, if you asked most men, they would agree to call the ladies' toilets for what they are: sacred ground for women's business. When you're out with a few friends and the girls go to the loo, you know you have time to get another beer or two.

To men, the toilet is just a tool. You go, do your business, and get out – and you do all of this in silence.

When I was growing up, many pubs had men-only sections, but these spaces are gone now, challenged into oblivion by women. But I'm okay with female-only places. I feel women should have their own space, where they can go and do whatever. Yet at the same time, I believe that the mental health of men would benefit from having places where only men could go.

A place and time to unwind, to laugh with – or be laughed at by – your brothers, who you can heal as they heal you, without any woke psychologist ever comprehending how they're achieving this.

"I don't get it. They don't even have deep conversations. They just whinge, brag, and joke, all while taking the piss out of each other."

But that is not true. The language of men is subtle and learned. It's spoken in barely imperceptible nods and in cuss words used to convey affection. For they are all aware they have the ability to conceal more trauma than one soul should ever be allowed to bear – under nothing other than silence.

This is some of my learned mythology of men.

But now, thanks to the actions of my brothers in these last few years, I am questioning it.

Never in my time have I experienced such a level of compliance. I have seen and heard men who previously questioned everything now telling me that sometimes you just don't question – you just do what you're told.

At first, I managed to process this by seeing these men as soldiers who saw Covid as the enemy. The mask was their shield. Their own houses, where they were locked in, their foxholes – from where they fought to defend their families and community by being obedient.

And I get it. I was briefly caught up in this battle plan too, until very quickly certain things stopped making sense.

And as one thing stopped making sense, suddenly – like tumbling dominoes – everything began to fail. Suddenly, I was locked up and watching as all our liberties were removed without a murmur of resistance.

It was then I called my father and asked what he thought of the unfolding events. He said, with a tone deep in thought:

"I think they are intending to cull us."

Me too, I said. Me too. And we were connected.

Then, a short while later, he went and got himself – and my mother – jabbed. Twice. Thrice they cancelled their first appointments. But on the fourth, they did it. Since then, I've heard him holding onto two conflicting views in his head – congratulating me one moment for holding out, then urging me in the next breath to get jabbed, because he doesn't want to see me in hospital on a respirator.

I didn't realise then how lonely I was becoming, as around me men began doing things I never thought I'd see them do. Driven by fear, they started ostracising family and friends. Mates who I'd fought in union campaigns with – who I took for granted were natural-born renegades – not only decided to comply, but attacked or cut me out of their lives because I wouldn't.

And no day highlighted the severity of this ostracisation as much as the first Covid Christmas.

Before then, Christmas was a day where family members, even those who spent the entire year out of touch, would come together for a few hours – like an awkward prayer to the power of love.

But that year, in houses decorated with illuminated Christmas trees and crowned by the Star of Bethlehem, love – or if you prefer, God – was defeated by fear.

A few months later, on Anzac Day, the forces of fear defeated God again, as fear – proudly wearing all the medals of our fathers and grandfathers – rested its hand on our betrayed hearts. Those soldiers, and the families of soldiers, who refused to comply were not allowed to attend the Dawn Service.

And although many women were a part of this too, the tragedy to me was that the men not only allowed this to pass, but insulted the ultimate sacrifice of those who had fought and died for our freedom with three words, spoken repeatedly and condescendingly: "Just get jabbed."

But another remarkable Christmas Day happened during World War I, when along the line men from both sides emerged from the trenches and played soccer.

If you put 100 red ants and 100 black ants in a jar, they will just get on with their lives.

But if you shake that jar, the red and black ants will attack each other, believing the other side is attacking them.

This analogy carries over to all our demographics – black and white, Muslim and Christian, vaccinated and un-jabbed.

The solution is to pause and try – as a team – to ascertain who is shaking the jar.

And on that Christmas Day, on the frozen mud of no man's land – coated with the broken dreams and blood of their brothers – those men must have realised that they weren't each other's enemy. That they weren't the ones shaking the jar. That somewhere people they'd never met – the rich and powerful who would never visit these trenches – were the ones shaking it.

And as they watched each other kick the ball, they must have realised too that their noble sacrifice was actually a communal betrayal. They must have also understood that they had all the guns. If they wanted, they could have agreed to stop fighting each other there and then, and after turn their weapons on the generals. They could have all returned to their loved ones.

On the Russian front, this happened – yet it still all went to shit.

I believe French soldiers also rose up. But not our boys. Like the Germans, they got back into the trenches and started fighting and killing and dying all over again.

Why?

A good friend who initially was on our side – to the point of coming onto early episodes of Café Locked Out, where he called the pandemic for what it was – suddenly vanished.

When I finally got hold of him, he had gotten jabbed. He was almost 60, in great health, and didn't need a job – his house was paid off. And all he could say – the last time he spoke to me – was: "Well, I've always had bosses. Eventually, you have to do what they say."

Since then, I found out his real boss – his sister – threatened to excommunicate him from his only family (her and her two kids, whom he adored) unless he complied.

Everywhere I've travelled in the last few years, I've been asked one question: "Where are the men?"

Our men have been duped – given a false enemy to fight (Covid-19), a uniform to don (the mask), and a weapon to fight with (the vaccine). They were given what most men crave: a purpose. Save our community.

But I believe the lie runs deeper than this.

Men have been fighting another world war for decades – a war aimed directly at them. And they've fought this war silently, with their hands tied behind their backs.

If you used the word "toxic" to describe any other demographic, there would be an uproar. But masculinity? Knock yourself out.

We've had mothers saying how they're retraining their little boys not to become rapists.

We've forced our young men to stand up in front of all the girls in school and apologise – not just for being boys, but for the sins of their fathers.

This war is the real enemy. Mature white males have even attempted to remove the word "man" from our language and universities. In some universities, you can lose points for using the word "man" in your essays.

And this war has been relentless and effective. Its victims are measured by our outrageous male suicide rate, and the men who drink or drug themselves to death. The survivors? Most just stay silent.

In The Art of War, Sun Tzu argues that the most successful type of war is one where your opponent doesn't even know he's in a war.

Right here, right now – it's our time to enter no man's land and play soccer as we ponder who is actually shaking our jar.

All through history, these moments have happened. What they are is a rare point in time where you, my brothers, can choose not to be a nameless statistic, but a member of a movement that came together and redefined history.

Covid was an act of marketing genius that blew away all the mythology of this country. Currently, we have no identity. All our souls are up for grabs as the next war – the one that promises to reclassify most of us as redundant – is already here.

But you have a choice. You can continue to be compliant and let whoever is shaking our jar shake us deeper into totalitarianism, where we all become a shameful stain in the history of this land. Or you can accept the responsibility of our communal destiny and help us take back our beloved country and all our God-given freedoms.

And your reward for achieving this future is that once again, you will be able to call yourselves men.

I believe there is a God. What form He takes, or if He has an agenda – what it is – I don't know.

But what I do know is that you were not born to be a slave.

You were born to be the tested hero that one day the sons of our sons will celebrate. For history is not pre-written. It is a series of decisions.

And right now, my brothers, that decision is ours – and it is crucial. This is why I implore you – not just for the future, or for the present, but for yourselves – shrug off this long, marketed anti-male campaign, and join your brave women, and together we can fight our way back to a place where we can once again stand proud as we sing our national anthem with gusto.

For its words – thanks to you, and your decision to act – will no longer be a lie.

And more importantly, since we all know that boys have always learned how to be men by observing older men, you will once again become what our communal sons need: mentors, destinations, or – like my Uncle David, the delivery driver once was to me when I was a small boy – a hero I could see, a hero who was a man.

15 June 2023.

HAS DAZELLE BEEN SENT BACK TO US FROM THE LIGHT?

As the rest of us were journeying through lockdowns and mandates, one young girl in NSW was battling leukemia. After going through chemo, she was offered a bone marrow transplant—and she briefly won – until the DNA of the donor attacked its new host, and this new battle saw all of her organs shut down as Dazelle descended into a coma.

On life support her family was told to prepare for the worst. She was not expected to live. Her father, who like her mother was unvaccinated, was finally allowed in to see her.

He found his daughter sprouting tubes, surrounded by machines. As he pleaded with her unconscious spirit to fight, he was unaware that somewhere Dazelle was walking in a place free of pain.

Above her, shooting stars streaked the sky – and she felt so very tired.

Eventually she came to an illuminated bridge. Figures she couldn't see clearly – blurred by the blinding light – called to her from the other side. But as she stepped forward to cross, a man with long hair, his face too radiant to make out, rested a hand on her shoulder. "Not this way," he said. "I want you to go back."

Somewhere in their exchange, he told her his name.

Following this, she immediately woke up – and the first thing she asked her relieved mother, once the tubes were removed, was, "Who was Ely – or Elohim?" She then recounted the whole dream to her.

But despite returning, her body was still in the wars. What she needed now was a double lung transplant, and here is the second part of the story.

Her surgeon told her that not only did he doubt she'd survive until the transplant, but that unless she agreed to take four Covid shots, she wouldn't even be considered.

Following this, he asked her father, in her presence, what he did for a living, for even if she did survive, her medication would be very expensive.

And this is where Australia heard about Dazelle. Ironically the hospital is a Catholic hospital.

I went to visit the family for an in-person interview rather than over Zoom. What I found was a household scraping by in poverty – their every ounce of energy and time poured into saving their daughter – yet brimming with love. The family was bound so tightly it felt like invisible glue held them fast.

"And in the middle of them was this lovely young woman, who explained to me that she simply didn't want the jabs. It wasn't her parents, it wasn't us – it was an inner voice and her own critical thinking."

As I travel through Australia's unprepossessing country towns – under the shadows of their own humble and heartbreaking shrines of remembrance, and past the banners proclaiming "Get your Flu Shot here" – I think about the freedoms we have previously risked and sacrificed our young men and women for.

One of those is freedom of choice, and here's where it gets complicated.

If there is any part of you that still believes, then it appears that God sent this young girl back to us – but to do what? Die because she refuses to comply with our vaccination requirements?

From my point of view, I see a young girl – aglow – standing before the giants of Big Pharma, our medical establishment, and our government, all demanding her compliance. With defiant voice, she stares back up at them and declares, "I want my freedom."

The other issues this sad tale has uncovered are that it appears that society will take the organs of the unvaccinated and give them to the vaccinated.

Their reasons are that there are very few organs to go around, and due to autoimmune issues, they have to be respectful to the family who allowed the organs of their deceased family member to be shared.

While I understand this, it appears our unvaccinated organs are good enough to be harvested, but we unvaccinated are not worthy enough to receive them. This is why, after having been on the Organ Donor registry since I was a young man, I am removing myself.

Other unvaccinated people are telling me they are doing the same.

26 June, 2023.

DR BRUCE PAIX IS AN AUSTRALIAN ROGUE BULL

FROM BEHIND HIM the horse rested its great chin on Bruce's shoulder and lit the veteran's face with a smile born of simple appreciation. Later his two little cats will do the same, settling on his lap because dinner-time is near.

With these hands – now stroking the ginger tom called Mao – he has, for 32 years, pulled strangers back from the lip of death. An anesthetist by trade, he spent most of those years in rescue helicopters: the doctor who dropped out of the sky when you were trying not to drop any further. A stranger who joined your fight armed with skill, a gently disarming wit, and a heart so big you could see its warmth beating behind his focused eyes. Seven war-zones, volunteer fire-grounds, more, much more – sucking the marrow out of time by living on the edge where, ironically, most of us met him.

Then Covid struck and he had questions, pages of them, emailed to his local Member of Parliament. The MP sent the police instead.

Bruce filmed the visit. The officer explains the emails "have come to our attention" and are "drawing attention to you, which you probably don't need or want".

Paix pushes: "So I'm not allowed robust discussions with my MP?"

The cop admits no crime has been committed; he's simply "letting you know we're aware".

Bruce hasn't shaved since they jailed him.

Mandates arrived; he lost his job. To stall the incoming tsunami he pointed his ute toward Canberra and the biggest protest the capital would ever see. While others camped in the library car-park, Bruce was arrested en-route to the airport – accused of trying to run over a man building a road-block.

Six days in a shoebox isolation cell, strip-searched, cut off, exorcised by the State from the country he'd bled for.

Eventually the charges collapsed; every testifying officer was shown to be lying. When they finally released him he climbed on the back of a truck and toured the world's first temporary anti-vaxxer city – Epic Park in the north of Canberra – received as what we all knew he was: a hero.

Now he's self-exiled on a scrap of a farm that lets us borrow tools to patch Florence the Freedom Bus.

How do we as a country benefit from stopping Bruce doing what Bruce does best – saving people's lives?

How did we reach the point where living national treasures, medical specialists who question the reigning orthodoxy, are punished? Parallel, anyone, with early-stage communist states that shoot their giants first to frighten the rest?

Last year on a remote cattle station Luke White, another hero, ran down a defiant rogue bull with a Mad-Max four-wheel-drive buggy. Trapped beneath, the beast snorted fury while cowboys bound his hooves, leaving him under the vast afternoon sky until the meat-truck arrived at dawn.

Luke told me, driving off in search of more bulls, that farmers must root out the rogues. Born wild, never handled, they've spent years believing they own the scrub. That freedom surges through veins and balls. Left intact they'll sire a herd ready to fight rather than walk politely into the final yard.

The Brahmas we ignored – big showy things with no fight in their balls. They breed compliant cows and father slaves.

Slaves are easier to handle, Luke shrugged.

Another year into documenting what looks like the orchestrated decline of my culture – I sit on the porch listening to a rogue bull – this man, this great doctor – sure the cowboys masquerading as police, maybe even the Australian army, will come for him soon.

History, he smiles, read it. It's all in there.

Ever heard of a country that stopped totalitarianism while it was forming? I ask.

He answers with a wry smile. The cat purrs in his ageing, healing hands while he watches the storm dressing itself in shades of darkness across his land.

The sad thing, Bruce says, is that in the face of this gathering storm all they have to do is say no.

It was raining when I wrote this; drops tapped the bus roof as I tapped the keys.

Tomorrow we leave at first light – the road to whoever-knows-where calling in a tone that makes sleep impossible.

21 September, 2023.

BUDGIE DREAMING

OUT HERE, ON the edge of the Little Sandy Desert that flows into the larger Gibson Desert, the land – to my eyes – appeared averse to life. From the safety of our spaceship, Florence the Freedom Bus, everything seemed to be struggling to survive. On the verge of death. The anorexic trees didn't grow very high, and we rarely saw any animals. The few creeks we drove over and stopped to explore supported not fish, but the footsteps of all the thirsty ghosts – both animals and birds – that had scoured the damp mud, now dry and cracked with the fading memory of water. The sky, too, was a distant and indifferent ceiling, owned by the sun, who – with little else to do but burn – was using this land as her anvil.

We would not survive out here for long – not with our eyes. But when we pulled over to interview four Indigenous elders, who were sitting around a large campfire cooking kangaroo tails, they tried to show us the same land through their eyes.

To them, this was not a wasteland, but their mother's pantry. To them, the clues to food were everywhere – even the little finches, frantic and perched in the emaciated trees, were guides who would lead them, if needed, to water.

They had no fear of being lost out here. It was questionable whether they could be lost – whereas I, after almost fifty-five years of living in this country, realised that this was why I would always be a tourist. For despite their gentle, warm laughter as they tried to point out the tracks of bush turkeys, I couldn't see them.

Then again, perhaps the fact that the kangaroo tails they were cooking hadn't come from kangaroos they'd hunted themselves – but from the only shop in their town, an IGA, where they were wrapped in Gladwrap, complete with barcodes – perhaps that was a clue. Could they really still read the land? Or had they come out here to sit on their milk crates and have a picnic with the memories of their ancestors?

But then, as we were driving to the next town – down a highway guarded by crows, confidently perched on the summits of the roadkill kangaroos, each a demigod who would only bother to fly away lazily as the road trains (four trailers each) barrelled past – we started to see large flocks of wild budgerigars.

Like punks, they were tearing through the stunted trees, as though, as one, they had broken free from some chain gang and were now communally on the run. And it was clear, by their speed and their joy, that they had no intention of being caught.

As I watched them I wondered how hard their life must be out here – where probably everything wanted to eat them. These wild chicken nuggets, whose only defence was speed and the safety of the flock.

But what did they eat? Where did they drink? Where did they build their nests, and how did they defend those nests when they were so small?

I wondered if any of them knew that millions of their kin were spending their lives safe and warm in small cages, where their seed – mixed and balanced for a healthy diet – was always supplied, and their plastic water bowl never ran dry. Jammed between their bars would be a dried cuttlefish for them to sharpen their beaks upon. Some would be kept in bigger aviaries, where they'd be allowed to breed. And over the years, their keepers had bred them into various colours – some so rare they were entered into competitions at local fairs, even national ones – as breeders competed to produce the perfect budgerigar.

And all of this came free of charge – for the budgie. In fact, each time they spoke or sang, they were rewarded with the smiling face of a human, who, in turn, would talk to them through the bars.

Chances are, these pet budgerigars lived far longer lives. And all these benefits came at the minuscule cost of one concession: the freedom to fly.

And until I watched these flocks of green hoodlums tear over this harsh landscape, I never knew that budgies were capable of flying like this.

And by this, I mean: as though they were the princes of all they could see. For despite the sound of my bus's engine, I could hear the joy in their tiny voices, celebrating as they vanished into the distance – unaware that they were the legendary source and destination of all those caged budgies' dreams.

1 October, 2023.

A VISION FOR AN ALTERNATIVE AUSTRALIA

When I close my eyes to the mess we're in, I can see the other Australia waiting – one brave heartbeat past the edge of sight.

Its streets look like ours, only every camera has been ripped out.

Schools stand there hungry – not to stuff kids full of answers but to teach them how to think, how to use the free tools life handed them so they can push every border of who they might become, then stitch their own bright patch into the national tapestry.

In those schools teachers will be revered because they live by one core lesson:

Nescis quam potens sis, sic disce.

"You don't know how powerful you are – so learn."

When we get there, our kids' sexuality will be theirs to discover at whatever pace they need, no pressure, no judgement. Childhood will be allowed to stay innocent for exactly as long as the child requires.

Cafés, bars, restaurants look familiar, but listen: people are talking – hot, pragmatic, wrestling the country's problems out loud. Free speech is the crowbar they use to crack open issues and fish for solutions hiding in the common ground that still joins us.

I see our men: heads up, chests out, striding the developing streets.

They've shouldered the job of nurturing and guarding this new Australia, soldering freedom and culture into place with work so worthy the worth itself tells them they matter.

Young mothers choose – office or home – neither side sneering at the other. The community long ago decided kids' health beats material gain, so cost-of-living is kept in check. Families won't be punished by poverty for wanting to be the parents they dream of being.

Medical clinics resemble ours – only doctors and nurses are allowed the time to build private relationships with patients. Government is absent from the room; the healer's pledge is empathy and truth, and people revere them for it.

Teenagers snap proud selfies with cops – police respected because they volunteered to be the heroes, ready to die for the creed "serve and protect."

Fresh places of worship: spiritual leaders free to become navigators for any soul needing solace or direction.

And journalists – larrikins, trouble-makers – guard the gate, yanking political correctness gags from politicians' mouths and hurling them into a museum we'll call Regret. Inside: lockdown photos, masks, rubber bullets – reminders of how fear almost herded us into an Australia we'd have been ashamed of. Lesson learned.

I can't map the problems they'll face once we get there, but I sense they'll meet them with courage, critical thought, and a reflex that always leans toward defending individual freedom.

Finally I see the natural leaders among us stepping up as politicians – driven to unite, to give us purpose through vision, communal and bold enough to make the other Australia real.

A Vision for an Alternative Australia dreams that the public are encouraged to be actively engaged in, as together they forge the policies that will affect us all.

Look further too and you will see businesses selling products that are manufactured to last, because the tradesmen have relearnt their community building skills, and will now teach these crafts to those who want to learn.

And there are flags flying everywhere, declaring how proud we are of what we have built and are building, and our national anthem is sung with gusto, for our lyrics are no longer our lie, but a foundation to build upon, and a dream to reach.

Can you see it? It is glowing in the distance, and reflected like a candle of hope, flickering in your children's eyes.

It is beckoning us towards it, for it wants us to paint its streets with all the miracles of our humanity.

And if you don't reach it, if you fall on the long journey there, then your courage, for at least setting out towards it, will become a guiding light for those following to navigate by.

Those who will one day reach this awaiting land; this revitalised Australia, that the rest of the world will look upon as proof that when determination uses courage for fuel, and love for measure, then we are all capable of amalgamating our hopes and dreams into a culture, so vibrant and inclusive, that each of our souls will know, that this is more than a country, this is our home.

7 December, 2023.

THE HARD BUT NECESSARY PATH

A post on X the other day got me thinking about who we are as Australians. Not the shallow stereotypes of barbecues and beaches, but something deeper, something we've lost in the noise of the last few years.

The pandemic didn't just lock us down, it fractured our sense of self. We were told who to be, what to think, and what to fear. Café Locked Out started to fight that, but it's become more than a fight – it's a search for who we should be.

We're not the same Australia I grew up in. That Australia was rough around the edges, but it was free. You could speak your mind, call out nonsense, and trust your neighbour. Now, we're divided, censored, and watched.

The digital leash tightens every day – cameras on streets, apps tracking our moves, laws creeping in to silence dissent. But I believe we can find our way back, not to the past, but to a better version of ourselves.

This path isn't easy. It means facing truths we've been trained to ignore. It means admitting we let fear override our principles. It means rebuilding trust, not in institutions, but in each other. Café Locked Out is trying to do that through stories, art, and conversations.

We're collecting the voices of Australians – truckies, nurses, poets, parents – who still believe in freedom, who still believe in us. These stories aren't just nostalgia; they're a map to something stronger.

The post on X asked, 'What makes us Australian?' I don't have the full answer, but I know it's not compliance or silence. It's the courage to question, the stubbornness to stand up, the mateship that binds us when things get tough. We're at a crossroads.

We can let this new Australia – timid, controlled, divided – take hold, or we can forge something else, something worthy of the sunburnt country we love.

Café Locked Out is all in on this. We're not just resisting; we're building. Every podcast, every poem, every rally is a step toward that deeper identity. But we can't do it alone. Talk to your mates, share the stories, make art, and sing songs. Be Australian, unapologetically. The path is hard, but it's necessary, and it starts with us.

Together, we can find our way.

13 December, 2023.

WE STAND WITH BARRY AND ALL WHO HAVE STOOD UP

BARRY YOUNG, A 56-year-old IT worker at New Zealand's Te Whatu Ora, became a global figure in December 2023 when he leaked a terabyte of Covid-19 vaccine data, alleging it showed significant vaccine-related deaths.

A mild-mannered database administrator, Young's act of defiance stemmed from his belief that the public deserved transparency about vaccine safety.

His leak, shared online and discussed with journalist Liz Gunn, suggested mortality rates far exceeding the official claim of only four vaccine-related deaths among 12 million doses in New Zealand. Young's data, analysed by figures like Steve Kirsch, indicated a potential 27% increase in all-cause mortality for vaccinated individuals, sparking worldwide debate.

Arrested on 3 December 2023 for "dishonest" data access, Young faced up to seven years in prison but pleaded not guilty, declaring, "I can't wait for the trial."

Released on bail, he was hailed as a whistle-blower by supporters, who rallied outside Wellington District Court, chanting for freedom.

The New Zealand government, led by Health Minister Shane Reti, dismissed his claims as misinformation, while Te Whatu Ora's Chief Executive Officer, Margie Apa, denied clinical validity.

Young's courage – risking liberty to expose perceived truths – resonated with me. I saw him as a legendary figure driven by love for others. His case, still pending as of April 2025, underscores the tension between individual bravery and institutional silence, galvanising the global freedom movement.

Café Locked Out is more than a group of independent media streamers; we are voices from the front line.

We are veterans in a strange war. Our greatest adversary is the apathy of our brothers and sisters. Australians whom we now know are being injured, or even worse. Australians who would probably say nothing if we were all imprisoned and/or removed from view. The Achilles heel of hubris is that it's blind to the power that has seen many tyrants fall. It is the power that can drive an apparently powerless individual to sacrifice their dreams, their liberty, and even their life for others.

It is the power of love.

Sometimes their sacrifices are recorded, but not often. And while history is not populated with such tales of success, our stories are.

From David and Goliath, The Lord of the Rings, to Braveheart, we crave to believe that those who seek to dominate us can be toppled by one act of bravery.

Barry Young – thanks to the circumstance giving him access to the data, and thanks too to his love of others – found the courage to bring his discoveries to the public. This is why he is already the stuff of legends.

A mild-mannered, law-abiding man, Barry slipped deep underneath the trust of the powerful, despite their passport to their better jobs; their jabs, not being in his veins.

They must have taken it for granted that he would keep their dark secrets silent, because, like many, he would be more interested in protecting his own mortgage, and all the other commodities that create his own little hill of beans.

But the soul of man is unpredictable. Its companions are the deeper voices that haunt it through intuition – voices rising from wherever we came from – and often all it offers in this realm, for listening to it, is misery and loss; but underneath that carnage a profound peace is waiting.

An inner place of peace those who would strive to subjugate us cannot recreate. In fact, they fear it, for they know that the only force that can show you this map, that can guide you to this place of solace, is the force they continually fail to erase: Love.

The future is always unwritten, but we have the tools to create a better one. All we need to do is control our fear, and learn the lesson that a love of the material will never decorate your heart like a love for each other.

I stand with Barry.

12 January, 2024.

THE SILENCE MUST END

The silence is a prison, and every day we choose not to speak, we build its walls higher.

I was reminded of this recently while interviewing Barry Young and Liz Gunn.

Barry, the Kiwi whistle-blower who risked everything to expose the truth about the mRNA shots, stood before us not as Winston Smith, the broken man of Orwell's famous dystopian novel Nineteen Eighty-Four, but as a man of conviction, declaring, "I am Barry Young."

His courage is rewriting the story.

In New Zealand, the data he shared screams of excess deaths, yet too many still turn away – just as we sidestep the homeless or ignore the suicide rates.

This avoidance isn't new. It's how we've been trained: to see the truth but not acknowledge it, to let the evidence pile up while we cling to the comfort of denial.

But the evidence is all around us.

From the young men collapsing on sports fields to the sudden heart attacks, and turbo cancers, the stories are mounting.

Friends and family, once healthy, now gone – and still we're told to look away.

The silence is not just deafening; it's deadly.

Barry Young saw the data in 2021 – patterns that couldn't be ignored – but he waited, hoping for a moment when the truth could break through.

When he finally acted, contacting independent journalist Liz Gunn, he didn't just share numbers; he shared a warning.

And yet the response from many is to double down, to attack the messenger rather than face the message.

This is the power of silence – it protects the narrative, not the people. But there's hope.

I see it in the older Australians, those who've lived through enough to know when they're being lied to.

I see it in the younger ones, too – the kids who are waking up, asking questions, refusing to swallow the script.

Just the other day, a group of young Aussies approached me, aware of what's happening, unafraid to speak.

They're not the majority, not yet, but they're a spark.

And sparks can ignite.

The digital prison being built around us thrives on our silence.

Every time we choose not to question, not to challenge, we hand over another brick for its walls.

But Barry Young didn't stay silent, and neither can we.

His act of defiance – standing up to say, 'This is wrong' – is a call to all of us.

We don't need to be heroes; we just need to be honest.

To talk to our neighbours, our friends, our families.

To say, 'I see it, and I won't ignore it anymore.'

The silence must end, not just for us but for those who come after.

If we let this prison stand, our children will inherit its chains.

So let's speak – loudly, clearly, and without fear. Let's rewrite the ending, not as Winston Smiths, but as Barry Youngs: People who stood up and said, "I am here, and I will not be silent."

16 January, 2024.

AUSTRALIA DAY SPEECH

NATIONS AREN'T COUNTRIES, they are stories.

And the Story of Australia – the one anyone over 35 grew up with – has been torn up.

That story was based upon the sacrifice of those who fought for our freedoms in the great wars. Great sacrifices for which most of us willingly sacrificed, almost on a whim, when they threatened to take away our right to go to a pub.

This showed the world that the story of Australia was a myth most Australians no longer believed in.

Trouble was, when we allowed our fear of Covid to sweep away the belief that we were a brave nation, what we were left with was the realisation that the majority of us were self-serving, materialistic cowards.

Now, by enforcing their uber surveillance, the CEOs of our supermarkets, supported by our Prime Minister, are trying to rewrite the story of our nation – one in which we are ashamed of ourselves.

And through our silence we are not only complying with that story but communally agreeing to live by it.

We are passing a story in which we acknowledge that, fundamentally, we are worthless cowards, down to our children, so that they can be cowards too.

And it's not a story we will sing the praises of, for when cowards sing about bravery they mumble, because even they know it's a lie.

But the story of every nation is never fixed. And each of us, just by being here, is a writer.

The ink of your country resides in your heart, and your pen is your mouth – and your willingness to speak out and be heard. We could start rewriting the story of who we really are today. So what do you think the story of our country – of us – should be? Do you yearn for us to continue writing this story, where as a community, we compliantly proceed to silently shrink into the shame of our ancestors' shadows?

Or should we rip that up and start a new page – where, as a new country, we forgive ourselves and once again strive to write a story in which our country becomes a beacon of hope and liberty for the world?

A country that, after finding itself besieged in a strange cultural war, found the courage to identify the values we wanted for ourselves and the next generations, then rose up and cemented those values and freedoms into the foundation of the new novel known as Australia.

A story in which Australians are a brave people, fair and tolerant people, who encourage their children to follow their dreams.

A people who learned the values of liberty only once we had our freedoms removed.

A people who learned that liberty can always be taken back – by the people and for the people – and that the prize of learning that lesson is the only victory that will make our country, and our people – us – great again.

And it all comes down to one word: Choice.

That choice is: as an Australian – which I know you know should be a privilege to be – do you want to be lost in the herd of the passive and disillusioned readers, or are you ready to stand up and join the writers who are willing to try and rewrite history – a new novel for a new country in which we shine.

26 January, 2024.

THE BROKEN BONES OF GOD

At the eulogy, from the pulpit, two of his "closest friends" – that's what they claimed – smiled as they said how much they loved him, regardless of his little conspiracy theories. In unison the congregation giggled, and in that giggle they declared, again, that victory had been achieved.

This is why facts don't work: these people never wanted truth; they wanted status. That condescending giggle was the prayer of their new god.

I'd wager that if you got most of them alone, secretly they'd admit doubts about the weirdness of the world. Brilliantly, the powers-that-be worked out long ago that to defeat them all you simply turn their lives upside-down – while they tumble – stand stoic on the telly and offer the security of a fresh communal belief, even if it's an obvious lie.

Australians were offered a new god, one accessed through a needle; and because they were terrified of the fall, they converted on the spot.

The dogma was simple: keep your doubts quiet and you stay safe. Remain silent while they lie around you, or even better sit in the pews and giggle along with the mourners as you gently mock the man who loved you and whom you claimed to love back.

This dogma is why people refuse to defend their fallen family. The new sin is letting the community know you have doubts. Speak the truth – that the jabs, or the state, injured or murdered your kin – and the punishment is exile from the Church of the Frightened.

So, as the dead man's clear eyes tried to reach us from a video screen beside the altar, the real victor – the pope of this new religion, Fear – basked inside the church. It was his now; everyone had agreed to huddle around his comforting lies and giggle. That condescending giggle evicted God.

I was born Catholic. I knew every ritual, but I practise none now; they're worse than meaningless. Each psalm-response, each sign of the cross, is an insult to whatever God we once had.

Then, to make sure the few of us still listening got the memo, the priest in his theatrical gown preached that we must all be a light for others.

I almost stood up and asked: How exactly are we meant to see your light, Father? When the lies were conquering our streets you locked God's doors.

Jesus – man or myth – is the poster child of the best in us: courage, love, wisdom, grace, hope, and more. A man who shone so brightly some claim they still see it.

Humanity's light. The bulb that lets us believe that, no matter how dark, goodness – through integrity, physical and moral courage – would guide us back to the foundation stones of a healthy society: decency and truth.

But what if that light is deeper than God, older?

What if it's more precious than the promise of eternal life? I once watched a video: an archaeologist was asked for the oldest proof of civilization yet found.

She answered: not a pyramid, not an arrowhead, not cave art – a healed femur.

Deep in our past, someone broke a bone – and someone else, maybe a whole tribe, risked starvation, predators, worse – to stay and heal them. Fear must have screamed: "Leave them for the greater good!" But they stayed. They left us that healed bone, not as metaphor or hope, but as fact – the womb of God, a sliver of divine empathy and the cradle of our shared mercy.

God isn't a building, a ritual, a man in lace repeating words while statuettes stare at nothing.

God is a young atheist-raised bloke in the midst of the Melbourne struggles who, as police morphed from protectors to oppressors in one afternoon shift, walked their line holding a crucifix to their visored faces, forcing them to look at the suffering face of Jesus.

I watched him move along that line again and again, giving every officer a chance to ponder.

That was courage.

A tribe of one, risking everything to pause and heal a fallen stranger.

He controlled fear to do what he knew was right, switching on the light that separates us from animals: the ability to create gods.

That's what we need now. The old god – cathedrals, funny hats and all – has been evicted by communal fear, fed by the silence of priests and spiritual CEOs.

The god we grew up under is dead.

We killed him.

But outside the churches, on the battlegrounds, the new faithful are everywhere, knitting the broken bones of our communities. Every day they fight, lose, rise, fight again. They never stop because, in this war, they have chosen a side: the army battling to save humanity itself.

Inside their courage, inside their spiritually wired, growing global womb, a new god is growing.

20 March, 2024.

CAFÉ LOCKED OUT COPS 3649 DAY FACEBOOK BAN

KEYBOARD WARRIORS AROUND Australia have worn their Facebook bans as a badge of honour. Over the years various internet groups, after spending hundreds of hours building up a following, have been banned for breaching government agendas, most particularly on gender and multiculturalism.

There is a long and scandalous history of the Australian government interfering with and manipulating the public narrative by using American big tech platforms to delete, manipulate and censor Australian citizens. Uncannily, the cut-off point has always been around 100,000 followers. We had just hit 106,000 followers.

The collusion between the Australian government and Big Tech companies, most particularly Facebook, to manipulate the Australian public narrative is an open scandal, and one of the very reasons the country is in such a mess today. Unaccountable bureaucrats have enacted their divisive agendas without fear of blowback because they know the voices of the people will be silenced the minute grassroots movement becomes too powerful to ignore.

It is a sad indictment of the politicians of our era that none of the major political parties have ever spoken up about this issue, and are thereby complicit—all to benefit who, exactly? Certainly not the Australian taxpayer. Certainly not the so-called Great Unwashed, Australia's rough-around-the-edges working class. The ones doing all the grunt work that keeps the country going.

Café Locked Out has joined the internet Gulag, setting something of a record in the process.

This is the notice I received: "Your account is restricted for 3,649 days. Your account activity didn't follow our Community Standards, so you can't do one or more things you usually do."

Almost ten years!!! I think the real concern is that people won't care because it doesn't really affect them. But this restriction is a giant step towards silencing you, your children and your grandchildren.

Most will probably stay silent, but the ramifications are profound. We are a free speech platform, populated with the thousands of interviews of ordinary Australians having their say but obviously YOU need to be PROTECTED from THEM.

And so here we are.

Thank you to all who have bravely supported the Facebook page. Curiously, my phone died yesterday, and we also copped a brief Twitter and Instagram ban.

Also my speeches have been removed.

All that's left now is to move from the net to real life, where I won't be able to post this for I'll be in a camp I guess, being re-educated.

This is your time.

They are not coming, they are here.

Why is Café Locked Out seen as a dangerous Australian voice?

Thousands of interviews with ordinary Aussies – an alternative Covid history, filmed in real time – now live inside Facebook's archives. The page had morphed into a multi-headed beast: streamers from every corner of the country, all under individual shelling from mainstream media and the paid troll brigade.

Why?

What is so dangerous about hearing alternative opinions from Australians?

What is so dangerous about free speech?

Despairingly, I wrote: "We've spent four years trying to wake our brothers and sisters, but are we the ones still asleep? Why keep selling a product no one wants to buy – The Truth? Is it time to re-write the marketing plan?"

But that old saying, "the truth will out", is coming true in the multitude of voices streaming from Australia's heartlands. You cannot silence everyone, you cannot censor everyone.

We rest our case.

21 June, 2024.

THE ARMY OF LIGHT

WE ARE THE grandchildren of Gallipoli who, despite all the pointless deaths, galvanised our Australian spirit through the heroism, empathy and love of one man – Simpson and his donkey. Then we added a healthy dash of Paul Hogan until we all agreed that, as a rule, Aussies are easy-going life-lovers who value mateship.

Covid was a Pearl Harbor attack so successful in destroying our core myths. We no longer know who we actually are. The shooting at the Shrine of Remembrance is the perfect example: There we sat with placards demanding freedom – on one of our greatest altars to freedom – while our Victorian brothers and sisters, dressed and armed as storm troopers, stood before us.

We represented the Australia we thought we were; they were the willing henchmen of a fresh fascist state, announcing that their story is the new Australian identity.

A country where courage is replaced by compliance, integrity by silence, and any act of empathy must be state-approved. One high-ranking VicPol officer told a cop who resigned on principle, Craig Backman: "Craig, in the future there will be the oppressors and the oppressed. Better to be an oppressor."

Then, from my hospital bed, I saw the true depth of their censorship.

Algorithms have built social-media echo chambers around us; millions don't even know a resistance exists.

Brady Gunn, founder of the quiet protest movement Stand in the Park, points this out often. His rants can score a thousand shares – great, we think, I'm helping – yet when he tracks the shares, none have likes or re-shares.

Online, we are being corralled by code. (It's why I never see Taylor Swift posts.) So what can we do?

The hippies are still a household name – and they never had Instagram.

The Amish are famous without Rumble.

Sikhs are known for turbans, not Facebook reels.

Practising Jews wear skullcaps.

Trump's army has MAGA caps.

Trans kids fly rainbow hair like battle flags.

You may not agree with them, but one glance tells you who they are and what they stand for.

Uniforms, voluntarily worn.

We, after five years of resistance, still don't have a uniform. We drag out the old rally T-shirts for events, but every other day we blend so well we may as well be invisible.

We roll town to town and the only way we spot our own is when they hug the bus.

Isolation does not breed hope.

Imagine one of us designs something so cool we all find the courage to wear it.

You hit the mall and bam, there we are: buying milk, sipping lattes, paying cash.

Garment by garment we start taking back or re-defining our culture.

Step one: write a short description of who we are. Trouble is – who are we?

I've crossed the country dozens of times and I'm always stunned. We're not united by sport, hobby or dogma – we're united by a love of freedom.

PhD scientists, stay-at-home mums, broke poets, wealthy farmers – every shape, every size.

If Covid and the podcasters hadn't yanked us together, we'd never have found ourselves: the Cookers, the anti-vaxxers – slurs worn like the ancient graffiti Romans would etch into their empire's walls.

The lions are gone; the Christians remain.

But we're not them – we're something new.

Battle fatigue, online acid, zero big wins – we forgot how rare and beautiful we are.

I believe we're in the early days of a great spiritual exodus: humans everywhere – sensing the overlords herding us to a place where our souls can't breathe – hunting a new way to live.

We indie-media types are surfing that wave, documenting, entertaining the troops.

But we're more than that.

We are the Army of Light that rose organically to meet an invading darkness.

No generals, no brigades, no tanks – no uniform.

What we do have is open-door recruitment:

Ignore the self-serve till and queue for the human cashier? Welcome to the Army of Light.

Pick up a discarded protest sign and let me photograph you holding it? Welcome to the Army of Light.

"My only skill is violin."

Recompose the national anthem so it sounds like it has a broken heart? Welcome to the Army of Light.

No silver bullets; this is a marathon relay. We're the first runners.

Job description: defend the baton of freedom, lay the foundation of who we actually are – our dogma, mantra, code – and recruit like hell.

We must be seen: a brave, resilient, diverse, passionate community defending human rights and the best bits of the human spirit.

There is no cavalry.

No other tribe is waiting to adopt our orphans.

There is only the slow awakening of brothers and sisters who haven't joined us yet.

Café Locked Out was born in Victoria's darkest lockdown days – one live broadcast a day to defend free speech.

It's now a nationwide network of podcasters dropping shows seven days a week, often several times a day.

Despite the fractures, CLO is still here – still passionate, still growing.

My wish: use courage, art, innovation and relentless commentary to turn this exodus-without-a-destination into a genuine human renaissance.

We don't need to find a new home – we already have one. We just need to win enough hearts and minds to dethrone the wolves who let the wolves in.

That day is coming – because they've made the same mistake they always make: they underestimated you.

In conflicts like this, the side that never gives up wins.

Victory is a choice – your choice – so I suggest you never, ever, ever give up.

15 August, 2024.

FREE SPEECH

FREE SPEECH IS a weapon to stave off tyranny. Conversely, hate speech is a weapon designed to destroy free speech and enslave you under the pretense of protection.

I had a friend, a social worker with twelve years of experience, who posted on a Facebook page she managed under a pseudonym, the vile lie that only women can give birth. She was reported by someone and subsequently fired. The reason for her harsh dismissal was to deter anyone else at her company from challenging the new narrative that men can give birth.

If you are pretending to believe something you know is not true, just to keep your job, your friends, or whatever else, you are willingly choosing to live under tyranny. Your warden isn't the Human Resources Department or Facebook censors; it's fear. Fear is ultimately not a giver but a taker, seeking to make you surrender your greatest asset: yourself.

You are being groomed to be meek. They want you to realize, to your own shame, that you have willingly given up your liberty. The only solace is knowing that many around you are propagating the same lies for the same reasons, thus paying the same price. Tragically, the true losers will be our children, who will look to us for guidance and learn through observation that lying is the only way to prosper.

Can men give birth? No. Should men be allowed to participate in women's sports? No. Did the jabs work? Are we still a democracy?

I watched a documentary on Stalin, who inflicted a reign of terror upon his people. Every night, he signed off on quotas for people to be killed or imprisoned. The lists were indiscriminate. He'd instruct:

"Today, take 1,000 people from Ballarat. Execute 500 and send the rest to the gulags." Did the people unite to defend themselves against this terror? No.

The most chilling moment of the documentary was when it was revealed that despite the appalling crimes, people in the city continued with their lives as if nothing was wrong, hiding their pain and fear behind a mask of apathy.

Every day, I hear of people dropping dead – grandparents, parents, friends, kids.

Were these the ones chosen to be executed? Or do I meet others who have been incapacitated by the jabs, struggling to find doctors or even family who will acknowledge their plight? Instead, they are left alone with medical bills to cope. Are these the ones sent to the gulags?

Lies are rampant, and our brothers and sisters, who are not as brave as you, are so confused that they perceive the truth as dangerous. Since truth equals freedom, they have become frightened of it, justifying their cowardice with statements like, "We were never free." They are so scared of the truth that they have willingly betrayed their loved ones to be seen as good, decent, lying citizens. Ironically, if you believe a man can give birth and are passionate enough to debate it on social media, that is free speech, but when you threaten people's jobs, social status, or cancel them to force others to propagate your beliefs, that is not free speech – it's hate speech and tyranny.

Telling a few lies or staying silent while lies trample over your rights might seem wise in the short term, but in the medium to long term, you are committing slow euthanasia. Your body might still exist, but your soul will scream as it suffocates behind a polite smile.

We met a woman from Hong Kong who saw "Free Speech Defense" on the side of a bus and asked if she could share her story.

She had left Singapore for Hong Kong seeking freedom but now found herself silenced by the new regime. She told me that the price of her silence was an internal fading. When I asked if she wanted me to share her story despite potential trouble from China, she said, "Post it. I'm already dying."

There is a mathematical equation for lies upon lies: it equals loss. You will remain lost and powerless until your inner pain surpasses your external fear of repercussions. At that moment, you will use your inner compass, the one you were born with, to navigate through the gray towards True North, towards the light of truth and freedom.

But here is another truth: many people do not want liberty. They want stuff, status, comfort, and power. If lying will get them these things, they will freely choose to be modern-day slaves. The latest lie is that digital ID will be voluntary. Tragically, even if we collect and share videos of politicians claiming it will always be voluntary, few will care when it becomes impossible to function without a digital ID, because they knew from the start it was a lie.

We know it's not Canberra that wants this; it's the corporations, banks, and those above them. But they are not our enslavers; our compliant brothers and sisters are. The most chilling part of the Stalin documentary was a film of a child reporting his father, an act that would see his father jailed or killed. The crowd celebrated the child's courage, but I couldn't help but think of how similar this is to urging people to report their own to authorities. Now, we are mocked, as they display their power by disrespecting Jesus at the Olympics' opening ceremony, beating women, and praising abusers. We are all being taken somewhere, and many are heading there voluntarily, silenced by fear, to a place where humanity struggles to flourish. But they have one problem: you.

Awakenings. Division isn't a problem; it's a weapon. We are like a brush fire, hard to control. If we had one leader, they'd be easily corrupted or killed, and soon we'd run out of leaders. We've never been here before, and we are all finding our way through darkness to a better place. Let's have various groups throwing ideas against the wall and benefit from those that stick.

We are not divided; we are conscripts in a great Army of Light. An army with no visible leader, generals, or medals, but we are powerful and rising. It starts with doctors and scientists sharing their thoughts, spreading globally through major podcasters, then shared again by others, reaching down to a grandmother placing light in a café or a young man in Perth highlighting the rise of myocarditis in young men.

We are an army fighting with and for the love of humanity, using beauty and truth against fear and lies. You can join our army with one simple word: No. But before we move forward, we need to address a problem: What is freedom, and what will our victory look like? Understanding these will give our paths a destination. We are resilient and entrepreneurial. If we visualise what victory is, articulate a destination, our focus will narrow, and we will become an unstoppable force for good. I don't have these answers yet; they need to be discussed rigorously.

Even if you don't feel it, you are an essential part of the most important movement in human history. Relish that. Celebrate it. You have the chance to ensure the future's foundation is built on the best of humanity: love, faith, fairness, integrity, honesty, and health. A world where our most valued assets are our children, and technology serves us.

So, don't stop. If your current path turns out to be a dead end, shrug it off and explore another. As Dr Bruce Paix, a war historian, said, this is an asymmetrical war, and the side that refuses to quit will be the side that wins.

So, are you intending to quit? Are you intending to quit?

August 20, 2024.

MY BROTHER, MY BROTHER, MY BROTHER

In September 2024, I premiered my play My Brother, My Brother, My Brother at the Alex Theatre in St Kilda and the Red Rock Regional Theatre and Gallery. This 90-minute, two-act work – depicting three young men adrift in a dingy fishing boat amid stormy seas – emerged not just as a survival tale, but as a defiant response to the authoritarianism that defined Australia's Covid era.

The poster captured its raw heart: "If you treat our young men with shame, what do you think will happen to their souls?" In a nation where mandates turned mates into informants and stripped away personal sovereignty, this play became my cry for the sacred masculine – a bulwark against the overlords who herded us toward a world where souls couldn't breathe.

The story follows Isaac, Connor, and Jesse – three straight young mates who wake up drugged and stranded on a disabled vessel, phones gone, radio smashed, land nowhere in sight. Their grandfather has vanished, leaving them with scant food, dwindling water, and the relentless pound of waves. What starts as a tense fight for survival – bickering, laughing, clinging to stoicism – unfurls into a mirror held up to our fractured society.

As the ocean's isolation closes in, they confront not just the elements, but the deeper peril: a culture that shames boys into silence, brands them as toxic, and discards them like yesterday's threat. Starring Odysseus Pollock, Joshua Bruce, and Tom Dray, the play crackles with humour, profanity, and unfiltered mateship, celebrating the courage that binds men even as the world tries to break it.

This wasn't born in a vacuum. Australia's Covid response – those vaccine mandates enforced with the cold precision of a police state – exposed how quickly we sacrifice our own. I saw it firsthand in the protests, the job losses, the family rifts: young men, the breeders of our future, treated as disposable resisters, oxygen thieves in the eyes of the compliant. The play weaves this in without apology.

Connor's raw outburst nails it: "They tell us to man up, but when we do, they shoot us down. Mandates, jabs, rules – it's all about control, not care. Out here, no one's forcing a needle in my arm. I'd rather die free than live like that." It's allegory as weapon: the sea's tyranny echoing the state's, where "resilience camps" ringed with razor wire became our modern gulags, and freedom of choice – a divine gift, as I argue in my essay Your Greatest Gift – was criminalised. Like the wild scrub bulls I chronicled in The Scrub Bulls of Mildura, these brothers refuse the cull; they're the hope, not the problem.

Writing it just months earlier, I braced for rejection. In a theatre scene captured by woke gatekeepers – where a script honouring unapologetic masculinity risks cancellation – who would touch it? Yet resilience, that stubborn Aussie trait mandates couldn't drown, pulled us through.

One actor, living abroad, read the draft and flew back from Canada just to audition. Another jetted in from South Australia. The cast who landed the roles – Odysseus, Joshua, and Tom – dove in eyes wide open, determined to voice these lost souls despite the social blowback.

Even now, the South Australian actor is staging his own version down there. Rehearsals have been electric: not just honing lines, but forging bonds in a "woke environment" where marketing a non-compliant play feels like smuggling contraband. We've leaned on grassroots fire – Rumble streams, Substack shares – after Big Tech's boot (my decade-long Facebook exile, YouTube's scrub of Café Locked Out's Kulture page in October 2024) slammed the door.

As I told the FreeNZ Podcast, "Life is not about not falling down – it's about getting up. And you get up, and you're stronger."

Audiences felt it viscerally. Over four nights, fathers brought sons who left whispering, "They get us."

One Substack reader nailed the resonance: "It made me laugh, cry, and think about what it means to be a man today. You're not afraid to say what others won't." Mateship – that cultural bedrock mandates turned to snitch-lines – shines through the banter and loyalty, a reminder of what we lost when fear herded us apart. Critics were split, as expected.

The Unshackled hailed its intensity: "A survival story that doesn't shy away from big questions. The script is tight, with dialogue that crackles with humour and pain, reflecting the real struggles of young men today." They praised the trio's chemistry but flagged the second act's lingering on societal critiques – like mandate coercion and jab dangers – without tidy bows.

The Blurb echoed that: superb setup in the first act, but the back half grew repetitive, "spit-balling ideas without solutions," my personal axe to grind laid bare. Fair cop; art isn't therapy – it's provocation. Mainstream stats (Australia's Covid death rate a mere 4 per 100,000) clash with my protest-scarred truth, but as The Unshackled put it, "It's not subtle, but neither are you. You're a voice for those silenced, and this play screams their truth."

My Brother, My Brother, My Brother isn't just theatre – it's my artistic rebellion, a spiritual exodus from the shame machine. Like my plays before it (Marooned on suicide's shadow), it's self-healing through story: for the brothers told they're toxic, the resisters branded disposable.

As I wrote in A Sense of Place Magazine, "This is a play about three boys lost at sea – three mates who have to fight to survive, not just the ocean, but a society that has forgotten how to honour its men." And in that fight, amid the mandates' long shadow, we remember: men aren't the problem. They're the solution – if we let them be free.

18 September, 2024.

THE PERSECUTION OF DR MY LE TRINH

Dr My Le Trinh's life story is one of triumph over adversity, of a doctor's fight against systemic injustice. Escaping the horrors of the Khmer Rouge regime at the age of five, she endured the devastating loss of her mother, who was killed by the regime.

Sent to live with her aunt in Vietnam, she spent several years under communist rule before making a daring escape as a boat refugee. At the age of 12, she arrived in Australia, determined to build a new life.

Despite the challenges of adapting to a new country, language, and culture, Dr Trinh excelled academically, graduating third in her high school class. Her hard work and resilience earned her a place at the University of Sydney, where she pursued medicine – a career she envisioned as a way to serve her community and honour her mother's legacy.

For 27 years, Dr Trinh was a highly regarded General Practitioner in Sydney. She cared for her patients with compassion and dedication, while also volunteering her medical expertise in rural Cambodia, offering free care to underserved communities. Her career remained exemplary until September 27, 2021, when two complaints were filed against her on the same day through the AHPRA portal, marking the beginning of an extraordinary and unjust ordeal. AHPRA: The Australian Health Practitioners Regulation Agency.

The first complaint stemmed from Westmead Hospital, where a Covid patient Dr Trinh had treated for severe complications later presented with psychosis. Dr Trinh believes this was likely caused by the virus or the high-dose steroids – a calculated and medically necessary decision that saved the patient's life.

The second complaint came from an anonymous "John Smith", alleging inappropriate prescribing of Ivermectin for Covid patients.

The complaint lacked credibility – the contact email bounced back, the phone number was disconnected, and no address was provided. Despite this, the HCCC – the Health Care Complaints Commission – treated the complaint as legitimate, disregarding their own policy requiring verified communication and documented patient consent, which neither Dr Trinh nor her legal team had ever seen.

On October 27, 2021, following a rushed inquiry-style hearing, Dr Trinh's medical licence was suspended indefinitely under emergency powers meant only for genuine crises.

While Dr Trinh does not know if her indefinite suspension was orchestrated, she believes the rushed inquiry, coupled with the decision to suspend her indefinitely, raises serious questions about the process.

After her suspension, Dr Trinh was referred for investigation. However, internal documents suggest that the outcome of this investigation – her indefinite suspension – had been predetermined, raising doubts about the fairness and transparency of the process.

Seeking justice, Dr Trinh brought her case to the Court of Appeal, where the focus was on the legality of indefinite suspensions under existing legislation. She believed her case could set a vital precedent for other health practitioners.

Instead, her case was dismissed – a decision she found deeply troubling.

Dr Trinh also found it unusual that the judicial panel comprised two retired judges and one newly appointed judge. This composition raised questions about the impartiality of the proceedings, especially in light of the significant precedent her case could have established.

Meanwhile, the financial toll of her suspension mounted. Her medical indemnity insurance company refused to cover her legal costs, citing her indefinite suspension as grounds for non-support. Over three years, she spent more than $200,000 of her savings on legal battles, leaving her financially drained.

The Health Care Complaint Commission's actions did not stop at suspension. They initiated a four-day prosecution hearing, seeking to revoke Dr Trinh's medical licence for three to five years and demanded that she pay for the costs of the prosecution hearing.

These proceedings exemplified a relentless pursuit, targeting a doctor who had spent her career saving lives and supporting her community, now being forced to bear the financial burden of a process that aims to strip her of her livelihood.

Dr Trinh's ordeal is not just her story; it is a cautionary tale about systemic flaws in the regulatory and judicial systems. Her case raises critical questions: Can anonymous, unverifiable complaints dictate the fate of professionals? What safeguards exist to ensure fairness in disciplinary actions?

Despite the immense personal and professional toll, Dr Trinh remains steadfast in her fight. Her courage and determination serve as a call for reform, challenging a system that prioritises bureaucracy over justice.

Dr Trinh's story is a reminder of the importance of standing firm in the face of adversity and fighting for a system that truly upholds the principles of fairness and accountability.

9 December, 2024.

LEUNIG'S LAST CLUE

Michael Leunig was one of Australia's greatest ever cartoonists. One job of great artists is to navigate our human soul and bring back any clues they find for us to ponder. Back in a time when our perceived identity could support us all, like an indomitable perch in time, this saw him embraced by the governments, mainstream media, the arts, and the people. Every quirky image he produced, that we published, bred hope for us all, because it was clear that, whether we believed him or not, or whether we ever understood the clue, as a people, we were willing to look.

He was already falling out of favour with Australia's chattering classes with his endless War on Woke, only to see his public standing completely annihilated for his stand on Covid measures, including vaccines.

Leunig's studio announced his departure on Instagram.

"The pen has run dry, its ink no longer flowing – yet Mr Curly and his ducks will remain etched in our hearts, cherished and eternal. Michael Leunig passed away peacefully today, in the early hours of 19 December 2024. During his final days he was surrounded by his children, loved ones and sunflowers – accompanied, as ever, by his dear old friends Johann Sebastian Bach and Ludwig van Beethoven."

It was Leunig's scepticism towards Australia's ultra-woke cultural agenda – and the censorious, humourless, totalitarian instincts behind it – that led to his cancellation. He was reportedly gobsmacked at the news he was being sacked, or "let go", from *The Age*.

The same ultra-woke "news" outlets – including the $1.2 billion Australian Broadcasting Corporation and *Guardian Australia*, set up with contributions from Bill Gates, were happy to celebrate his unique style.

Guardian Australia reported: "In recent years, Leunig's views critical of no-jab, no-play vaccination policies, sometimes apparent in his cartoons published in *The Age*, drew controversy."

What a very nice, gormless way to put it.

His parting with the publication was bitter; the cartoonist told *The Australian*: "It's almost embarrassing now to say that I worked for *The Age* – it's become like a tacky tabloid."

Then, post-Covid, he started bringing back clues that hinted at a cold shift in our combined core. Because the powers that be didn't want these clues published, and because we, the people, had lost the strength to look, he was cast out. We wanted to categorise him as old and irrelevant. What we didn't realize was that his greatest clue was yet to be produced.

He had to leave us that one, by leaving us. Australia, our souls are in dark times, and our greatest canary – the one who sang with a voice so light and deep it connected us all – has died. But just before dying, we tried to smother him. And that's the clue. For today, many will actively ignore our cancelling of him in order to celebrate his work.

Like trying to glue his unique wings back on to the soul who has now found a way out of our grip.

And that is the final clue he is leaving us.

Leunig was Leunig before many of us were born, a national living treasure, and whilst in the future he will be ever more revered, the image he left our generation, is a portrait of us.

There we are, looking up at the space he left, with his wings in our hands, the wings we silently let *The Age* clip.

20 December, 2024.

CAFÉ LOCKED OUT IN BENDIGO

We have been moving so fast for so long, we haven't had time to reflect, but in November 2021, Damien and I went to Bendigo. Our plan was to set up a table and see if anyone wanted to come out and chat with us. And they did.

And we streamed it live. It was raw, unpolished, but real.

People came with stories – hard, cathartic stories of loss, defiance, and hope. Like drummers announcing an approaching war, they spoke of barricades being erected, trenches dug, not because they wanted conflict, but because they refused to hand over their liberty. I remember a woman, a nurse, who had lost her job for refusing the jab.

She wasn't angry, just resolute. She said, "I'd rather lose everything than betray my patients."

Then a bloke, a builder, told us how his mates turned on him for questioning the rules.

These weren't rebels; they were ordinary Australians, pushed too far. That day in Bendigo showed me what Café Locked Out could be – a voice for those the mainstream ignores.

One of the people we interviewed told us how horrible the op shops were being. For international readers, in Australia charity-based outlets selling second-hand clothing and other basics, such as cutlery and plates, are known as "op shops".

People who worked there, who had grown up with them, were barring them from going in.

This led us to do the two op-shop protests, which, a week later, saw the op shops drop their mandates. After this we would do a few more towns, unaware, as we did, of how long the battle was before us.

Looking back, Bendigo was a turning point. It wasn't just about recording stories; it was about building a community that wouldn't bow. We're still doing that, every podcast, every post, every rally.

The war's not over, but we're still here, still fighting.

21 December, 2024.

THE PERSECUTED CARDIAC NURSE

Courage takes many forms. We at Café Locked Out recorded many powerful stories and profoundly moving interviews. Below is the transcript of just one of them.

I was fired from my job as a registered nurse on September 21. I was at Castlemaine Health for nine years. I have over 20 years nursing experience. I have postgraduate qualifications in cardiac nursing.

Besides being a nurse, I was also an Occupational Health and Safety representative for my ward, which gave me additional responsibilities when it came to safety. It gave legal responsibilities.

All I did was question the measures that were taking place once the so-called pandemic was called. I questioned masks especially.

Once the mention of a "vaccine" was touted, I became very wary. I started questioning it and talking about it among my peers. Very quickly, though, I was being told to be quiet. I was then warned not to discuss it at all and to not talk to patients about the jab. I refused to get it myself and the pressure on us to get it was intense. We were being treated with disdain by other staff.

The environment was hostile.

I stood my ground. I had a duty of care to myself and to my patients to keep questioning.

I was told by Human Resources on the day I was stood down, "We are all replaceable, Bernadette."

Nine years of hard work and I walked out without one thank you or goodbye. My legal battle with the Victorian Government continues.

26 December, 2024.

THE SILENCE OF BROKEN HILL

It's morning, and the breeze rising off the desert has a crisp chill to it, as though the night – full of unreachable stars – is trying to cling to the last of the dark while the sun rescues this iconic town once again with the warming brushes of dawn.

The only thing missing from the streets are the giants who built this town. We heard stories of earlier generations crossing this desert with all they possessed piled into wheelbarrows. No GPS, no servos with toilets and cold bottles of Coke – just lean, sun-tanned dreamers chasing the possibility of a new life built on a strike of gold or silver.

A family born and bred here told us how the town was multicultural before the word had entered the vernacular. The Afghans came, ferrying water on camel trains. The Croatians, the Italians, the Irish, and the Celts came too, vanishing down holes in the ground, seeking – through risk and hard work – a better life for their families, a life simply not available back in their old countries.

The mining giant BHP was born here, and the union movement was formed here too, to protect the miners from the greed of the mine owners. The evidence sits in the children's names on the shrine dedicated to the fallen miners. A 12-year-old boy's name is there.

Other shrines are planted around the town as well, dedicated to the men who left to fight and die in battles not their own, lured by the tales of valour, glory and the importance of nationhood spun by Australia's politicians. Those they left behind would never see the battlefields on which so many of them died. Even from the top of the hill, all that was visible then – and now – is the desert, keeper of secrets, ghosts whispering in this morning breeze.

The wheelbarrows have long been replaced by large four-wheel drives with bull bars, CBs and air-conditioning. A mobile-phone tower looms over the town-hall clock, and the locals and the tourists – the majority of them overweight and unusually pale despite the sun treating the town like her anvil.

That your bus? a woman asked.

Yeah. I'm an indie journo out here looking for the current Australia.

Hmmm, she replied, and walked away.

Another man asked me the same thing, but with his family waiting in the car he nodded as he took in the images on the bus, then shook my hand and whispered, Keep going – even though there was no one here to hear him but me and the ghosts.

Wokeness was here.

Planting its flag in the middle of the town is a poster of a joyous young man with Down Syndrome playing with the rainbow braces holding up his jeans. It reads: "Positive Social Change." We've seen these banners in most towns, yet most of the people don't appear to be transitioning. They are instead just quiet.

One young man spoke to me off-camera about how he'd been violated. To keep his job he'd taken three jabs. Before Covid he had been relatively healthy; now every week he suffers crippling migraines. And while he didn't want to talk – didn't want to risk the job he'd already risked so much to keep – I could see in his disquiet eyes the vast amount of water he wanted to spill.

The police had a chat with us in Broken Hill. They were cool, but this actually happened:

So, we were asked, "Where are you from?"

MGG: "We live on the road."

"Where have you come from?"

MGG: "The road."

"Where are you going?"

MGG: "Back on the road." And we got a laugh.

Something has changed. We've seen it in other Outback towns.

The warm "G'day mate, how ya going?" has gone.

The "she'll be right" attitude has been blown away by Covid, and when I ask anyone here who will talk if they think the Covid years have stolen our identity, they all agree.

Once, men left here again and again to fight an enemy who never stood a chance of reaching this town. They weren't defending the pubs or the cafés; they were defending the freedom the people had built their town upon – the freedom their own government, and other forces, have since compromised. Their soldiers march the streets in invisible brigades, their subtextual signs reading: if you speak out there will be retribution. Better to remain safe by remaining silent.

And this is how it's done.

The weapon to defeat such invaders is the God-given right of freedom of speech – but if you can't summon the courage to draw it from its sheath, your town slips away. It's no longer yours: just a museum piece, a diorama of lost Australia, its streets haunted by ghosts who once bellowed against the bosses, the banks, the bloody mandates. Inhabited by who? Shadows, mostly – compliant echoes in the empty shafts.

How will we ever know you again, Australia – if your true voice hides in these silences, the same merciless hush the red desert has always pressed against Broken Hill's outskirts?

2 January, 2025.

WHAT RUKSHAN ACTUALLY CAPTURED

In late 2024 Sri Lankan born Fernando Rukshan came under surprising attack on social media, a fair amount of it racist in tone. He was one of the true heroes of the Australian Freedom Movement, and as events unfolded one of Australia's greatest journalists and social commentators. He had always been well accepted and indeed much admired within the Australian community. Formerly a wedding photographer, Rukshan's unflinching eye as he filmed Australia's Covid protests was seen around the world. He aimed his camera squarely at exactly what was in front of him.

Perhaps, one can only speculate, the attacks on Rukshan were engendered by the historically high immigration rates, initiated in 2022 by the Labor government, the so-called Indian inundation, which stretched the bounds of civil tolerance, contributed to social fragmentation, raised serious questions about Australia's multicultural experiment and were an underlying factor in everything from the housing crisis to depressed wages.

Whatever the cause, I decided to speak up in defence of Rukshan and pay tribute to his historically significant work.

Rukshan Fernando aka "Real Rukshan" gained prominence in 2020–2021 for his on-the-ground live coverage of Melbourne's anti-lockdown protests, which he streamed primarily via Facebook Live before archiving and cross-posting clips to YouTube. While Facebook was the powerhouse for real-time reach, with peaks of 60,000–70,000 concurrent viewers per stream and cumulative totals running into the millions across his broadcasts. His YouTube uploads of highlights, full streams, and protest footage also racked up hundreds of thousands of views individually and collectively pushed into the millions over time.

Here is what I wrote.

The courage it took to continue streaming, while capturing the moment Victorian Police, before a huge worldwide audience, lined up with their new weapons and passionately fired upon our country's identity, cannot be overstated.

The footage from the Shrine of Remembrance is hard to watch. Not just because the officers – dressed like stormtroopers, masked to hide their faces – are shooting fleeing protesters in the back, but because they take aim and fire repeatedly, as if relishing the hunt. They were enjoying themselves; getting off on it. It's there in their stance, their rhythm; you just have to look.

One protester summed up the moment perfectly, by crying out during the stream, "This is Fucking Australia?"

It is a day I will never forget, and was a transformative moment for me.

In the morning, the streets of Melbourne were being patrolled by armoured cars called 'BearCats'. Victorian Police Officers were hanging off these vehicles, many holding rubber bullet rifles and firing indiscriminately at those they assumed were protesters.

A dramatic picture I took of stormtrooper-style police with a military tank in the background confronting protesters should have been published in a major newspaper with the headline: Is this weapon truly required to police protesting Australians?

But the mainstream media outlets, hostage to the government through advertising budgets, all colluded in the official lies and refused to publish either the story or the dramatic pictures of a military tank confronting unarmed protesters. They buried, ignored, or distorted the story, the images, and the truth. They betrayed the very citizenry whose lives and grievances they were meant to document.

Before I understood the true depth of the media's treason, I believed their failure to publish the dramatic image of unarmed Australian protesters did not fit the perception most people have of Australia. It's like a piece that somehow got into the frame, but is actually from a North Korean jigsaw puzzle – a piece we want to hide and forget.

But the shooting of protesters went deeper.

Not only were Victorian Police shooting fleeing protesters, but they were shooting them as they were protesting at the Shrine of Remembrance – a building built to commemorate those who fought and died in the belief they were protecting our freedoms.

And what were these protesters protesting about? Government-generated agendas such as climate change? No. Black Lives Matter? No. The Black Lives protest, held only weeks before, had seen Victorian Police officers dropping to their knees, pledging to restrain themselves in the future.

No, these protesters were defending what they believed were our enshrined freedoms. The only reason they were there was because their politicians wouldn't acknowledge their concerns, mainstream media wouldn't publish them, and social media was actively censoring them. So, because they lived in a democracy – where even the Deputy Police Commissioner had been quoted on video stating, "Protesting isn't against the law; it's a fundamental human right" – they were on the streets, airing their grievances.

When confronted by stormtroopers in black, the marches became full of powerful religious symbols.

In their eyes, it was an assault on the sacred, freedom of choice and freedom of speech, enabled by Covid terror: the fear that the virus would wipe us all out, peddled against mounting facts that proved otherwise. Time has vindicated the protesters. We were right to rage.

But being right wasn't enough. Perhaps what the majority of us didn't understand was that this was far more than a protest. This was a clash of identities. A battle between the past and the future.

On the Shrine itself were the ragtag protesters, ambassadors of an Australia which many naively believed we were still in. They looked like spectators at the cricket or people coming home from bingo.

Except their chants weren't sport-related; their chants were for freedom. At one point, they sang the national anthem with a defiance I'd never heard before. A beauty, for in their voices you could hear their love for the country they believe they were defending.

And before them, dressed like stormtroopers, were their brothers and sisters – who had initially joined the police to protect and serve the community, but were now enthusiastically taking on a new role – oppressors.

The shooting was only part of this oppression. On the steps where they arrested us, there was no tapping on the shoulder asking us to "please stand". Instead, they leapt on us in packs, punching us and smashing our heads into the concrete with their new plastic shields.

As I recorded earlier in these essays, the officer who did this to me repeated three times, "Stop making me do this." There was despair in his voice. But he wasn't saying this to me. He was pleading with whoever was making him do it. Because I believe, on some level, he knew what he was doing. He was betraying his oath as a police officer and his duty as an Australian, who had grown up under the banner of Lest We Forget. He was betraying himself.

This was not about forgetting our promise to the ghosts we built the Shrine for. This was him using his shield as a weapon to say, "Fuck your sacrifice, Granddad. These people won't do what the government wants them to do, so I'm allowed to hurt them, in order to frighten the rest of the public into doing what they are told, so I will."

While he was doing this to me and the others who were arrested with me, his colleagues lined up and shot at the other protesters. Then, once they had dispersed them, in their black uniforms and fully armed, they marched up the stone steps and conquered the Shrine like a human black cloud, as the world watched via Rukshan's livestream.

There were grandmothers in the crowd, fathers, mothers, young people, and even children – defending not just their own freedom but all that was good about who we thought we were as Australians. Armed with nothing more than their presence, speeches, and as I stated before, the national anthem, they stood against this battalion of officers who embodied the country's new identity, where integrity would mean compliance and questioning authority would see you labelled a conspiracy theorist, a second-class citizen – a leper. If they could, they would have you fired from your job. Cancelled.

Better to comply.

That's why this wasn't a protest; it was a battle. An assault on who we thought we were, by those who were willing to work for those in power, somewhere high above us, who had decided who we, as Australians, were going to become.

And to show their commitment to establishing this new identity, they ordered their officers – these Victorians – to shoot their fellow Victorians, the stubborn ones who still believed that they could cling to the Australia we all thought we were, by simply standing up.

This is what Rukshan captured; Australians whose badges pledged to protect and serve, serving instead a government that ordered them to shoot. And they did shoot. And they enjoyed it. And the echoes of their weapons can still be felt today.

Yet, while they won that battle, they have not won the war.

That victory is still up for discussion. Sadly, even though many Australians are aware that great change is coming, many have lost their larrikin courage to speak out.

4 January, 2025.

MILDURA POLIO

WE WERE ON a farm in Mildura, working on the bus when two women turned up. One of them, Wendy, was a lifelong sufferer of polio.

She told me: "When I was four I had polio. In my early 20s I was hitch-hiking across Africa."

In the inverse snobbery of contemporary Australia, where to be a victim is to have status, Wendy, in this interview showed that she was never once interested in being a victim of polio even though she still wears a metal brace on her leg. She just wanted to live, and so did.

This begs the question, in these easier times, in this great country, why do so many crave victimhood?

Australia has never remained the same. Throughout our brief history, it has constantly changed, yet somehow, it has always remained Australia. And we have always remained proud Australians.

That was until the Covid years, when a tsunami of fear washed away our communal identity, leaving us silently trying to ignore an undercurrent of shame.

This left us with a question that it is not polite to ask: Who are we now?

Despite living in what should be one of the richest countries in the world, many are struggling financially, and in the face of great change, we feel powerless – even worthless.

Why?

If we, as a people, through conversation and action, don't find a way to agree on our current identity – or on an identity of who we should strive to be – then big business, the Government, and the mainstream media will create an identity for us that suits their needs, and we will have to live under that.

So, before that happens, we decided to hit the road again. Like modern-day apprentice street historians, we are willing to record anyone who will speak and ask them questions about our culture.

Who are we now? Where are we going?

And if we don't want to go there, what other options are open – or can we open?

Our goal is to travel from town to town, posting the voices we record in an attempt to foster this conversation.

For how can we defend ourselves from those who would oppress us if we don't actually know who we are?

5 January, 2025.

THE SCRUB BULLS OF MILDURA

THE STATION WAS so vast and remote that chances are the bull had never seen a fence or a house. Now in his prime, he was the king of this harsh terrain – a king who took his freedom for granted, unaware that, somewhere, he was known by another species, humans, as livestock.

When he finally met mankind, he was fighting three four-wheel-drive buggies, each wrapped in bull bars, all striving for the trophy of running him over.

The buggy I was in was the winner. Still holding my camera and full of the adrenaline my ancestors must have felt on a hunt, I filmed the cattle muster as his legs were roped together.

He was, with most of his great shoulders and head pinned under the buggy, in a state of rage and confusion, trying to make sense of what was happening.

The last time I saw him, he was lying on his side, struggling to get up – a fight he would never win. As the cowboys returned to mustering other cattle, he would lay there under the full, unforgiving sun, a gift to the flies and the ants, until the stars returned to look at him one more time.

In the morning, the musterers would return with a truck and, after dragging him into the rear, he'd be off to the meatworks, en route to your plate.

He explained that the station owner wanted these scrub bulls removed to prevent them from breeding with his cows. If the king did, the resulting bulls and cows would be too hard to handle. They would inherit the seeds of hope so precious to them that they'd have the audacity to fight for their freedom.

Instead, the owner brought in a beautiful Brahma bull. Despite his noble appearance, he had been bred to be passive. His offspring would walk into their final pen, where the trucks waited, without so much as a whimper.

I witnessed this.

Back at the farmhouse, I watched these cowboys being tender with the farm cats. Why? Were these bad men pretending, via a purring cat, to be good men? Or were they good men with a job to do – men who had bills to pay?

With a few beers and full bellies, we started recalling the day. It was a novelty for them to have someone around who had tried to document what they did for a living. Capture this part of the story that ended up in the city in your hamburger. The dirt of the day was still on their clothes and matted in their hair. There was no talk of transitioning out here, not tonight; these were men. A few weeks later, one of them would end up in the hospital with a broken arm, after another bull managed to gore him.

But tonight, as they gently petted the camp cat, who would curl around their shoulders like a living stole, Luke, my host, told me he had only spent one day in school. The rest of his education had been over the radio. He'd grown up in these stock camps and was still here. He was also unvaccinated, as were his little team and a few of the musterers. They were working out here, on the harder properties, the more isolated ones, because the station owner couldn't recruit anyone else.

I'd met Luke on the lawn of Parliament House in Canberra. He and his mate and son had driven down there, all the way from Mt Isa, to participate in the great march. In their cowboy hats, they had stood out from the crowd, and with his warm smile and infectious laugh, he had attracted a lot of fans.

We were here now to see what it was that would motivate these men to undertake such a journey, just to attend a protest. They had driven down here to try to remind the government and anyone else who would listen that this was a free country, and that our precious liberties were under attack. The freedoms our forefathers had left their country to defend.

But that was then, and this was now. A time when our government and their propaganda machine were working together, like these musterers, to convince their fellow Australians to compliantly walk into the vaccination centers, with their children, to take what even Health Minister Greg Hunt had declared was an experiment. A time where the same machine attacked anyone who challenged this insanity by calling them anti-vaxxers and conspiracy theorists.

Millions of Australian children were vaccinated with a poorly tested product which stopped neither infection nor transmission and for which the long term consequences were unknown. Millions of Australian parents, a significant number now filled with deep regret, failed at the time to raise a single word of protest.

For the last few days, I've been in Mildura, and there are scrub bulls here – people who defied the mandates. They've learned the lessons of the last few years and now talk online, in chat groups, or quietly with each other.

A few brave ones spoke to us, but most shied away from the camera. "Cowed" is the correct word.

Instead, they told me stories of the carnage: friends and family dying of sudden heart attacks and turbo cancers. Friends who, nearing death, would only admit they suspected the jabs were to blame.

But we are not scrub bulls, for we are not livestock – unless we volunteer to act as though we are. What we are is unique slivers of the divine, each a possible hope for all of humanity. But that hope can only be seen if we allow it to shine. The best way for it to shine is to speak.

11 January, 2025.

THE CUCKOO'S NEST BLUES

Florence the Freedom Bus growled eastward from the sun-drenched citrus groves of Mildura, where the Murray River irrigates a patchwork of orange and lemon trees under vast Victorian skies, into New South Wales' rice-bowl plains, where Deniliquin's merino sheep dotted the floodplains amid the faint echo of ute engines revving in the distance. It was a stretch that traded fruit-laden abundance for the raw, flood-fed fertility of the Riverina, each mile peeling back layers of urban conformity.

We interviewed many along the way. Once you might have called them salt-of-the-earth types; now we called them warriors.

One teacher we met had finally clawed her job back after burning through all her long-service leave – the nest egg she'd squirreled away for the holiday of a lifetime. Instead, she'd rationed her days like wartime, waiting for the mandates to crumble so she could return to the classroom.

Now, in the staff room, she eats alone, weathering the occasional jibes from colleagues – including her extremely fit, early-fifties principal – who, with grim irony, suffered a heart attack not long after.

After another teacher joined us, she told me how they never have full attendance anymore. Either the kids are sick, or the teachers are sick – or both.

But then, this is a very dangerous place to live, with the Murray River ebbing through the town like a brown artery, supporting a spread of endless farms, most of them growing food and wine. The sun nurtures the earth with an abundance of vitamin D, which, apparently, we are all deficient in.

Her own grown children have their issues, and her son-in-law, who has turbo cancer, still refers to her as an idiot.

I feel like I'm Jack Nicholson in One Flew Over the Cuckoo's Nest.

Later that day, a farmer arrived at the place where we were staying. He had the same baffled tone so many of us have. One of his lifelong friends – whom he had pleaded with not to take the jabs – succumbed to fear and jabbed himself, along with his entire family.

Recently, this friend reached out to the farmer, pleading with him to look after his children if anything should happen to him or his wife.

When I mentioned this story to others in the town, a few told me they'd been asked to do the same.

Oil floats on water, and this is a metaphor for our country now. The upper echelons are still singing the praises of the jabs, the mRNA factories, and how they're "helping families" in these harder economic times. Meanwhile, underneath, the currents are stirring, as questions that have haunted the troubled eyes of Australians for years begin to take shape.

One man, who managed a car wash, wanted to hear my thoughts, then shared his.

He'd taken it to keep his job but was now convinced it was just a money grab, with all the politicians in on it.

To him, the country has been needle-raped and pillaged by overseas corporations working in league with the blessing of our government. And the people don't want to talk about it – like the altar boys who kept their sexual abuse secret, drowning their pain in drugs, rage, and alcohol until they either took their own lives or spoke out.

The last man I met told me his story. A farmer, he'd had a great marriage and a load of kids. While Covid didn't kill any of them, it destroyed his family all the same. His wife was a believer in the vaccine and didn't want to lose all her friends, as he had, by refusing to conform. Now he's trying to establish a new life while grieving for what he's lost – his family, and friends who ostracised him but are now falling sick. They struggle with heart issues or are diagnosed with turbo cancers.

And then it's Monday, and we've just pulled into another town. The carnage is being handled as neatly as the churches handled the sex scandals: with the help of loyal parishioners who fill the Sunday pews, then drop to their knees before the man on the Cross who died for their sins, and tell him, through combined prayer – we believe.

13 January, 2025.

THE DOWN SYNDROME ORPHAN WHO CHANGED MY LIFE

HE WORKED IN the circus as a performer, a natural-born clown. He had the talent to make you erupt into laughter, using a goofy smile, despite his good looks. He adored what he did, that's why he took the jabs. Now, today, his mother is fielding calls from loved ones and friends because her son, her only child, is being placed into an induced coma. Since the vaccinations – and he's had six – he's been having seizures, but instead of the CAT scan revealing the dodgy switch, it uncovered a brain tumour so large it's inoperable.

Further down the road, as my partner searched an op shop for new clothes, a woman approached the bus to say hello. Finally, she revealed that she was the local funeral director, which saw the conversation quickly move to excess deaths. Last year was their busiest year on record.

I asked her if any of the mourners had queried or even come out and stated that the jabs were behind the loss of their loved one.

No, she said. They say nothing.

Then I asked her who was the youngest she'd buried. A newborn baby, she said, and I saw the pain ripple through her eyes.

Is that common? I asked.

No, she said. It's rare. But the young mother was all jabbed, she said. She had to take it to keep her job.

What was her job?

She worked at the local IGA, part-time.

A flock of corellas cracked the sky above us as they flew over the town like the last custodians of our rebel souls.

The next morning, I interviewed Mika from Finland, and we went through the tyranny checklist – digital ID, end of cash, chemtrails, you know the rest – and it's all the same. What's happening here is happening there, which leaves you sensing this dark cloud spreading across the world as the people look into the light of their phones, as though it were an umbilical cord to a safe place. Nothing to see here because everything's fine, their downcast expressions claim.

A day before, another woman started talking to me. Quiet and gentle, she talked about a time in 1974, when she was working in a hospital in Carlton.

"The little boy was Philip Marmo. He was a perfectly healthy baby up until nine months old when he was given his third triple-antigen injection – which caused catastrophic brain damage.

"This was the first time I had ever heard of vaccines causing any harm," she said. "In those days the doctors and nurses talked openly and freely about the damage caused by vaccines.

"When I knew Philip, he would have been about ten years old. It was 1979 and he could not walk, talk, or feed himself. He was totally reliant on others to do everything for him – but his face used to light up whenever I walked in.

"This little baby was a Down syndrome baby who had been dumped there by his parents because he wasn't perfect! But just a few months old and he was already giving me the most beautiful smiles. He touched my heart.

"No one ever visited these children, ever," she told me. "We were their family."

Maybe this is evidence that defaulting to silence and looking the other way is a cultural norm.

Is it how we manage to drink our coffee and shoot our TikTok dance videos without being affected by all the excess deaths and injuries?

There was another orphan there too, in 1974. He had a touch of Down syndrome – just a touch, she said – but it was enough for his parents to dump him here. They too never returned. But regardless he was full of joy and he also had this beautiful smile, she said.

"In fact, it was his smile that inspired me to have my own children. So I did, and now they are all grown, and jabbed, and they call me an idiot, as I pray every morning for them not to be harmed."

It's Friday. Tomorrow, around dawn, we'll be heading back on the road.

17 January, 2025.

MY SAVIOUR THE JUNKIE

It was not a question of not wanting to take it; Tom was adamant – he was not going to.

His wife felt the same.

Trouble was, Tom was a young Australian father with a young family to support, a mortgage, and the other usual bills to service, which he routinely honoured by working hard at the job he was about to lose if he didn't take it.

Up to this point he'd also been attending most of the rallies in Melbourne and had been constantly outspoken on social media, to the point of being censored, perhaps even having his details recorded by our country's ever-growing and secretive surveillance network.

So, when he finally reached the date where he was expected to provide proof of vaccination, he did so – an achievement his unjabbed friends, the hesitant few, did not believe.

Together they set about grilling him until he revealed his secret.

There were saviours among us.

People who, either coping with unbearable pain or simply unable to authentically act in the script we call normal Australian life, had opted to create a new reality to survive in: a counter-culture supported by illegal drugs.

In a previous life, Tom had run a business, and one of his employees – a nice bloke in his early thirties – had, for unknown reasons, turned to drugs and, as yet, displayed no interest in returning to the hamster wheel.

So Tom approached this ex-employee with a deal.

"Would you take the jab for me for a thousand?"

"Yes."

And the deal was done.

After giving the junkie his Medicare card and another form of ID, Tom helped the junkie memorise his birth date and the first names of the family members listed under his name on the Medicare card.

Prepared, the junkie entered the vaccination centre; a while later he returned with Tom's proof of vaccination.

A few weeks later, for another grand, the junkie would repeat the procedure so that Tom would be officially recorded as double-jabbed.

Tom was now a Jew pretending to be a German in pre-war Nazi Germany.

But there were many other Jews desperate to remain hidden too, and so – after identifying an opportunity – capitalism created, as it always does, a new business.

Those Australians attempting to cope with life by remaining high have a constant problem: a need for funds, lots of funds. But now a new income stream was becoming available to them – Australians who, for their own reasons, did not want to take the jabs.

When I interviewed Dr Hobart and Dr Borsos – two doctors both suspended for handing out exemptions – they recounted how their surgeries were besieged by desperate Australians.

Doctor Hobart told me he had people at his window, crying while waving wads of cash.

Cash was what these junkies craved.

Tom set about becoming their secret manager.

With everyone invested in keeping it secret, he began to recruit other junkies and even created a coded language – such as the Mafia would use when talking shop on the phone, knowing they were probably being bugged.

It was an egalitarian business.

He had everyone applying: Chief Executives of powerful multinational corporations, police officers, prison guards, shop assistants, teachers, nurses, tradies, truck drivers – you name it.

And since this was capitalism in its purest form – supply and demand – the price kept rising, driven up, too, by the amount of risk Tom was taking.

In the end, people were paying five grand a shot: one thousand for Tom, the rest for the drug addict.

"What will happen if you are arrested?" his partner asked him once, when they were both unable to sleep.

"I don't know," he replied, listening to the dark suburban silence for an approaching siren – or sirens – "I don't know." The sirens never arrived.

Willing female drug addicts were especially difficult to recruit, so they became the most expensive.

One client required his junkie to be of Indian descent – a requirement Tom finally managed to fill, and once again the transaction took place.

Thanks to the fresh victory of Trump, Tom does not think the Australian Government will try it again.

"But they are building mRNA factories," he said, "so I do not, and will never, trust the Government again."

Tom's children are beautiful, strong and healthy – each a part of the foundation of the next generation of Australians.

A foundation Tom is not only determined to protect, but now regrets ever giving them any vaccines.

When I was growing up, I always sensed there was something amiss about our country.

It shifted in our own silences, that sense of strangeness.

Lurked in the shadows underneath the Paul Hogans, the tourism posters; it underwrote the conversations of men talking about footy as though footy was all that mattered.

It left clues in the suicide notes of people who decided to leave our lucky country before their time.

It was like there was a fault in our otherwise perfect diamond, an open wound that many felt but few mentioned.

Covid liberated this secret.

It was the fear that we knew we were not who we thought we were. To a degree we were all acting – pretending to be brave and free when it turned out we were debt slaves who, thanks to an endless propaganda attack, showed the world how easy we were to control and subjugate.

Many of us have not got over this shock, nor have we dealt with the consequences, for the fear we used to smother with bravado is still out, liberated by our responses, and now it is busily redefining our character.

For years now we have lived in a world of lies, thanks to a refusal to accept responsibility for any of it, or even to acknowledge those who have been injured or worse.

A world of lies that is devouring our identity, feasting on our culture; its appetite supported by Government policies and corporations determined, for their own reasons, to prise our grip free – our love for our country – with their crowbars of shame. Ironically, our new unspoken ghost – the splinter of our quiet spaces, visible often in the troubled backwoods of our eyes – is the truth.

Or, as the state calls it, "misinformation".

Stirred by Trump's victory, will it now rise to the surface? Drawn back to our lips by fear's nemesis: courage.

One by one we are all learning that fear has an Achilles heel – one those who have tried to oppress throughout time, using fear, cannot rectify.

Despite its endless appetite and promises to keep you safe, no matter how much you feed it – including your own identity – in return Fear will always give you this amount: nothing. Nothing but shame.

We then talked more about the junkies.

Since they are all still alive, perhaps Big Pharma should use them as models for their posters:

"See, we told you it was safe."

Or were their veins so toxic that whatever was in the jabs fizzed up upon entry?

Or is it, as Tom fears, too early to tell?

20 January, 2025.

THE LONG ROAD TO A FADING DANCER

IT'S EVENING, AND the day has succumbed to hiding in the streetlights, the IGA, and the Laundromat, where Kelli waits by the dryers. Fruit bats flail overhead, their leathery wings sounding as if they're forgetting how to fly. In the bus, I prepare the podcast gear for tonight's show. Our studio is the back parking lot of this small string of shops, where Florence glows under the security lights.

The next day, we head to Ipswich, unaware of the Aussie diamond we accidentally kick out of the shadows of time. Myra is the first to seek us out. In her mid-eighties, she tells us how she ended up in the hospital for weeks, sent there, she claims, by a problematic vaccine that gave her a double pneumonia. That was the reason she said no to the Covid vaccine, and she told her husband of 60 years that he wasn't taking it either. And he didn't.

Then she invited us to camp outside her house, which is what we did. Our first night in Ipswich. We'd found little today in the way of interviews. Several were booked online, but the goal was to find the alluvial jewels scattered down the country towns' quiet roads and the suburban streets, each house with its widescreen TVs and theaters visible from the road.

Maurie has a large ulcer on his leg that won't heal, and initially, the conversation is about the slow and ongoing train wreck of his physical health, from fractured hips to an eyelid that won't close. He then went on to talk about his childhood, which was poor and tough, and I won't elaborate unless I receive the OK from Maurie later.

But to round it up, after surviving that, he became a pastry cook in a bakery in Ipswich. Pies, sausage rolls, cakes, and cookies, all made fresh daily. Being a cook would be his life's work, but his love was ballroom dancing. Both children of the war, their adolescence was in the fifties. Before the Beatles, before Chuck Berry, when Frank Sinatra and the Rat Pack were all the rage.

"I loved it," Maurie said. "I could have danced all night."

"And he would," said Myra. "I was OK at the quickstep, but I couldn't waltz for quids, so I would let him go dance with all the girls who knew how to dance properly, but the last dance was always mine."

He went on to tell me how Ipswich had a great dance hall with a floor built upon springs, which just allowed you to float across it. But on weekends, they'd pile into their cars and head to the smaller towns and their halls.

I often notice these halls. Each like a forgotten museum piece, all with the "Hall for Hire" signs outside, and inside, the memory of a golden age imbued in the well-worn boards of their small stages and their pressed-tin roofs.

So here, Maurie was populating these halls with the ghosts of his youth, whose FJ Holdens and the like were parked outside. But then a question uncovered that day's diamond.

"So how did you learn to dance?" I asked him. "Did you do lessons?"

The smile that emerged on this old man's face briefly lifted his soul out of his pains and took us to a memory that few, if any, had seen. He'd been sent to work in a bakery in Toowoomba for three months. There, he struck up a relationship with another apprentice, who was a dancer. And when the cakes were all baking, and in those moments when the shop had no customers, this apprentice would say, "Come on, then," and together, in their flour-dusty aprons and boots, they'd waltz along the kitchen floor.

And even though that actual moment is gone, and even though life had many other challenges waiting for him, including the underrated mediocrity of a suburban existence that over time can douse all the fairy lights of your soul, time didn't get this one.

Can't you see the morning sun pouring through the sash and cord windows, as maybe with the radio on, its tinny sound filtering Mel Tormé, these two young men, arm in arm, dancing as they honed their skills, all in order to go searching on the weekend for a good time and love? Maurie found love with Myra. Soon they would be celebrating their 60th anniversary.

But under the promise of that, I could see Myra's fear of losing him. For with no one in her immediate circle agreeing with her stance not to get vaccinated, who would she talk to once her dance partner had left?

The next morning, some of their little group turned up – people who had lost their jobs in the mandates and found each other in other groups, which had evolved into this group of twenty or so non-compliers.

I asked Maurie what happened to these dance hall days? Did rock and roll end them? But he said he couldn't remember. Because Myra hadn't been that fond of dancing, he told me, they hadn't been to a dance since they'd got married.

Later that day, I interviewed Lindsay, a psychologist, who has her own views on the current state of the world.

Out here now, with a new day of mining stories before us, I was writing this in our mobile home we call Florence, who is parked in a golf course car park. And as my fingers typed, all I can still see is Maurie and his mate dancing in that bakery, as though the miner in my soul was turning this diamond over and over in its hand.

22 January, 2025.

AUSTRALIA DAY IN CORAROOKE, 2025

Once upon a time, on a lonely road, fudged by night and a thick mist, Andrew suddenly found himself outside of his car. It took him a long moment to understand what had happened.

Another car had missed a give-way sign and hit them.

As he started to piece this together, he heard a voice calling. It was his wife, Mary.

Everyone in their car had survived, except their baby, Carolyn.

Andrew was a shrewd dairy farmer who had built a dairy empire on the foundation of a small paddock he had bought from his parents.

The town was called Cororooke, a speck on the map near the larger town of Colac.

The town had died in Andrew's youth. He had grown up amid its decline, and the abandoned factories were still here, slowly being dismantled by time.

In the town, too, was a church that no longer had a congregation. When it came up for sale, Andrew bought it and initially converted it into an art gallery and theatre. He called the theatre Carolyn, after his daughter.

But he did not stop there. Now he had added a restaurant and an old tram. And not only can you dine in the gorgeous tram, but it also acts as a backdrop to the amphitheatre he had built at the rear of the venue.

Over the years, I've staged a few plays here, but this weekend we brought the Kulture artists for their first concert.

Sadly, few people turned up, and we knew most of those who did. They were all from our tribe – no one from the town, no one we didn't know.

Meanwhile, online, over a thousand watched the stream, and chances are we knew most of those as well.

Graciously, Andrew let us camp in a neighbouring paddock, where our red 8:32 flags blew over the roofs of our caravans and buses. "8:32" isn't some cryptic time stamp or arbitrary number; it's a direct nod to John 8:32 from the Bible: "And ye shall know the truth, and the truth shall make you free." It became a rallying symbol for breaking free from lies, mandates, and societal control. The red flags were badges of that collective yearning for unfiltered reality and autonomy, hoisted by people who had been kicked out of normal society but had found deeper bonds in the process, wanderers united not by blood, but by a shared hunger for what's real.

It was like we were a brief gathering of gypsies, and maybe we were. In the evening, David Ricciuti kept singing his songs – the ones we knew all the words to – as we climbed to the crest of the hillock Andrew had built behind his amphitheatre.

This was the eve of Australia Day, and while we were proud to be Australian, we were also keenly aware that we were a minority within a minority.

We were those who came together regularly to try to stem the dismal tide that most people seemed unable or unwilling to see. It was here, listening to the music and listening to my tribe passionately sing along, that I watched the last pink tendrils of day dissolve into the night. For the long night was where these people – and my country – were headed.

Beyond the view from this hill, many appeared resolved to this journey. Meanwhile, here, this small group of apprentice gypsies, part of the great tribe cast out of society and their families for not taking the jabs, were smiling, hugging, and dancing on the dirt. And this, I knew, was the only chance we had to attract more numbers to our tribe and our cause: which is to remain human and free.

Despite the reality of all our lives besieging the bottom of this hillock, thanks to Andrew – and us – we had erected the briefest of forts. One where the walls were built from our love for each other and mortared by our organic ability to have fun, and to share joy.

I don't know if we will win, for the mountain is steeper than this dark is deep.

Our brothers and sisters whom we don't understand seem determined to continue this cultural descent. And I'm wondering now what it is they are after – what treasure they can sense below – that has so much worth that they have chosen to no longer see what we can see, which is the beauty of defiance and hope.

We have been igniting lamps in their darkness since the beginning, none brighter than the light of Epic. But even though there were only a handful of us here, we still shone our light as brightly as we could from the top of this tiny hill, as those in the nearby towns, for their own reasons, pulled down their blinds and turned their backs to their windows.

27 January, 2025.

HEART OF DARKNESS

I know why you're silent. I know how difficult it is to remove that spot.

Their son was beautiful. His eyes would blossom with joy, and he would laugh – that silent baby laugh – every time he found you smiling at him. A smile that let him know he was safe because you were letting him know, just with your smile, how wanted he was.

But he hated needles.

That was why, when he was receiving his second MMR vaccine, I sat before him, twiddling my fingers in a way that left him enthralled. Then, as they withdrew the needle, I watched him – and felt him – spiritually vanish into himself, and to this day, he has never returned.

I was called an idiot. I was told to move on, that I just got unlucky. I got told it was just one of those things. But I know. I know.

These were the stories that haunted us all.

I met her in a caravan park. She approached the bus as we were parking it. She told us that she knew she was going to see us. She just knew.

Later, she sat with me in an outdoor communal kitchen and told me her story – one I'm curtailing to keep her identity safe.

She was the CEO of a home-run Family Day Care business. She managed sixty homes, four students in each, all cared for by trained educators.

"I'm a hypocrite," she said as trouble, like a current, washed into her eyes.

"All the funding comes through me, so it's my job to make sure that all the children are up to date with their childhood vaccines. In fact, one of my duties is chasing parents up to make sure their children's shots are up to date. Your child cannot attend unless they are up to date."

She continued: "My children are all unvaccinated. I don't believe in them, but I have so many people relying on me. What do I do? What do

I do? For you see, if we get caught with having one unvaccinated kid, or insufficiently jabbed, I could cop a five-thousand-six-hundred-dollar fine.

"That's why I'm resigning.

"And the kids," she went on in that smiling despair, which was full of stubborn disbelief. "So many of them are affected." "How many?" I asked.

"A third to half of them," she said. "From autism – so much autism – to allergies, and you have no idea how many allergies they have. And many others are just not right. Asthma, eczema, developmental issues, and when we were kids there was none of this. None!

"Then we have to cater for the integration specialists. These people are sent in by the Government to help the sick kids adjust. And they achieve nothing. They'll put a picture here or a sign there, and then they'll tick some box on some form. Nothing. They achieve absolutely nothing."

"So let me get this straight," I said. "Instead of trying to discover what causes all these ailments, we just exonerate the vaccines, whose manufacturers are indemnified, and then, upon the misery of these children and their guilt-ridden parents, we build industries."

"Like mine," she said. "And the NDIS is worse."

I knew most of this before she started talking, but to hear it all condensed into one woman in her sixties, who now makes a living pushing vaccines despite her wallet constantly wrestling with her morality, left me feeling like I could suddenly see deeper into all of us. For a moment, I understood the great silence – the same silence that haunts our suicide rate and the industries we've built upon them.

No, we are not bad people, but all through history good people have been responsible for atrocities.

Now, instead of protecting our children, which we love – and you can see this love everywhere – yet still we put them forward to be jabbed so they can go to daycare, so both parents can go to work in the hope of paying off a house that their autistic child can haunt. And we do this so often, and with such little pushback, that business people have realised each of these injured children is a golden goose. Which adds to the communal incentive not to discover or reveal the cause of our autistic pandemic – because if we managed to make all our children healthy, what, all these people would lose their jobs?

Can all of this truly be traced back to Ronald Reagan deciding that all the vaccine manufacturers are protected from prosecution, which meant he created a perfect business model for a pharmaceutical industry that is now out of control?

And all they had to do after winning indemnity was wrap these vaccines in a dogma that claimed they are miraculous.

A concocted belief that is now so strong that even the daily visual evidence of all our ill children can't penetrate it.

It was now, as she continued to talk, that I realised this was a Heart of Darkness story. Except instead of a river in the Congo or Vietnam, this river was our society, and the deeper you travelled, the darker and quieter it became.

I can't recall when I first saw a yin and yang symbol – yang being white, the light, and yin its opposite. But I wonder if that's who we are now. We live, work, and play in the yang, with its bus stops coloured with the posters of smiling young people selling phones, as we try to ignore the yin – like that teenage boy, sitting on the bus. The young man who is only partially here. The one sucking his well-sucked knuckles, between occasionally banging the side of his head with his fist, as though, somewhere beyond our view, someone was torturing him.

20 February, 2025.

AUSTRALIA: THE GREAT SILENCE

"I'm a paramedic," he said. "Forty years. And do you know how many cases of myocarditis I saw in that time? Zero. Pericarditis? A few times, not many. But now it's everywhere."

He had refused to take the jab, so he lost his job.

"They still won't let me back. In New South Wales they've dropped the mandates. They even put out a media release stating that the Covid shots cause myocarditis and other things. But here? Here they still want you to be fully jabbed."

His wife was in the health industry too, as were his grown children.

"All unjabbed," he said, with a smile. "But they're still working. We paid a pharmacist – someone we never even met – to pretend they'd taken it. He organised their MyGov records so they could work. Cost a fortune, but it was worth it.

"I begged my brother not to take it. Almost succeeded. Then his doctor told him it was safe, that he had to have it, so he did. His wife too.

"After his second shot he had a massive heart attack; a few days later he was gone. She ended up with severe blood clots at the same time. They put her on huge doses of warfarin – she got through."

He told me there were loads of paramedics like him who still couldn't work.

"So even though they're desperately short-staffed, they'd rather let the public suffer – even die – than allow unvaccinated paramedics to work?" I asked.

"That's it," he said. "And my daughter, she works in a fertility clinic. When the jabs first rolled out she couldn't believe the number of missed abortions and stillbirths they were seeing. Off the charts. But no one talked about it. No one."

"Would she do an interview?" I asked.

"No, she can't. She'd lose her job."

"How about you?"

"No," he said. "I can't. Could endanger all their jobs. My son – he's a nurse. Took two, to keep his job, but now he's told them: no more. Sack me if you want, I'm not taking them. And they haven't sacked him. Think they're so short-staffed now they're looking the other way.

"And the cancers my son's seeing now – through the roof. Lots of them young. They come in with stage four and they're gone within weeks… weeks.

"I tried to get a job with a private ambulance company. During induction they wanted me to have a flu shot. I said no.

"Sadly, though, there was one young man there – half-Indian, half-Australian. Training to be a paramedic. Only young. Then I heard they'd found him. Died on his bedroom floor. Suddenly. Mid-twenties."

It was all so sad.

"Oh, I don't know how you do it, Michael," he said, patting my wrist.

"Before he died, was your brother aware it could've been the jabs?" I asked.

"Oh, they were both aware. Their doctors had told them – secretly."

"Were they angry?"

"Oh no. No, I think they just thought they were unlucky."

"How about you? Were you angry for your brother?"

He smiled and tilted his head, turning the question over in his mind. In the end all I got was a slight shrug and that same smile.

"It's so good to see you," he said. "I went to all the big marches. Got a selfie with you somewhere on here." He brought up his phone.

As he scrolled through images of himself with those who'd made names for themselves back then – most of them silent now – I asked: "Do you know why they ignored the marches? Strategic. Their way of telling us – and everyone else – that what we thought and felt didn't matter anymore.

"No matter how many turned up. Look at Canberra – all those people, not one politician came out to talk. Media lied about the numbers. All on purpose. To make us feel powerless. To make us quit."

Changing the subject, he said: "We went to France, you know. Paid a doctor to fake the booster. Cost a fortune – didn't think we'd get away with it. But when we showed the paperwork to our doctor here she said, 'Oh, and there's the batch number. Yes, this is fine.' So my wife could go back to work. I could've too – but they wanted me to take the flu shot as well." He shook his head again.

"I was a good paramedic," he said. "Specialised. Could give up to thirty-two drugs."

And he cycled through every procedure he'd been trained to do.

We'd paid for all that training with our taxes.

So if you're at home waiting for an ambulance that just isn't coming – well, here's one of the reasons.

And that made him mad. At last I could feel it in him.

"What was the young man's name?" I asked. "The trainee paramedic."

He told me. Then said, "I've got a picture of him here."

He lifted his phone and showed me the young man's handsome, mixed-race face.

"He was a nice guy," he said. Then, rhetorically: "How do you keep going? Hmm. You amaze me."

"I think like a paramedic," I said. "Once I record an interview they're inside me – until I post it and share their pain, their fears, their thoughts with the world. Then they're out of me. Like I've dropped them at a hospital.

That's how you must have coped, right?"

As he nodded I watched his eyes, inwardly scanning views from the past he didn't share now.

"The only thing I haven't captured is anger," I said. "For all the carnage and the betrayal, no one seems angry."

He nodded to that too, but with less vehemence.

Then he asked if he could take a picture with me, since he couldn't find the one from the marches.

I obliged – while seething. He'd spoken to me for an hour but refused to record his story in any way. Now all his ghosts were haunting me.

They haunted me the rest of the day and the following unsettled night.

Until, parked up on a beach, Kelli making us a coffee and the morning walkers and cyclists streaming past – like Covid had never happened – I opened my laptop and delivered this collection of pain here.

But the question still remains, like a key secret lost so deep in my soul I just can't seem to reach it:

Where is the anger? I don't understand.

Or do I?

Could it be that under all our wealth we are slaves who believe they have the right to do this to us?

And that our duty – once they've ignored our complaints – is not to liberate ourselves or our children from our masters, but to find ways to avoid their wrath? To hide. Anywhere we can.

Even if that's only in the great silence supporting so many of our social smiles.

22 February, 2025.

FREEDOM

If you are studying Trump, hoping that he will save us, then your hope is the wish of a slave, praying that their new master will be kinder than the current one.

Think back to the moment when Victorian Premier Dan Andrews stated something like, "We will have to restrict your freedoms until this crisis has passed."

Online, I remember watching so many of us gratefully accepting this deal.

But what they didn't realise, out of fear of the virus, was that what he said wasn't an offer to help us – it was a declaration of war.

For unless we, as a community, had discussed this at length, then our freedoms weren't his to restrict. They were ours: both a gift and a burden that we, without a fight, handed over.

Initially, Dan took our Freedom of Choice and punished anyone who dared to defy him. But simultaneously, that army hidden behind him had already begun attacking, through censorship, our Freedom of Speech.

Recently, our own Government concealed their final affront on this liberty under the smokescreen of protecting us from Hate Speech.

This is why, inside of us, despite the poster of the world stating that everything has gone back to normal, there is a cancerous splinter – a lingering bad taste in our souls.

This is why no one celebrates the anniversary of "Freedom Day." Remember that?

That one day when your masters declared that those who could prove they had fully complied could leave their house and go out again.

I remember watching you cheer us, who were still locked up, from the tables, lifting your drinks like victors, when instead you were collaborators. Enslavers.

Now we are here. A community that has strayed so far from the story of who they believed they were, that they are now lost.

In the story of our country, we are no longer the "she'll-be-right" larrikins; those sun-bronzed heroes born of greater heroes. Instead, we are the obese and willfully ignorant enslavers of the coming generations.

The ones who, heads bowed, are consuming TikTok dancers, as our masters install our children's digital prison around us.

We are the generation who, instead of leaping into the cold current to pull our drowning brothers and sisters from the waves, turned our backs to the water. Then, when forced to acknowledge their despair, we condescendingly informed them, "It wasn't the vax." Now, stoically, we continue to look away, long after we've heard their voices fall quiet. Why?

Seriously, why?

Is money all that matters to you? Status? Just surviving – no matter the ideological cost? Or is it the stuff you've acquired, making you feel rich? Everyone knows the rich don't lose their freedoms. Freedom is the prize of riches. A prize that has asylum seekers risking their lives to reach our Golden Shores.

Inland from those shores, we find you now: in a supermarket, studying – with a baffled expression – the latest prices. And all the while, you know that beneath your feet lies mineral wealth enough to spare you, your kids, your kids' kids from taxes forever.

A wealth corporations are stripping away now, leaving you and your offspring with a bill you'll never service.

Not only, out of fear, have you opened the door to the wolves, but you are hiding this truth from everyone under the only barricade an apprentice slave has left to protect the integrity of their soul: Silence.

A silence that will also, for a time, hide your shame. Quietly, in that space no one can reach, you are watching Trump, Elon, RFK Jr., and all the rest, hoping they will come here and liberate you.

But they can't liberate you, for you were never enslaved. You see, our culture's crown jewels – our invaluable Freedoms – were never stolen. You gave them away.

You even pressured the reluctant, us, to give up ours too.

Trump can't liberate you; he can only, maybe, replace our corrupt current rulers with his benevolence.

That is not freedom, that is the philosophy of slaves. Not citizens, but victims to the moods of the powerful.

Democracy is where the people rule, and the government serves. We no longer have this.

Which is why we need, for the sake of our own identity and pride, to restore all and enshrine in our constitution our freedoms.

This federal election will be the touchstone.

We all know Liberal and Labor are two cheeks of the same arse, unable to fix themselves because they are all deeply invested in the system.

A system that is heralding in the robots that will replace you and a cashless society that will be used to control you.

It's here.

It's happening.

And somewhere inside you, you know it.

Ironically, our only hope now lies in your soul, for it possesses one real and incredible quality: the ability to self-heal. The first step to this cure is to stand up, and the second is to embrace change – to be the change.

And once engaged, you will see the hope, for you will be the hope. For inside you, your soul will fill with all the fuel it needs to repair not only itself but your country, and your country's future for the next generation.

An ancient fuel that, throughout history, slaves have acquired through choice. And that chosen fuel is redemption.

24 February, 2025.

THE WAR OF MANUFACTURED DISILLUSIONMENT

What happened?

In our naivety or idealism, did we place too much faith in the weight of our beauty?

For in the face of tyranny, we were beautiful.

Did we really think the armoured cars were morally incapable of running over pieces of cardboard we'd scrawled freedom and love on?

Still believe that if we could only get them to read one perfect document – every amendment, every clause – they'd lay down the pepper-spray, eyes wide, join us, maybe even beg for forgiveness?

If nothing else, how about this: we didn't die.

We're not sick.

Surely they can see that? Why doesn't it resonate?

They are.

Surely that will make them see.

We reach down like hands to drowning men. Why won't they grab on?

Why protect the thing that's drowning them?

The world turns, oblivious – species blink out, nations slip from liberty into totalitarianism simply by choosing to believe what they're told instead of what's there.

And then there's us.

Our trench never held weapons – only courage, defiance, grief, shock as they shoved and pepper-sprayed our grandmothers.

The only army we raised was a Free-Hug Army; I watched it melt into the arms of soldiers.

Our soldiers were often grandmothers offering solace to the same cops who'd brutalised them.

Still nothing.

"Move on," the trolls crow. "It's all over. Move on."

I felt a tightening in my chest, a sense of foreboding that clawed at my ribs.

Time passed. Most of our ideas, campaigns, court cases failed or stalled. Our protests – which achieved little – thinned as engines ran low on enthusiasm.

Before us, our opponents' defences hold: high walls of apathy. Some still yell "Cookers!" "Anti-vaxxers!" from the battlements, but most are silent – some of their own personnel revolted by their bosses' efforts to ignore the sick and dying, not just in the general population but amongst their own friends and family members.

Pointless? Hopeless?

Then another petition lands in your feed.

More paper rolls across no-man's-land, signatures dissolving in puddles – or rolling through the mud of Covid's storm, or melting in ignored puddles.

A realisation that hits when another petition lands – and in your head, you see the old ones rolling through the mud of Covid's storm, or floating in an ignored puddle, where your lists of signatures are melting.

But what if this was planned too?

What if the resistance playbook was predicted, gamed, weaponised against us?

Do we really think they didn't budget for push-back, or that they stopped learning?

Doesn't it make sense they planned for dissent? Prepared to tackle resistance with new weapons?

They learn on their feet, too.

The shooting at the Shrine was the catalyst for Epic.

We came together, bled a little, were largely ignored.

Half the country still hasn't heard it happened.

The violence of the shooting at the shrine was a mistake, for it became the catalyst for Epic.

But how they covered it up, marketing us as the pissing villains? Genius.

They hid the Canberra weekend: the country chanting prayers for love and freedom, injured by modern weapons. After brutal incidents, they convinced Australians to ignore us – obediently forget.

But check your memories. They've ignored us since the start. Even now, re-entering family groups we were kicked from, the price is silence.

They ignore us everywhere – even in the family chats we've been allowed back into.

Price of re-entry: don't mention the war.

Our groups constrict as weary soldiers melt back into the herd – shepherded by poverty and the crows' calls to "move on."

Our platoons are shrinking.

Soldiers drift back into the herd, shepherded by rent, groceries, the polite injunction to "move on."

Now we stay silent in staff rooms, swiping memes from our people, smiling gently as others whisper of turbo cancers – then hide concern under condescending grins.

Now we stay silent in staffrooms, swipe our own memes, smile thinly while the others whisper about turbo cancer before hiding their fear behind the condescending grin they save for us.

Us, who are not dying.

Throughout history, oppressors wield two weapons.

First: Fear.

After five years Fear is toothless – masks stay in glove-boxes, boosters rot on shelves.

Even their soldiers ignore its calls. Masks stay boxed; boosters degrade on pharmacist's shelves.

It all feels too hard. Or does it?

Second: Disillusionment.

What if that hopelessness isn't yours? What if you're a victim of their other weapon: Manufactured Disillusionment?

Side-effects include frustration, infighting, division, the cold realisation that we are powerless.

This has sundered movements through history. Side effect: frustration. Which breeds infighting, division – how many campfires have we watched doused, feeling powerless?

They inch ahead, dragging us toward a future unfit for human souls.

They, meanwhile, inch ahead, dragging us toward a future unsuitable for human souls.

So here we are. Quietly studying Trump and Kennedy, hoping their revolution reaches our shores – liberating us as our banners gather dust in cupboards.

So we sit here, quietly tracking Trump & Kennedy, hoping their revolution will wash up on our shores and save us.

Why wait for another country to save us? Better to liberate ourselves.

We won the Covid War. Only 5% take boosters now. We – with jab injuries they couldn't hide, the deaths, our endless shares – won that battle. Hollow, though.

We won the Covid War. Only 5% are now taking the boosters. We, along with the jab injuries that they eventually couldn't hide, and the deaths, and all the posts we have shared and keep sharing, won that battle. Though it is a hollow victory.

The war's far from over. Here, despite awareness, they win again.

But the war is far from over, and now here, in this country, despite many being awake, they are once again winning.

They don't care if citizens know – as long as we shut up and do nothing.

For you see, they don't care if citizens know anymore, they can know everything, as long as they shut up about it and do nothing.

This is why Australians don't join our ranks. Why should they? What can we do against determined change? AI, robots replacing us; rules shifting on purpose – hard to fight disillusionment on a virtue-signalling waterbed.

This is why, despite the rising awareness, Australians are not joining our ranks. Why should they? What can we do in the face of such determined change? With AI and robots amassing to replace us, and with so many of our brothers and sisters attempting to adapt to their new rules, which keep changing? And that is on purpose too. It's hard to face off disillusionment when you're standing on a virtue-signalling water bed.

They've accepted powerlessness. See us not as saviours, but old homeless men yelling "The End is Nigh" from bus-stop homes.

Welcome, veterans, to the battleground of the New War.

The new war where we are still humanity's hope.

If you feel disillusionment now, their weapon is working.

Welcome to the New War.

The first step to halting disillusionment's advance? Realise it's not real – just propaganda.

One weapon against it: humour (we know that well). Lift your chin, show how strong you've become.

You walked streets maskless once. Now the country's masked in apathy, strapped by silence. Pull out the old T-shirts – wear them proudly?

Or make new ones?

New ones spotlighting their weapon's fakery – it hates the light, prefers quiet conquests.

Could you craft a plan to remind people they're not powerless? That they're the true architects of our future – if they find the courage?

Under corruption and cancerous morality, this country holds promise: a beacon for the world, waiting in its DNA.

Renovated by the people, for the people. Transparency and common sense as foundation. Integrity and respect as walls. We man the battlements against subjugators. Ranks full of soldiers fighting for liberty – for children, and children's children.

Momentous times. With one hard-won victory, knock on fate's armory door. Answer:

"Is what's happening now right or wrong?"

One answer opens it. Inside, beyond disillusionment and inconsequentiality, a gift.

Before knocking, read this aloud:

"Greatness is not a destiny,

It is a choice.

And even deciding to strive to be great

Is greatness in itself.

Currently, humanity is under attack.

The Meek cannot save us.

What we need is an Army of Greatness.

So, choose well.

When you're ready, look inward – below frustration and un-cried tears. Find that door.

Can you see the warm light streaming from its rim, as if light itself breaks free?

What if this is the room God wanted you to find? A storeroom of your soul's inexhaustible fuel. Where your heart's illuminated armor awaits – or, in old speak, weary soldier, where the Gods wait with a gift: Your Destiny.

1 March, 2025.

LIFE IN THE CARPARK BENEATH AUSTRALIAN PRIME MINISTER ANTHONY ALBANESE'S CLIFFTOP MANSION

It's 5 a.m., and while Kelli sleeps – murmuring in her dreams – I'm writing this in Florence, camped in a forgotten car park in the beach town of Copacabana.

During the day, David pointed out the Prime Minister's house. "It's one of those on that hill," he said. "Four point six million dollars' worth."

The Prime Minister was in town the other day with his entourage, including his security team of Australian Federal Police officers. The media filmed him in the pub, declaring with his characteristic lisp, "This is my new local."

David has been living in the car park.

Next to him, in his son's station wagon, lives Max, his son's German Shepherd.

Once, Dave flew the world as a charming and handsome Qantas air steward. And that smile of his – the one he can still wield to disarm anyone – is alive as he rolls off stories like the town's oracle.

When lockdown hit, Dave took off. Unvaccinated by choice, he lived on empty regional highways and back roads, camping here and there, always expecting to be pulled over. But that never happened.

I found him at the Canberra protests. Well-dressed, he'd separated himself from the great herd of protesters and – looking to all the world like a stylish tourist – approached a line of masked police officers, blue gloves and pepper-spray canisters at the ready. He asked the most senior cop he could find if this was where he joined the tour.

"Tour?" the copper asked. "What tour?"

"The Satanic Tunnel Tour. I've just done the one in the Vatican, and they recommended it."

Yes, he actually asked that – which still makes me smile as I type this.

Across the road, the waves pound the beach like an artillery barrage from a discontented war. They kept firing rhythmically last night as Dave and two other men sat in the car park, where we shared our stories from this war.

The rain fell as gently as angels' tears, and Dave opened up about the daughter he lost at seventeen months old. He believes it was the MMR vaccine – her death certificate simply read SIDS. That was all he said, and the anger still corrodes him.

"But I'm trying to be happy, you know. What else can you do? But then this government… They owe me four years. People keep telling me to move on, but I can't get past it, you know. I'm owed retribution. I want it."

One of the guys – who is vaccinated – clearly can't comprehend the foundation of Dave's discontent. Out of kindness, he offers the same advice: move on. He urges Dave to focus his energy on preparing for the economic collapse. "It's coming," he says, hands painting a mushroom cloud. "It's coming." But I get it. And so does Peter, the third man, as I try to explain, calmly.

"It isn't the fact that we were ostracized. It's that for the majority of these past few years – especially early on – we lived under the distinct possibility that they would come for us."

"The pandemic of the unvaccinated," sang the choir of puppet journalists fronting Mainstream Media – as Queensland's Health Minister branded us oxygen thieves. And never forget: all over the world, and right across Australia, amid this supposed apocalypse, they raced to erect so-called resilience camps – rows of IKEA-flatpack huts ringed by walls topped with rolls of razor wire.

We heard the hate – and saw it too, through the windows to their souls: them closing their doors in their hearts. It was that glimpse that told us, plain as day, if the authorities came looking, you – our loved ones – wouldn't hide us. Chances are, you'd be the ones pointing us out.

Move on, they say now, as if we could swallow the lie that the darkness we saw has simply vanished.

Move on, they toss back over their shoulders, from under those apathetic masks – required to protect their souls in this new normal. The one where a Monday diagnosis of the Big C sends you back to the gods by week's end. Turbo cancers – who had even heard of them before?

Move on. How?

We saw you not only cave to the fear, but quietly agree to sacrifice us.

That's why you stayed silent as we lost our jobs. That's why you agreed to ban us from Christmases and christenings, weddings and – of course – funerals. We watched you swallow their lies about us, then vent in those hate-filled Facebook comments they wouldn't censor: wishing the police had used real bullets.

This is why we're so close. For in that time, we strangers – we black sheep – were all we had. That's why, when we hugged, we hugged like people who'd found someone lost in the wilds. And still do.

"Fucking right," says Dave. "If they did come – and it looked like they would – I had a contingency plan. Lots of us did."

"I was shit scared," says Peter. And I can still see and feel the fear haunting his eyes, as those unseen waves pound and re-pound the beach – promises from a war that hasn't forgotten us. We were the ones who, as those around us lost their minds, drove straight to meet this tyranny head-on. In our protests, on the steps of their parliaments, our unmasked faces breached those waves – until their army of fear retreated into the shadows haunting their conquered souls.

"What are you talking about?" said my partner Kelli, her eyes as wise and wary as an owl's. "They could still come for us," she said, leaning alone against Florence – her home – as her resilient elegance, those protective wings, sheltered all her unspoken and active wounds.

But once again, the sun rises. As I write this, I'm watching its hope rescue my keyboard from the darkness.

Soon, we'll be packing up and heading north. We're en route to another 8:32 Gathering – like a modern-day corroboree, a joyful meeting of orphans who found each other by having the courage to challenge their suffocating night. By holding up our souls like streetlights illuminating Goodbye Road.

14 March, 2025.

WELCOME TO THE REAL BATTLEFRONT

When I bring up the belief that we're under attack from a weapon called Disillusionment, people respond: "It's a war of attrition." But I think the two are different.

There's no perceived war now. No lockdowns, no vax passports, no cops cracking skulls for mask offences.

Most now file the Covid years under "unfortunate events" they were powerless to control; their only duty was to endure. Which they did – so, if they kept their job, house, and pulse, they congratulate themselves on having "won."

The Freedom Warriors are still out here banging on about Truth, still hunting one golden, irrefutable fact that will flip the script. And convince everyone else – all those people who turned their backs, all those people they cared about.

But what if that fact is already in front of our face and we simply don't want to see it?

Robert Roach fronted his Murray Bridge Council with the Port Hedland DNA challenge – that Pilbara bombshell from October 2024, where a remote hub town's council voted 7–2 to suspend mRNA jabs over lab-proof DNA contamination in the vials.

Peer-reviewed studies showed plasmid fragments that could hitch-hike into genomes, spiking cancer risks or worse; the motion demanded the feds, the Therapeutic Goods Administration, and the World Health Organisation investigate, halt the rollout, and pay up for the fallout – calling bullshit on the ignored emergency.

It was a smash for the Freedom crowd: not just owning the botched vax-push as unscientific, but snowballing copycats across South Australia, Victoria, New South Wales – a dozen-plus by mid-year, all drilling the same irrefutable lab nail.

Port Hedland cracked the "unfortunate events" facade, proving Warriors could flip local scripts with cold, hard data.

Yet even there, status reared its head. Roach lined up one councillor to table it, another to second – but a third, eyes on his community perch, whispered, "I agree, but I can't be seen as an anti-vaxxer."

Five years of noble truth-hunting... and maybe that's the rub: the majority just wanted what we forfeited by bucking the line – status. Something we can't hand back, 'cause in their eyes, we've got none left.

It poisons us too. Jealousy, infighting, clique snobbery – our scramble for pecking-order scraps shreds the unity that once made us dangerous.

"Viral vid's gonna change everything, bro." Nah – it's dopamine in a dead scrimmage. Likes and shares fizzle in the echo chamber before the whistle.

We chant "freedom" online, but can't boil it down to a ten-word T-shirt. Go on – define it in thirty seconds, under ten words. Can't? That's the trap.

The real battlefield's status. Daniel Andrews nailed it: Victoria, now a "vaccine economy" – in-crowd or leper. So, against their gut, most just obeyed the boss.

Why? Easier gig, promotion, fatter cheque, stitched identity in a job title. "What do you do?" sets the room temperature.

"Doctor" lands differently than "delivery driver."

Doctors and nurses now drown in vaccine-injured patients – yet stay silent, gaslighting ("It's just anxiety") to keep the badge. Some whisper, "I took two for the job – no more." Speak up? Lose the gig. Survival elbows status aside.

The condescension – Kochie on telly urging us to exile the un-jabbed, stoking fear for Pfizer sales (bribes or fees? The era's great unanswered question) – was perfect priestcraft. Millions did it: scrubbed "vaccine" from eulogies, smoothed ripples at funerals we watched online, because saying the culprit's name would've been impolite.

We awaited a grief-powered uprising. Instead, victims cremated, status restored. Void inside? Only they know.

Tribes shrink, grey, fragmented.

Many slip back into society, swallow the lie, crawl to us only when the cognitive hunger pangs hit – then crawl back to the paycheck. Even Novak Djokovic – the world's number one tennis player, living proof the juice was optional – was caged in a dingy Melbourne immigration hotel with asylum seekers and refugees before being unceremoniously deported from the country, while most Australians shrugged or accepted the word of their grandstanding, politically motivated Prime Minister, Scott Morrison, that nobody was above the law. Not even the world's most famous tennis player.

All his aces couldn't outrank the label: anti-vaxxer.

The metric isn't safety or efficacy; it's: Did you take it? How many?

Simple pecking-order arithmetic.

Most of us have had bosses.

Those without the itch or gear to climb the corporate ladder gripe, moan – then do as we are told.

We the anti-vaxxers, the freedom fighters, we're the black sheep; herds chafe us.

We can stand alone, but allies make it easier – yet allies are evaporating.

Then I was dragged to a new church meeting in a borrowed conference room.

Full house: inked tradies, penitent power-lads, adored toddlers, hope.

No stained glass, no mortgage-sized cathedral – just a crucifix and folding chairs.

I scanned for status-hunger; couldn't smell it.

They'd left it in the carpark, or at home.

The great shrines proved expendable when tyranny peppersprayed our lives.

But a simple Cross still says: you're always at war; good and evil watch your choices.

The genius: they framed "no" as weak, selfish, bad-people choice – status killer.

Possible only because we'd let the presence of God in our societies erode to almost nothing.

That great military strategist and philosopher Sun Tzu wrote: "Supreme art of war is to subdue the enemy without fighting."

Fear lost its fangs; Disillusionment now gnaws the bone.

Time for self-audit:

What do we actually want?

What are we selling?

Where are we going?

No destination, no map, no arrival.

Maybe the clue is in that room: hope, shared, bigger than self.

I'd seen it before – Camp Epic, status stripped, lepers birthing human beauty that still raises goose-bumps.

Offer the world moments like that: strangers, smiles, hugs, generosity – worth you can't buy, only earn by turning up and being you.

The victors will keep drifting into lonelier corridors of themselves, pleasant masks bolted on, Anne-Frank-quiet in the cellar of their souls until death signs their release.

We can't yank them out – yet.

So we get busy living: start businesses, hire each other, build commerce, seed traditions, honour folk-heroes – Doctors Oosterhuis, Bay, Patterson…

Become, slowly, the alternative society where status is granted for growing into the greater part of ourselves.

We don't yet have the resources for a full parallel world – but zoom out: what choice is there except to start building something better?

The organic growth phase is over.

Options: give up, or grow up.

If you choose grow-up, step one is evaluation:

What worked? What didn't? What do we believe? What do we want? What can we offer the poor soul who finally flees and knocks on our door?

Answer that and we might become the foundation-builders of a community far more conducive to the human soul.

16 March, 2025.

RATTY AND THE BOAB TREE

By the time we were heading into the Kimberleys, we had all found a new love – the country itself.

We'd also found our grooves. Kret drove, and he was an incredible long-distance driver. Wendy kept our growing network humming along, phoning ahead to let each mob know we were coming, while I rode in the back, editing and posting from the table.

Because I was sitting sideways, in front of me was a small rectangular window through which my whole country streamed past like a living Albert Namatjira painting. Once we entered the Kimberleys, it was obvious that this land had been Albert's muse.

At one point we passed three strange, large hills. They looked like piles of enormous rocks, capped with a few gum trees and flattened summits. All three were exactly the same height.

We didn't have a drone then, so I told Kret and Wendy that a cracking shot would be Wendy's Winnebago threading between them. All I had to do to shoot it was climb one of these hills.

This is what I did.

I took my camera, my tripod, Ratty, my microphone, and my phone.

Let's talk about Ratty.

Barry Hargrave, a professional sound guy, gave Ratty to me way before Epic. He said the windsock would let me interview people outside without the wind ruining the audio. He'd then used the handle of a handbrush as the pole that I could hold onto.

Now every time I pointed this out to Barry, he'd call their microphones crap.

"Yours is the best," he says. "So don't worry about it."

Which was fine for him to say, seeing how he wasn't travelling the country interviewing people with a rat stuck on a handbrush.

He was right – it worked a treat. Trouble was, from the back of Wendy's Winnebago, I watched all the other podcasters brandishing sleek, professional mics, and all I could think was how amateurish I looked with the Rat.

I was determined that once we hit a proper town, I'd find the cash to replace him. I wanted the world to see Café Locked Out polishing its public face.

So here I was, scrambling up this hill of stacked boulders, when – thanks to the height – I suddenly had reception again.

I put some gear down and had a great yarn with the mate who rang, then made a few more calls, sending photos of where I was. Trouble is, when I talk on the phone, I walk around. When I finally hung up—and it was a long call—I looked down and found only rocks; I was on the summit now. And I realised I had a problem. I still had my camera around my neck and my tripod was slung over my shoulder, but where was Ratty?

I scanned the rocks I'd climbed, but they all looked identical.

An eagle glided overhead and I wondered: what if he – or she – thought Ratty was an actual rat.

With no way to reach Wendy and Kret (down there the signal was dead), I hunted harder, driven by something I hadn't expected: the possibility of grief.

Now that I couldn't find him, it hit me how used I was to having him around. Even the people I interviewed called him Ratty, as did plenty online.

Suddenly I wasn't looking for a Rode mic wrapped in a hair-sock thing; I was looking for a mate, an ally who'd stuck with me through everything. No way was I leaving without him.

But where was he?

The longer it took, the more upset I got, then the more I laughed at myself for being upset about a microphone. Still, whether laughing or stressing, I tore across that hilltop.

That's when I saw it.

In the middle of the summit, invisible from the road, stood a single immense boab tree.

From its pregnant trunk to its stubby branches – each stretched out as if praising the sun – the thing looked sacred, magical. I wondered how many people had ever seen it. How many other passing idiots would be stupid enough to climb this odd hill?

There was no human rubbish, no graffiti – just me and this secret church of a tree.

That's the odd thing about this life: in the flow of time, these extraordinary moments carry no more weight than the mediocre ones on either side.

The moment a baby is born, or you fall in love, or you win something, or you have a great orgasm – even your final breath – the following moments are already busy devaluing the beauty. Maybe that's why, now our phones have cameras, we photograph everything. We try (and fail) to trap the awe of these stand-alone slivers of time.

What pulled me away from my audience with the holy tree was the need to find a microphone that looked like a rat.

Finally, I accepted he was gone for good. Years from now some other adventuring tourist might trip over him and wonder how the hell he got there.

I was so down I couldn't even be bothered filming the drivethrough – the whole reason I'd climbed up.

Apart from the tree, I seemed to be the tallest thing in the landscape. Beyond the other two carbon-copy hills, the flat land ran to a horizon that melted in a heat mirage.

It was a grand but lonely perch, made lonelier by the simple act of misplacing a rat.

And then – there she was, curled on a flat rock, waiting patiently. Or loyally. Me, who had never been happier to see him. Or her.

After that I filmed the boys driving through, then started down – but I didn't come all the way down. I left on that hill every scrap of animosity I'd aimed at Ratty.

Ratty is my mate. I still use him, here and there, and when I pull him from the bag the veterans grin: "Hey look – it's Ratty."

My good friend and great contrarian Richard D. Wolstencroft won't touch him. He claims Ratty's interviewed so many unvaccinated people he's now the world's most infected microphone.

Maybe, when I finally stop, I should have him framed and put that in the description.

But then, who knows when – or where – I'll stop?

20 March, 2025.

AUSTRALIA: LAND OF SLAVES

In the Kimberley, I saw the broken backbone of a mountain range – time had spent millions of years pruning it down to here. Its rocks were cracked and angry, too hot to touch, for the sun was using the entire landscape as an anvil to cook everything into submission.

I saw a thin line of trees bent into a dry creek bed as though time had frozen them in their last, desperate search for water.

I saw crows, like the living shadows of the birds they chose to escape from, overlooking it all – like Princes waiting for their cook, Death, to serve up today's meal.

There were broken ballerinas, dressed as kangaroos lying on the side of the highways, with more ants and flies dining upon them than there were stars forever flooding this endless sky with questions.

This land will kill you. Suburban man. This land, which is your land, Australia. It's waiting out there for you. And you know it. Every time you're squashed into a bus, heading to a job that you know is killing you, you can feel it. And you want to go too, for dangerous or not, you know she wants you, whereas this concrete jungle has, as yet, not even realised you are here.

The first white people to come out here built churches from the cracked stones.

Fringe fortresses for God, where they taught the black people how to be ashamed of themselves.

Because shame is how you defeat a people.

Rather than rising up, they'll stay silent, trying to hide their regrets and pain in the grog or the drugs, until the rage escapes and sees them break the houses they live in, the cars they drive, and the people they love, until…

Too often, their lonely souls suggest a more permanent escape.

Same for the other races now, as the corporations make it clear – with their policies that, despite all the freedom this harsh land has to offer the brave, you are a slave.

If you say something – or post it – they don't like, they'll sack you. And even if, in a desperate bid to prove you're a dedicated, valued employee, you swallow every offensive word, they'll discard you all the same. With all the pomp and circumstance a road train offers a kangaroo.

I once sat at a public table, near a trio of painted silos, and watched for a few hours as these discarded men, in their shorts, T-shirts, and obese bellies, parked their four-wheel drives and caravans. As their bored wives watched, they took pictures of the silos. For who?

Would they look at them again? Would they show their grown kids? Would they even wonder, why am I taking this?

Or is it for those they left behind at work – evidence that they were free? Many of them were born here, some are several generations old.

Yet if they parked out here, near the last of this mountain, and walked off into the desert, the land would take them.

But the black man lived out here.

He saw the land, for it was – is – his mother.

He can read the hard ground for the clues to where life, where food, is hiding, as his woman dug up sustenance from the baking earth.

But not our tourist.

That's why he spent his life in the city, hunting for sustenance in fast food venues and shopping aisles.

Why he spent the best part of his life paying off bricked-up air.

Creating a cave from a shed, filling it with the greatest discoveries he'd found, his best kills.

A fish.

A signed jersey.

Within the concrete forest we built ourselves. Only to become its seasons.

We are the weak ones.

We are the ones who take the abuse – who whine if our abuse is not recognised. We are the ones who scan our own groceries so the supermarkets can make more obscene profits, as our kids look for work.

We are the generation that future generations will curse.

If they ever talk about us at all.

The generation whose most famous battle was for toilet paper in supermarket aisles during the Covid panic.

The generation that forgave those who violated them by saying, "It's all over now. It's gone back to normal."

Except in this new normal, you can die of cancer in a week.

A baby can be aborted within sight of birth. And if it survives – this gift from the gods – we'll leave it to die, without painkillers, on a bench in a hospital room most would call humane.

We use the word safety as though it meant bravery, and we rarely use that word anymore.

We are the ones that, if God could, He would reread His blueprints
and ponder: How did a generation I gifted with so many virtues
lead such inconsequential existences?

Then wonder why their suicide rate is so high.

We are the generation that stayed silent as they built the prison around us – the one we knew would one day cage their kids too. We could have been humanity's liberators: faces in some future mural, homage to love and courage and freedom. Did you make it this far?

Are you pissed off?

Do you want to find me, tell me off? Maybe punch, or hurt me?

I hope so.

I hope that somewhere inside of you, the stallion you helped them break so you could get a job as a pony, is snorting.

Attempting to blow out all these years of bridles and saddles and ropes until, with fresh free air in your lungs, you'll realise your soul has been waiting to perform its one trick… Redemption.

You are not a number in a corporate system. That is your chain.

A chain you are voluntarily locked in.

You are, instead, the most remarkable of creatures.

A child of the gods – able to create new people or kill them. It's your choice.

For if you put all your liberties into one pan, you could reduce all of them down to the core freedom you were born with.

Choice.

And currently, our society is slipping into a world where the powers that be are determined to steal that core freedom from you.

And these last few years have shown them that it's possible. What need of a God then, huh?

What need of a God when you have already chosen a master?

Greatness is not a destiny

It's a choice

And even deciding to strive towards greatness is greatness in itself.

Currently humanity is under attack. And the meek can't save us. What we need is an army of greatness: So choose well.

30 March, 2025.

SO AUSTRALIA, NOW WE SLAY OUR HEROES?

They weren't just playing by different rules. They were playing a different game – one where the things we were prepared to defend meant nothing to them.

Ethics, informed consent, the Hippocratic oath – all of it fell to one rule: just shut up and take the vaccine.

Or, if you were a doctor, shut up and inject every patient. No exemptions.

Denes' surgery sat down a long back street in Colac.

Born in Romanian-controlled Hungary, his family escaped and washed up on our shores, beginning a long apprenticeship called "adapting to freedom".

First lesson: supermarkets groaning with food. Abundance.

He became the go-to doc at the town hospital – anaesthetist, obstetrician, paediatrician, handyman of humanity.

Handsome, staggeringly clever, a dry humour ground in the grit of real life.

Initially pro-vax.

Four daughters.

One slipped into the autism spectrum and never came back – she haunts the house like an independent ghost, scanning benches for food.

Another baby daughter stroked out, left with Parkinsonian tremors.

He did that.

He can never undo it.

Year after year of jabbing newborns, he started seeing the cracks: the "religiously injected" kids chronically ill, the half-vaxxed or unvaxxed ones robust.

Then the historical data: infectious diseases vanishing long before vaccines arrived.

The slow boil of authoritarian policy robbed doctors of autonomy, ward by ward.

So he bought a farm, stocked it, and waited.

He knew the day would come when he'd have to run or be crucified.

That day arrived with the mandates.

Quit or jab – no middle ground.

Denes chose door three: a three-month exemption for anyone who asked.

No advertising, just word of mouth.

Monday: two people.

Tuesday: a dozen.

Wednesday dawn: a kilometre-long tailback down the country road, four abreast, kids playing with the goats, his wife hauling eskies of water to the queue.

Then the cavalry arrived.

Cops blocked the driveway; others knocked on the surgery door.

Waiting room packed, an hour from exemption time.

Denes to the nearest cop: "Are you here for an exemption?"

In that line – cars, driveway, gutter – sat desperate officers, local pollies, teachers, nurses, tradies.

Victorians who couldn't face losing pay or roof. Same choice Denes was making – except he was the one holding the pen.

Today he pays the bills six metres up a cherry-picker, lopping trees while Colac begs for doctors.

Channel Nine ripped my phone interview, spliced him into a ten-second villain hit-piece – ethics of press and government in perfect sync.

Heroes used to be easy to spot – society hoisted them aloft.

Now we operate on pre-war Nazi rules: shoot protesters, pepper spray nans, silence the stubborn, memory-hole the rest.

But I remember.

I remember the caller I never met, breathless with awe, calling Denes "our Schindler in a white coat".

May 2025 – after years of deliberate delay, long after public interest has cooled – AHPRA, the feared, hated, and discredited Australian Health

Practitioners Regulatory Authority, will haul Dr Denes Borsos before its Tribunal and deregister him.

Same playbook: wait until the crowd wanders off, then finish the job.

Question is: how does Australia benefit when brave, decent, competent doctors are struck off for upholding the Hippocratic oath – especially the bit that says: First, Do No Harm?

11 April, 2025.

THE BEAUTIFUL VIEW FROM THE SUMMIT OF SUFFERING

I'VE BEEN SUFFERING heart pain for a while, grinning and bearing the pain until it passed. And, to date, it always had.

Last night, it didn't pass. Last night, at four in the morning, after pacing the floor of my bus, Florence, burping and stretching, I finally gave up and woke my partner, Kelli.

We got dressed, packed up the bus, and drove to the closest hospital with an emergency unit – Redcliffe, north of Brisbane.

There, I was quickly diagnosed with a heart attack, and as I write this, I'm waiting to be transported to another hospital, The Royal.

But I'm writing this, under the effects of fentanyl, to talk about the view I can see from my hospital bed.

The community, whose stories I've been recording, has long had a deep suspicion of doctors and hospitals.

This stems from the fact that hardly any of those who worked in hospitals spoke out about the "unholy juice," or went public about the injuries we knew they were seeing.

But while one doctor pulled me aside to almost chat about the Covid time, and you could feel his anger, and another nurse shared how she took it and didn't want to, both of them – and everyone else I interacted with, or studied as they passed or chatted in the nurses' station – were clearly dedicated to their work. They were all interacting with each other with a foundation of fun and respect.

Basically, they were extremely cool and, for want of a better word, lovely.

In the morning, we made a short social media post to let our community know what happened.

And it was then that I was gifted with a stunning view of you.

While there were a few haters, the majority of well-wishes were warm, authentic, and humbling. The foundation of the vast majority of it was love. Like a family love.

But five years ago, few of us knew each other.

And in these last years, we have all faced numerous trials: court cases, police abuse, ostracisation from family and friends and community groups, job loss and so on. And, of course, we faced the frustration of having our warning voices ignored. We've had to become spectators, as those we loved not only participated, but many of them have died and been injured.

And let's not forget the trolls. These people, usually with false names and fake social media pages – perhaps they're not even human, perhaps they're AI bots – who knows?

A well-founded suspicion is that they are government-funded disrupters working for intelligence agencies.

Whoever they are, they spend their days hating us. Never debating, just derision and hyperbolic hate, as if they're convinced that, through hatred, they can finally get us to join them.

Which we haven't.

And while we were born in EPIC, and can still recall the beauty of those few days when, together, we glowed, the years of lost court cases, ignored petitions, and infiltrators causing division through infighting… Today, for me, the hardships fell away as the view from my bed was of the community I'm a part of, glowing through the bulbs of their kind words for me.

We truly are a unique and beautiful community.

But now, as I observe the beauty of those who took the juice to remain in the industry, for whatever reason, I wonder: who is it that is determined to divide us?

For these are good people – you can just feel it.

And we are good people. We know it. We can feel it.

So the gap between us hasn't been carved by either side, but by someone, or some ones, above.

If only we could see that, realise it, and start the bridge-building with the soul's tools of forgiveness.

Dr Nixon, who, after being suspended, reinvented himself by studying the jabs via his Dark Field Microscope, states that when he does his live blood analysis work, he can no longer differentiate between jabbed and unjabbed blood. Both appear corrupted.

We are one.

And we can be one again. This possibility is what I can see now from this bed, as my struggling heart ponders whether to allow me to stay here or leave.

Can you imagine the power of that? Of reuniting all these lights?

Or, if they don't want to know, then perhaps, through my struggle today, we can all see, through the outpouring of support, that we are still united.

We are more than anti-vaxxers and "cookers".

We are the children of EPIC, and we have the essential qualities we need to grow into a true alternative to the tyranny that is still attempting, through bureaucratic osmosis, to smother our voices and steal all that we hold dear.

And it is worth defending. We are all worthy of defending and fighting for.

In fact, in the words of Paul Lassig, we don't need a revolution, we need a renovation.

And we can do this, for not only are we great renovators, but from the possible edge of my life, and the perch of this hospital bed, I saw us living, working, and healing together. The one people who, weary from duress, simultaneously switched on their lights, and illuminated the world with a message that read: Australia is back, and keep watching, for we are all working our way back to the one word that used to define us… Lucky.

13 April, 2025.

THE JOURNEY I TOOK TO FIND WHAT I'D LOST

I AM AN immigrant. A refugee, whose family, when I was a kid, accepted the offer of this country – to come and offer your children a future that the social construct of the old country could not. They called us Ten Pound Poms, and whatever I came to believe Australia was, I lost that belief on the Steps of the Shrine a short time before Victorian police officers, dressed like updated stormtroopers, beat the hell out of me.

Earlier, on the streets of Melbourne, they'd shot me with rubber bullets, but here, one of the several officers on top of me was smashing my head into the sacred concrete with his plastic shield, while saying, desperately, three times, "Stop making me do this." I can still hear his pain, despite the years, and despite the fact that he had a black name tag covering the lower half of his face.

Perhaps we could both see then that this was the end of our belief of who our country was.

I did try to defend it, not with violence, but with a loudspeaker I was offered, and what I thought was a rational speech that went something like: "Officers, we aren't your enemies. Look at us – we're your brothers and sisters, your mothers and fathers, your children. And this Shrine is built on the blood of our ancestors who sacrificed their lives for our freedom. But if you come and attack us now, it will no longer stand for that."

But it didn't work, right there and then, as they beat us up and shot at the others: I lost my country under the cruelty of strangers.

Yet this commenced a long journey for me, as I went searching for and defending what I thought my country was, and those journeys are documented here and on Café Locked Out's various social media platforms.

Then, over a year ago, on the farm of Dr Bruce Paix, another violated defender of a country he loved, I was informed I should do something about these chest pains I was feeling, for they wouldn't self-rectify.

But since I had witnessed the health system refuse to give the 16-year-old Dazelle a double lung transplant, and since we had heard all these other horror stories about people's time spent in hospital during the heavy Covid era, I instead tried to fix it naturally.

I lost weight, I downed whatever health product Kel, my new partner, handed me, and I kept myself busy – even as, secretly, I felt the pain increase.

Sometimes it was so bad I would pretend I could reach those I loved through a soul connection and say goodbye, but then the pain would pass and I would wake up and keep working.

No one ever informed me that they received my message. In the end, it was my dedication to the work, such as it was, that kept me going.

Finally though, inside our bus, which was parked in front of Dr William Bay's townhouse, I felt the pain come on – as it had for several days. But this time all the old tricks didn't work, and with Kel asleep, I rested my hands on the edge of our sink and suspected that this was a heart attack, this knife that was piercing me from front to rear, with pain radiating down both arms.

Silently, I said goodbye to my loved ones again – but after I found myself still alive, though in pain, I woke Kel.

At first, I told her it might have been a major angina attack, and since William was once again a GP, perhaps he'd have some medication I could take.

But since he wouldn't answer his phone, being so late, I told Kel I thought we should go to a hospital. After packing up the bus – which meant putting everything back on the bed – Kel googled the nearest emergency department, and at around five in the morning we headed off.

Heading, as many in our movement still see it, into the lion's den.

A nurse of South African origin and weary after a long shift finally got to me – a grimacing, wild-haired old man who'd just been wondering if this was where I was going to die.

Kel was still outside trying to figure out where to park the bus.

The rest was a blur. Though this time several people told me they had woken up at 4:15 a.m. with a bad feeling.

The nurse took me seriously. She put me in a wheelchair and after wheeling me in, took my BP – which was 200 over something – and before long I was in a hospital bed having blood tests, angiograms, chats with doctors, you name it.

It was now that I started to notice that so many of these people caring for me were immigrants too – people who'd taken a punt on this country based on the same hopes our posters still sold. None of these people knew me, or had heard of Café Locked Out. Not one. And I didn't ask many of them, but I guess they were all vaccinated.

But what really connected them was that they were all clearly slaves to their own compassion. They simply loved helping other people. Even though they talked about weekend rates and the like, it was the work that held them.

Because this hospital didn't have the facilities to fix what they now knew was a heart attack, I was sent in an ambulance to a second hospital. Out of respect, I don't want to name them, in case that breaches some confidentiality thing. But it was the same where they took me – kind people, caring for sick people. Whether they were morbidly obese, under arrest, any age, colour or religion, unvaccinated and no one ever asked – they were respectful and kind to patients even when these sick Australians were rude to them.

In the second hospital, I met Jesús. He immigrated here from Peru. He had a radiant smile and soothing manner, and he would politely take my order for dinner, breakfast, and lunch.

And the deeper I travelled into the endless bowels of this infrastructure, with its posters on all its walls informing me of my rights and asking me not to abuse the staff – it was the same people I found.

Even the doctors – and I have interviewed lots of suspended doctors – weren't just dedicated to their jobs, but deeply committed to seeing if they could help me wrench from death a few more decades of time in this light.

Then, when I was undergoing the angiogram that I thought was going to lead to a stent, there came a cool young doctor informing me that I was going to need a triple bypass. Two realisations hit me. The first was as I left to wait in a wheelchair in a room full of very large Australians, realising my entire chest was going to be ripped open.

And the second: This wasn't nature. This was a trench built by humans to keep the inevitability of death at bay. From the people cleaning the toilets to the surgeon who ripped me open in order to help – they were all soldiers, and they were soldiers painted with every race in the world.

Even the anaesthetist – this man you wanted to stay awake to get to know, for he was such a character – was from one of the Germanic states.

Then the most beautiful moment happened.

This was Good Friday and the operation, we were informed, was booked for the following Wednesday, in yet another hospital, and they didn't have any beds. But I was getting worse, and despite all their reassurances I finally whispered to Kel that I knew I wouldn't reach Wednesday.

It was now, within moments of saying this, that a nurse came in and said, "We're moving you now and they're operating on you tomorrow."

On Easter Sunday, dressed in a hospital gown that read Queensland Government, I was walking around the Intensive Care Unit, with all my heart's plumbing repaired, my arm supported by a young multi-generational Australian physiotherapist who was talking to me about his young children.

Thanks to all of them, I was alive.

Now it is my eleventh day in hospital and my fifth day since the surgery, and this is the first piece I have written since the initial heart attack.

It's 1:30 in the morning and despite the pain from the healing wounds and the men in the ward snoring, I felt compelled to write this – for I know where I am.

This is more than a hospital bed.

This is a hospital ward in my adopted country – that I finally rediscovered, not through justice for a crime, and there have been crimes, nor the final victory of an argument about mandated vaccinations, that I will challenge, no, I rediscovered all that is still good about my country through the kindness of strangers.

24 April, 2025.

THE STRATEGIC IMPORTANCE OF TROLLS

In my live broadcast last night, I stated my belief that social media is the chessboard of culture, with each comment a move.

But it's an unfair board.

Café Locked Out just proved that by keeping my hospital journey live and interactive.

Not all, but plenty of the comments were from people who weren't far off from wishing me dead – hate speech.

Yet these comments were not censored by the platforms.

Meanwhile, Café Locked Out's main page was given a ten-year ban by Facebook, simply for sharing the stories of everyday Australians. Another example is the Batshit Crazy Cooker page, which is allowed to mock us at will without any retribution from the platforms.

Many of us also have fake pages set up against us, which the platforms refuse to remove.

This alone proves that Advance Australia Fair is no longer a goal for our leaders. But don't despair – because the people who have been hating upon us ever since Covid arrived can, surprisingly, be a great benefit to us.

Before we move on though, another important question: are they even real? Many of them have false profiles and very few friends.

They could be AI bots – but I think the majority aren't.

If AI were given the task of changing our minds, or shaming us into silence, then after a few days it would have reviewed its progress, realised that simple name-calling wasn't working, and would have started exploring other strategies.

Whereas our trolls just repeat the same old thing, over and over again, despite their complete failure to stop us.

Most also have silly false names and cartoonish profile pictures – whereas I believe AI would present itself more convincingly.

So yes, some could be bots, but many are just people.

Who they are exactly, who knows.

They could even be members of our own tribe – because most people are still unaware we even exist.

The other theory is that some of them are paid, either by governments or pharmaceutical companies, and that could be the case – for why, when you have such a short time to be alive, would you invest this much time pointlessly hating?

Finally, the longer they persist with their unabashed cruelty, the more we can have them start working for us.

I managed to grow my X followers quickly – not through my rants or live shows – but through my interactions with trolls.

I never expected to flip one.

Instead, I used our interactions to circumnavigate the algorithms that are shadow-banning us.

Because you see, once you start interacting with a troll, many people start quietly watching.

Think of it like an online MMA fight – and the prize is that they follow the winner. But I would strongly advise that you interact with them on our terms.

Meaning: we choose the battleground.

As you know, they are usually condescending and rely mainly on name-calling: Anti-vaxxers, Cookers, Grifters, Gropers. What's interesting though, is that many of us are now happy to publicly wear these labels – because we know it disarms them.

But I am yet to see one person, with a real face and a real name, proudly declare themselves a troll.

So, secretly, they must be ashamed. But, like I said, draw a line.

If they get too aggressive, ignore or block them.

Force them to set up a new email and a new profile just to come back. Train them to fight on our terms of decent interaction.

The importance of this is simple: it allows us to show the world how strong our characters are.

If we join them in name-calling, then they win a small victory. But if we ignore the hate and reply only when they offer us a decent and respectful challenge, then we can begin to instigate the very conversations our politicians don't want us to have – healthy debates about the issues facing our culture. And we can start now, by sharing this post.

And remember: There is no page out there, set up by us, where we mock them – unlike the Batshit Cooker pages. Which means the truth is simple: they need us, but we don't need them.

28 April, 2025.

YOUR GREATEST GIFT: FREEDOM OF CHOICE

I WAS IN Prince Charles Hospital in Brisbane, hooked to an IV drip of antibiotics fighting a staph infection in my chest wound after a triple bypass, when I wrote this.

A man I respected once read one of Brian's poems and told him he could be a great poet. Over the years, as our paths crossed on those dusty tracks, Brian shared that story with me – maybe half a dozen times. He'd arrived here as a refugee, seeking safety, and built a life in Australia over decades: a tram driver in his late fifties, with an Australian accent thick as the bush. But he'd soon lose his job after smashing his tram's computer screen. I remember him showing me the unbreakable plexiglass, embossed with the print of his fist.

That voice – his grade three teacher's – still haunted him. He never showed me the poem, or any he'd written since. Despite all those years here, the system that welcomed him as a kid turned on him in the end, shipping him off to Christmas Island's detention centre like yesterday's rubbish – a refugee all over again, stripped of the freedom he'd earned.

For the few times those faces made the evening news, the refugees looked like puppets with cut strings, collapsing in death. Our government had bought their contracts for free – they were only refugees, after all – and replayed the overhead footage of their final, desperate dance: face-down in the waves off Christmas Island, the ocean draining their brave souls of the last of their dreams. We didn't dump them here, just as we didn't stop Brian from picking up a pen.

These were choices they made. But unlike so many others, Brian had gambled on Australia and won a fragile slice of life – only to have it yanked away, not for a shrimp on the barbie, but because the powerful decided his dreams, and his right to them, weren't worth the risk.

That freedom was our gods' gift. Australia grew rich by letting its people realise theirs. So why didn't Brian – who'd fought to be born into it here, encouraged by the state to explore his gifts – ever fully take flight, even after all those years?

Choice. Your life's architect: Freedom of Choice.

For all our sacred texts and philosophies, across every soul who's ever lived, we have no proof of where we came from or where we're headed. All we have is faith – and its seed is Freedom of Choice. Ironically, most religions say God demands your fear and obedience, yet He hardwired you with the power to deny Him entirely.

Why would such a God build that freedom into your soul, only to demand submission?

Close your eyes now and picture your life as a sideways map – a brief, one-way trail. Below: the bottomless dark you emerged from, heavy with mysteries you carry and collect. Above: an infinite sky of possibilities, sirens singing us toward dreams.

So much to plumb and pursue. Yet too many of us skim the surface, flicked across life's pond by some lazy deity.

Why? Choice. Freedom of Choice.

Covid was the first time many of us – especially in Victoria – felt that freedom truly threatened. That's why the anti-lockdown protesters, the so-called anti-vaxxers, were so damn brave. Strangers from every walk of life rose up, willing to pay with rubber bullets, fines, lost jobs, even family exile, just to hold onto their right to choose.

Our country's still under siege. Corporations and governments wield fear to control that choice: cancelling artists like me, sacking journalists like David Southwell from the Daily Mail, deregistering doctors like Dr My-Le Trinh for honouring their Hippocratic Oath – though AHPRA's outlawed it. A migrant friend working in government got a memo: mention Israel or Palestine at work, and you're fired.

Now the so-called eSafety Commissioner, the nation's Chief Censor, stifles debate, censoring social media – the culture's chessboard. History shows this leads to silence, compliance. Feeling worthless, we skim through life.

A muzzled nation can't prosper, not like Australia once did. We're choosing silence now – clipping our kids' wings with crushing debt, shaming them through "Welcome to Country" rituals that brand them occupiers' spawn, hammering "toxic masculinity" and whatever else keeps us picking the powerful's script.

Call it what it is: voluntary slavery.

But we're not chained – we choose our path. If most pack away their dreams and obey blindly, we'll architect whatever bleak Australia follows – just as they did to Brian, after all his years.

Or imagine this: What if we chose a culture that cheers bold choices? One that blooms prosperous again, fears shed like old skin, our innate greatness unfurling into an abundant forest of Freedom – nurturing us all, and the generations after, no matter where they washed up from.

29 April 2025.

AVALANCHE

In an avalanche, silence is a sin.

An avalanche covers a mountain hut. Locked inside, two men – one religious, one atheist – are stuck. To survive the intense cold, they huddle together and stave off the long sleep by arguing who is right. After days of debate, the atheist wins – and kills God.

It is only then that the sun melts the snow low enough for the atheist to dig his way out. He emerges, breathes in the joy of fresh air and liberty, and waits for the religious man. But when he fails to emerge, the atheist crawls back down the tunnel into the hut, where he finds the religious man hanging from the rafters.

This is why I've never seen much point in arguing religion. In the easier times I was born into, God was an optional extra – usually exercised in moments of incarceration or illness. But now, times have changed. And the god we were born into is detrimental to our survival.

If there is a God – and I feel there is – then he is beyond our comprehension. The god or gods we believe in are shaped from our fears and limited understanding. A perfect God who knows all, whose son Jesus will return to liberate us from those who seek to control us?

Perfect? Perfect is a final destination. A place that doesn't exist in a fluid universe, immersed in the current of an unstoppable river of time. Besides, why would a god imbue us with the freedom to choose if he had already chosen everything for us? If every moment is preordained, then what is the use of prisons, or any punishment? All you're doing is torturing slaves – because there can be no sin without free will.

What if, instead, we have been created full of gifts – including a hunger for meaning – because he wants to see what we will do with them? Will we become serial killers or saints? Will we build bridges, start wars – or both? In fact, when you think about it, he gave us the ultimate freedom: the freedom to kill him. To believe he never existed.

No, it's clear to me that while God is profound – the genius of geniuses, capable of incomprehensible miracles, each woven into reality's impossible fabric – he is also imperfect. And always has been. And always will be.

The proof of that is us. For we are created in his image, correct? (By the way, I refer to him as He to keep this flowing. Personally, I have no idea what God actually is.)

What I'm challenging here is not God himself – but our interpretation of God. And the reason I'm doing this is because I know humanity is under threat. Before us lie two paths: one where we grow and flourish, and one where most of us – through inaction – will become redundant, both physically and spiritually.

We are the dodos, who – too impatient to wait for the Portuguese – have created the being that may see the majority of us slide into extinction. And it's not just unskilled workers in the firing line of AI. It's doctors, lawyers, accountants, movie stars, and more.

There's talk of universal income. But to believe in that, you'd have to believe that the corporations now embracing AI – because they see it as a way to replace their human labor force with obedient, tireless slaves – are suddenly going to spend the lion's share of their unprecedented profits supporting the very people they've classified as redundant. Not just them, but their children – born to pick up the mantle of meaningless lives, sitting on couches, playing the latest computer games.

In China, they have driverless buses running 24/7, hospitals with AI doctors, factories where robots long ago replaced people. Meanwhile, here, we have a growing debt we will never pay off. Especially if we don't have jobs.

Which is why I return to God. An imperfect God is an invested friend. Not only has he given you all these freedoms – freedoms most of us take for granted or shun, because we don't want the responsibility – but he has given us purpose. That gnawing hunger that there must be more to life than just paying bills. A greater purpose than trying to define your existence by some modern reinterpretation of gender. More than social media likes. More than fame itself.

An imperfect God is an invested friend because he does not know what will happen to you. For despite the sunny days and storms of circumstance, he gave you freedom of choice, so you could be your own navigator. Your own explorer. Not only that – but above and beyond the world he placed you in, he filled your soul with dangerous and magnanimous possibilities, loosely connected by your wondrously deep, uncharted territory.

Believing that Jesus is returning is, for some, an excuse not to strive to defend what you know is right. Believing that it has all been written by long-dead men is a reason not to develop your own unique relationship with God. Believing that he wants you to fear him in order to obey is the philosophy of an institutionalised slave.

And right now – staying silent, in a time where freedom of speech is our best hope of discovering the path that will see the majority benefit, including our children – is more than an act of cowardice. It is, at this moment, a sin.

Silence is a sin.

These are momentous times. We humans – every human – are beset by great challenges. From the lies of Big Pharma to the tsunami of AI. And our only saviour – or our destroyer – is us. Is you.

Take a moment. Sit back. Feel the enormity of the communal apprehension. What if that is God – and all the angels – sitting on the edge of their seats, wondering which path we are going to choose?

The courageous one, that will see us ascend to where he gave us all the gifts to reach – and maybe further. Or the other one – down into the dustbin of creation, where all our hopes and dreams drown in the inexhaustible appetite of time's indifferent current. Pulled under by a redundant interpretation of God – one man created, and recreated, to control you.

The avalanche is here. And to survive its hunger and its cold, we will need the warmth of each other. But perhaps… There is a third man in the hut. One arguing the case for a brighter future. Like a sales rep for a dedicated and imperfect God.

15 May, 2025.

THE CHEAPEST FREEDOM

He was from Sudan. Six foot something, he was built like a warrior – but there was no call for warriors here.

We were parked near a small oval. Some young men were kicking a football to each other as suburbanites patrolled the edge, spoiling their pedigree dogs with an hour of exercise.

All the dogs were on leads, in obedience to the sign. Many had their poo bags tied like bows to their collars. A few wore electronic training devices hanging from the same collars – ready to give them a mild shock if they stepped out of line.

The Sudanese man had just finished reading the words stuck to our bus, including the main banner: Free Speech Defence.

He told us how he'd grown up in a refugee camp in Sudan. He had gone there himself, searching for an education – because outside of the camp, that wasn't possible.

Years later, his asylum seeker application had been accepted by one of the bastions of freedom, decency, and fairness: Australia. Now he lived in the Western Suburbs of Melbourne and had a good job working for the government.

No militia here to drag him off to their army or just shoot him. No waiting on the Red Cross to deliver food trucks.

Instead, he was renting an apartment. He was building a life.

"We got sent a memo," he said. "Everyone received it. It stated that if we post anything about Israel and Gaza online – or even dare to bring it up in conversation at work – we will be summarily sacked." This was all he wanted to talk about. But the only ones he could talk to about it were us.

I asked him if he wanted to do an audio interview, offering to conceal his name and alter his voice so it would be impossible to trace.

Free speech is important, we said. He agreed. Then, after pondering for a while, he declined – choosing instead to exercise a rarely spoken about, but currently our most prevalent liberty: The Freedom to Endure.

On the east side of the Wheatbelt in Western Australia, we'd been searching for the Australia few ever hear from.

Taking the smaller roads, we came across a one-street town, bordering a lake being slowly besieged by the local desert. From the signage, it was clear the town survived on tourism – and this was off-season.

In the local Mitre Ten hardware store I was exchanging a gas bottle when the owner, who was not in a good mood, started asking questions about our bus.

"We're independent journalists," I told him. "We like interviewing people about what they think of the current state of Australia."

"We're becoming communist," he snapped.

These frontier towns come attached with a myth. You believe, initially, that people making a life out here must be self-reliant, tough – people who had decided they wanted to be far from government control.

I asked him if he'd do an interview. As he finished ringing up my bill, I watched him study our bus again.

Above the windows: Free Speech Defence, in bold red font. After our transaction was completed, he declined.

For now, I guess, out of all the tools of liberty he'd been gifted at birth, he'd chosen – just for now – The Freedom to Endure.

Our sky is large, our journey long. Sometimes, in the country, on these small roads, you can drive for what seems like hours before another car or truck passes you.

I see it as a land where only the dreamers can prosper – and even their hopes are not guaranteed.

Evidence? The brick ruins of houses that this old country is patiently dragging back into itself. Into its cockatoo silence.

But there is another silence here now – and it's been spreading in every town and city we've visited.

It's no longer contained by Covid. It's become the choice. The default setting.

Voluntarily disarming the majority of us by offering – in silence – a trade.

To sweeten the deal, those marketing the silence have spent the last five years tormenting the outspoken.

Formidable German lawyer Reiner Fuellmich, who did so much to expose the vaccine fraud through his series of expert sessions tagged Grand Jury – The Court of Public Opinion and was a hero to many around the world, is now rotting in a European jail. "The coronavirus hysteria is the greatest crime in human history," he declared. Fuellmich has become the new Assange.

Other whistleblowers – like Barry Young from New Zealand, who released data proving a certain medical procedure was dangerous – have been violently arrested. Young now faces seven years in jail.

And in one of the most dramatic images to emerge from the entire Covid debacle in Australia, a grandmother, who believed she had the right to protest, was pushed to the ground by Victorian police officers and then peppersprayed – twice – directly in her face before being left writhing in agony in distress. All of it was recorded. A mobile phone. An iconic picture. A miracle that she didn't have a heart attack.

A picture posted so we don't forget what the authorities did. But does that same image just sell the deal wrapped in this new silence?

Freedom of speech is a dangerous freedom.

Around the world, there are unmarked graves full of those who exercised it – under political regimes where truth is still seen as a threat.

Even as the truth eventually emerges and exonerates those who were once labeled conspiracy theorists – people still agree to the deal.

In the hospital, a few nurses asked what I did. When I told three of them – on separate occasions – they declared, in their own words: "There's no free speech anymore."

They didn't shout it. They didn't even say it through gritted teeth.

They just said it quietly, with the tempered sadness of someone well into the journey of recovering from grief.

And then, if anyone else came within earshot, they returned to the safe silence offered by what is, perhaps, the cheapest liberty of all:

The Freedom to Endure.

21 May, 2025.

PEOPLE B4 PROFITS

The world is changing so fast that you can feel breathless just checking the new AI updates on your social media feed. But the way people talk about it, it's like an inescapable destiny. Globalisation was the same, where politicians and the rich offshored every company they could to the Third World. Which is why our country hardly has a manufacturing sector anymore.

But we disagree that we, as a people, are powerless in the face of progress. We think AI should be used to enhance all our lives, but to achieve this, we need to change the foundation of our capitalistic structure.

Currently, even though our corporations employ good, hardworking people, the corporation itself is a psychopathic legal entity that has one goal: to create more profits. This mantra has seen us achieve wonderful things, but it has also seen us do terrible things, all of these crimes justified by the need to create more profit. There are numerous accounts of corporations knowingly committing crimes, knowing that if they get caught, the fine will be less than the proceeds of the crime.

But one thing that corporations have required is people. Over the past decades, they have worked them harder and longer, often making them work several hours for free, in an attempt to be seen as a necessary employee.

But now AI is here, and it's threatening several job types. Ask Grok for a list. And since, to a corporation, no matter how hard you work, you are just a number, you know that the moment they can, they will replace you. It's just business.

And since the government will not intervene, the future is up to you. For the truth is, you are the one with the power. It's your wallet. Support businesses that employ humans. When you are so busy surviving, living day to day, you can lose sight of one of your duties as a human being, which is leaving a better world for the next generation.

And the one thing the next generation needs, in order to be motivated to strive to build good lives, is a sense of worth. That is the War you are in now, even if you can't yet hear the guns. It's The War Of Worth, and with your help we can win it. With your help the Future will not be useless eaters and AI, but a human future enhanced by our inexhaustible desire to innovate. It all comes down to one decision you have to make now, moving forward: do you choose to be powerless or powerful?

Café Locked Out was born in the eye of great moral change. In a time when many followed blindly, frightened by the possibility of death, which was driven by endless propaganda, the podcast found its purpose in the storm.

First, by recording the stories of everyday people.

Second, by interviewing others who were questioning what was happening. This turned out to be frowned upon, and the podcast was heavily censored.

Now, though, we are facing new momentous storms as history contemplates the fact that, thanks to innovation, many of us could be forced into redundancy.

Elon Musk has been quoted as stating that the greatest challenge humanity will now face is "Meaning."

Infamous public intellectual Yuval Harari, author of Homo Deus and a WEF confidante, has stated that automation will create a "useless class." But we are children of the gods, creations of the universe, and I am interested in capturing the thoughts and experiences of people facing this unprecedented change.

If you can find the courage to speak, we have the courage to record you.

And despite the times trying to convince you otherwise, your voice is worthy of being recorded.

25 May, 2025.

AN AWOKEN, BROKEN MOTHER

I DON'T KNOW what her name was.

Early forties, she looked like the poster for white, middle-class Australia's pleasant, gentle, professionally working mothers. A teacher – that's what she'd scrawled in Sharpie on the back of her white T-shirt.

The woke crowd might once have called her "privilege"; if she'd dared raise her voice they'd have branded her a Karen.

Yet here, on the back streets of Moonee Ponds, I saw a fear in her eyes the likes of which she'd never tasted before. And it wasn't the fear of a virus.

Minutes earlier she'd been in Maribyrnong Park, bum on grass – correctly distanced from friend and son, and from every other silent protester and healthcare worker joining the nationwide park-stand.

When cops dragged one woman away, two coachloads of reinforcements arrived until there were easily two uniforms for every quiet mouth.

That's when she stood, gathered her family, and walked with the rest – still silent – across the grass, long lines of police shadowing every step.

What I saw in her eyes was brand-new terror: the instant you realise the rose-coloured lens has been ripped off.

Same back streets – manicured gardens, Euro cars, neat fences – but she no longer recognised any of it.

She was lost.

She and hers had dodged arrest, yet the sheer weight of badges had wordlessly announced: as an Australian she was no longer free to publicly question or protest her government.

Somewhere, while she'd been obediently locked down, the city – once hers – had been stolen.

Tolerance, common sense, liberty: gone.

Talking to her, I watched the penny drop: if she wanted the freedoms she'd enjoyed pre-Covid, she would have to remain what she was right now – a criminal on the run.

Her hideous crime?

Pleasantly, quietly, communally stating she wanted the right to say no.

And the shiver I saw in those blue eyes was this: because this once Safe City was still her home, the only one they had, she and her family had nowhere left to run.

27 May, 2025.

COMING HOME

It was late, and I was working in a nursing home. We had just finished our rounds, which meant we went bed to bed, seeing if people needed to go to the toilet, or cleaning them up if they had been, and turning the most fragile over. Most of those here had dementia, and once we were finished, I remember looking down the sub-lit hall, with its open doors, and all I could hear was old people calling out to return to their warmest home, and the word they used for this home was "mother." The hall was populated with the voices of the dying calling for the person who welcomed the majority of them into the world; their mum.

Once, the majority of us took it for granted that our mother would always be known as home. Even if the person you had grown into, the one who didn't match the blueprint she had for you, had seen her distance herself, somewhat, from you, still, if she was alive, she was Base Camp... Home.

Then Covid came. For those who took the juice, and weren't that affected, little changed, maybe. For those who were injured, lots changed. But for those who chose not to take it, an odyssey was waiting for them. This included being tossed out of families, being told they could visit their mother in the nursing home, or mothers being told they were not allowed to visit their grandchildren.

Covid was so terrifying it saw us betray what we once believed was sanctified. I know of mothers now who are still ostracised from their children. But then this was a remarkable time, full of firsts. I heard of a family who migrated to Russia because, for their children, they were seeking the freedom of their youth. They couldn't even speak Russian, though their plan was to be English teachers.

I interviewed one family of three; the father was a nurse, and they were selling their house to buy a caravan because they knew that, without a job, they would no longer be able to afford the mortgage. The second time I interviewed them, the couple was living in a layby near the Gold Coast. Their caravan was gone – I can't recall why – but they were now living in their car, alone. Their beloved son had been removed.

Another lady had been an inoculating nurse who had left her job when she was forced to take the goo. When I met her, she was working on an avocado farm and reading the death notices daily, hoping she would not read the name of anyone she had vaccinated. And her eyes were rimmed red with tears when she told me this.

Another nurse told me her story of how families weren't allowed into the nursing home – Health Department rules, ironclad. One asymptomatic carrier, and the vulnerable could drop like stones. That was the fear mongering of the day.

Many residents had dementia, already bewildered by the masked staff clad in their full rubber Personal Protective Equipment. These elderly people were dying in the midst of what must have seemed like a science fiction nightmare. Care grew clumsy with call-outs spiking, short-staffed shifts stretching thin. Families rang or rattled the doors, begging entry. But the rules held: safety's steep toll.

Tragically, many of these elderly people passed away alone. Loneliness, the price of the many spared.

Most grew cranky, understandably – they'd had enough. I sympathised. But we were mid-pandemic; the world had flipped.

One resident, though, always met the nurse each morning with a big smile that cut the gloom. Frail, fading, she never complained.

We assumed it was just her character, a silent strength. What we didn't know was she harboured a secret.

Every night, her 17-year-old granddaughter flouted the curfew, slipping unseen to the home. She'd jimmy the window, climb in quiet as a shadow, and spoon her gran till sleep claimed the old woman in her arms.

A true story.

I recall a retired journalist, sitting on a bench overlooking Perth, in tears too, as he wondered what had happened to his profession. He ended up being a prominent speaker at many gatherings and marches.

But it wasn't all gloom. Other people, who had seen their marriages fall apart, had met new lovers, and to date, these relationships were working. Dr William Bay had already remarried. Another man had purchased an organic fruit and vegetable store, and it was growing so fast he was already employing people.

The most remarkable fact was that out of all the unvaccinated people I'd interviewed, not one regretted not taking the vaccine. No matter how bad their current situation was, there was no one who regretted abstaining.

I did see one man who was severely injured by the jab, a successful musician, who had set up his own podcast, viciously attacking Big Pharma, then one day suddenly posted an apology to them. He said he had been taking illicit drugs at the time of being vaccinated, and they must have been the cause. He even congratulated Big Pharma on their work and empathy. Perhaps he believed it, or perhaps he was clear he had done it to try to reestablish his music career. I don't know if he succeeded at that.

I remember reading his sickly sweet, submissive retraction, and all I could see was Winston Smith in the café, in the last chapter of Nineteen Eighty-Four. He was in a café with other ousted dissidents, and on the screen above him, he was confessing his crimes.

But as the years progressed, other changes started to occur. The various protest groups around the country began shrinking as many people tried to return to their lives or began focusing on building new ones.

Sometimes at big events, you'd see strangers who were wearing the old protest T-shirts, and it would be joyous to see them. Asking, do you remember this? Do you remember that?

But then there were deeper divisions, the causes of which few knew. Some people blamed egos, and perhaps they were right. Others blamed it on the fact that we were black sheep and black sheep don't do herds. Ironically, this quality might have been what had protected us from the propaganda that saw the powers that be vaccinate the majority of the world.

Others questioned whether the leaderless movement had been infiltrated by people paid to divide us.

The more prominent anyone in the movement grew, the more they became like an unvaccinated Geiger counter. Hoodie, a former Qantas pilot who became a prominent speaker in the early days, and Topher Field, who went on to establish a popular podcast, are great examples. Take them to any public arena and if there is any unvaccinated there, they will recognise them.

This is a truth. In our dispersed communities, a few of us may be well known, but in the greater community, we are unknown.

In Adelaide, I did a speech before seven hundred and fifty people. I was actually welcomed to the stage with a standing ovation, which was overwhelming. But the next day, I travelled to Adelaide airport, then flew to Sydney airport. That day I passed through throngs of people, and nothing. I was just another face lost in a crowd. Which meant that the majority of my fellow countrymen passing by had all taken it. All of them.

There were moments, especially in the major shopping centers, where the crowds race around you like rushing water, that you realise just how successful the initial rollout had been.

There was no escaping it: we, the unvaccinated, were a minority. Just exactly what our numbers were, I'm not sure anyone will ever know, for those with the power and means to find out will never do the research.

Now, of course, the Tribe had also grown in number due to the vaccine injured, who had arguably been shunned worse by the greater mob than we had been.

Whatever our numbers were – fifteen to twenty percent of the population, who knows – all we knew was that after five years, the light of the great EPIC gathering was dimming.

Even if you collated all the people who watched the shows our community produced, you wouldn't find the crowds that had populated EPIC.

And this is a tragedy to me, for in my soul's rearview mirror, EPIC was still glowing.

And if I pause, I can hear the voices of children laughing, and people cheering as the newcomers drove into camp, their arms extended out of their car windows, shaking hands and high-fiving. I can still see the flags unfurling, some red, some blue, and many of them upside down, and people on phones walking around capturing everything, or at least everything a phone could immortalise. The actual feeling of relief and wonder and pure joy we all experienced was beyond technology to record.

The fact that everyone, and I mean everyone, claimed they just had to come was what made the event sacred. Often, they looked baffled when they said it, like the sensation was new to them. I know it was new to me.

I thought, at the time, this was the beginning of the end of the government's overreach. I believed that even though they used weapons on us. And I have documented several cases of people who were injured by some of their high-tech imported weapons, used for the first time against an Australian population. Burnt under their clothes, or just down one side of their face. People who were suddenly afflicted with such overwhelming fatigue, they had to pull over on the side of the road and wait. Some of these people, when they did make it home, were placed on iodine treatment, as their doctors claimed they were suffering from radiation poisoning.

Then there were the court cases, and the various groups, all over the country, that flourished and faded, and this goes for the podcasts too. And of course, the hardest lesson of all to learn was that losing a bond with someone you were close to in this new tribe hurt harder than losing someone from the original herd that had cut us loose.

But now, after all these journeys, when it comes to the Covid years, the war appears to be over.

Recently, all the Mainstream Media platforms returned to full-on fear mode and did a full-frontal attack on the entire country, pushing the boosters yet again because a new, more virulent strain was here.

But the attack floundered. It buckled at the knees, not because of us, but because of the vaccinated people. Check the comments of any of those posts, and the comments are ninety-nine percent ridicule and spite, as the once-onboard turn against those who arguably betrayed them.

And while we can take credit for some of this, I think our greatest ally, sadly, was the true undisclosed amount of vaccine injuries people suffered, either directly, or they knew someone who had. Out in the suburbs, horror stories abounded. They did not make it into our controlled and coerced mainstream media, but everyone knew nonetheless. It was impossible to hide. People who had lined up willingly to take the vaccines, believing the government propaganda, were now happy to declare: never again. They're culling us.

A truth too big for any government-controlled social media platform to conceal.

George Kesic, acting on a suggestion from Rosemary Marshall, managed to get on Chris Smith on Radio 2SM, a popular talkback radio, and to everyone's surprise, Chris Smith apologised for initially pushing the vaccine, and to date he hasn't been sacked for doing so, even though this two-minute section of his show is going viral around the world.

Then remarkably, the Government has come out and stated that people under eighteen shouldn't take the jab as the risk outweighs the reward.

All of this is why this week, starting Sunday, June 1, 2025, should be seen as Victory. But if this is victory, I doubt there will be any shrines built to honor those who resisted, or medals, or even an acknowledgement.

I doubt that even if those family and friends, who a few years back obediently cut you out of their lives, invite you back, that you will ever truly get home. That home is compromised.

Many who have been allowed back tell me how hard it is, because you can't talk about anything.

But we have a new home. Each other. This organic family of light, which formed when we found each other in the marches, the gatherings, the online groups, and the Zooms. This is your home. Which is why I find these persistent stories of division so troubling.

What's the point of it, for there is no other tribe out there waiting to adopt our orphans. Each other is all we had then, and questionably all we have now. And if some other questionable event does come along, and I know many of us believe that it will, then all we will have then could be each other, too.

So surely that makes strategic sense to remain in each other's lives, respectfully. Out here, now, surrounded by those who have long since disavowed themselves publicly from all that happened in those remarkable Covid years, you can feel like a soldier returning from a war to a community who is unaware that a war was even waged. They won't be able to, or more likely, won't want to see or hear about your war stories or scars. And if you persist in sharing these stories, they'll probably categorise you as crazy.

No, the only ones who'll listen are the ones who can or want to hear, and that's each other. Or should be.

Just think back to the start. To those days when around you nearly everyone believed the narrative, that to you didn't make any sense. Can you imagine how hard that time would have been if you hadn't found each other?

Or taking that a step further, how would all of us have reached here if we hadn't discovered each other? If we hadn't created this Tribe?

Perhaps, as the tide of Covid is pulled back out to sea, with all other inconsequential waves, we should spend some time reflecting, searching our soul's rearview mirrors, for those moments where as one, we glowed.

For me, finding a way to once again reach that radiance, would be the equivalent of Coming Home.

1 June, 2025.

ROUNDABOUT

It was Sunday, and we were looking for a park with a barbecue. The council ones were fantastic, but they didn't always work. If we found a park with a toilet close by as well, then we were being spoiled.

When you live in a bus, this is a morning ritual.

We were in one of the western suburbs of Melbourne. We were next to an oval, and while a few young men were kicking a football around, they were hemmed in by the dog walkers circling the oval. All of their dogs were on a lead.

We were on the carnivore diet, which had seen me lose my belly fat. As the steaks began to sizzle, I pointed out to Kelli how all the dogs were pedigrees.

In our fifties, we were now walking museums. We could both remember a time when there were no computers, no cameras, no ATMs.

If you wanted money for the weekend, you'd better make sure you got to the bank on Friday. There were no mobile phones. How did we stay in contact with each other?

We laughed as I told her about how Dad would load up the trailer with rubbish and take it to the tip where, in bare feet, we'd scramble over the rubbish already there, collecting any treasure we found, until Dad cracked it.

"Get that stuff out! I just emptied the trailer. I'm not taking back more than I brought."

Nearby the tip was the Swan River, and Dad would take us there afterward, where we'd jump off the jetty and vanish into the murky brown, while our dog remained on the jetty, his tail wagging as he barked at us each time our laughing faces emerged. There were pedigrees around then, but most of the dogs were mixed breeds, bitzas, and had their own lives that were entangled with ours via love.

One of our dogs adored Mum. Where Mum went, her basset hound shadow followed. He'd been a present to us all, bought off someone who didn't want him. But despite his adoration of Mum, whenever a local bitch was on heat he'd vanish for a few days, then turn up exhausted, beaten up, and starving.

One time he never came back. And even though Mum was always complaining about him, this broke her heart. I remember us walking the streets calling his name, as Mum called the pounds, but we were driven more to heal Mum than to find him. In the end, he became another scar her heart had to wear as time moved on.

Other times, we'd come home and find the front yard full of dogs who were hoping to get an audience with our little terrier, who was on heat. Despite our best efforts, one of them got her pregnant. She had six pups, and once they were ready, we all asked our friends and my father's work colleagues if anyone wanted a puppy.

As a family, we decided to keep the puppy no one else wanted, which turned out to be the ugliest one.

But despite his odd looks, this mongrel, who became Dad's shadow, managed to bury himself so deep inside my father that when he died Dad, who rarely cried, wept.

When we bought a cat off death row for my own family, the RSPCA vet asked if we were going to book it into "Kitten Kindy."

"Kitten Kindy?"

"It's a six-week course," she said. "It's to train your cat to be a more socially adaptable cat."

Socially adaptable? I thought. It was a cat. The reason we loved them was because they weren't socially adaptable.

Dad used to joke that this was cat heaven. Where else would they get a better deal than here?

"Look at him," Dad would say as the cat slept next to the dog. "He goes out when he wants, gets a hug when he wants, and has the audacity to tap your mother on her forehead at three in the morning, demanding to be fed. And she'll get up and feed him. I'd like to see how long the dog would survive if he tried that."

Socially adaptable? Why would this cat agree to such a demotion? I felt like suggesting that rather than kitten kindy, why not cat university, so he could become a feline lawyer and pay for his own whiskers.

A few months later, that cat got run over. We didn't know. The RSPCA called to inform us that he'd been found. They then informed us that they offered a range of funeral services, from a discrete, intimate celebration of his life to a forty-seat chapel. I told Rohana she should ask them if a bin was one of their options. And how about the chip they'd implanted in the back of his neck – could we use it in the next cat if it wasn't damaged?

Such a different time.

A treat was a ten cent bag of mixed lollies, and each long weekend, after hitching up whatever camping equipment he had – and it was all changing – Dad would throw us all in the car, and we'd leave just before dawn. So by the time the sun found him, Dad was already on the highway, one arm on the windowsill, and effortlessly ignoring all of us, as he went in search of anywhere to camp, where, from the step of the van, he could see houses, or even the road.

Newspapers were the news, magazines spoke of other worlds, where people were rich and famous, as we produced our own music tapes by recording songs straight off the radio.

There were divorces, there were murders, there was a neighbour losing his mind, striding naked up and down the street, screaming in his own language, with a piece of four-by-two in his hand. There were parents having affairs, and the Beaumont children were still missing. Evidence that amongst us, unimaginable monsters lurked, and yet on school holidays or on the weekend, my young brother and I were gone.

Leaving the house to vanish into the playground, which was a close and untouched section of bush.

If fear was here, it hadn't yet found the hooks it needed to control us.

But here before us now, one of the dogs had an electronic collar that would allow his owner to shock him if he misbehaved.

In the nearby playground was a modern roundabout. Small, it had speed inhibitors to protect the kids from falling onto the specially designed rubber-like floor of the playground.

For a long time, we grew up on caravan parks, and once, in one park, myself and a few other kids were trying to make our own roundabout, an impressive stainless steel cauldron, with handles.

Then, from nowhere, some grown men, fathers and the like, who must have been watching us struggle, came over and, with beer on their breath, said, "Hold on, kids."

Then they laughed as they used all their strength to spin this roundabout into the eye of a cyclone.

I can still remember the thrill of clutching desperately to a handhold, as the centrifugal forces tried to rip me off. It was a warm memory. A fun memory. A memory constructed by men; strangers, whose laughter I can still hear. It might have felt dangerous, but even as kids, we knew we were safe, for we didn't see these men as toxic monsters to be feared, but protectors who had decided to spoil us all.

Whereas here, in this small park, the playground had several young children playing upon it, as their quiet fathers watched on. The fathers weren't interacting with each other, only with their children, and that they did with whispers. Making the playground feel more like a library or perhaps a wake, for the more you studied these men, the more you noticed. It looked to me like the men were avoiding eye contact, even with each other, out of shame.

They were single dads, and this must have been their day with the kids, and the rules were clear: Don't have anything to do, at all, with any kid that wasn't yours.

But why the shame?

Was it the sombre wake of broken families? Was it the sense that they had failed their children?

The children didn't seem to share the shame. As our breakfast cooked, I watched these kids leaving the playground to run up to their fathers, and I didn't need to hear what they were saying, for despite all we've gained and all we've lost, I can still recognise the warm and ancient language of love.

It is that ancient language of love between people, between families, between communities, along with the pride we once felt to be Australians, the naive faith we had that our governments, our police, our churches, and our institutions had our best interests at heart. It was this naive faith we used to feel in our institutions, our politicians, and our fellow Australians, that was destroyed during the Covid era.

As I continue to travel around this deeply divided country, it is my hope that this book will, in some way, help to restore that lost language of love, those traditional faiths that once cemented us together, that united us as one country and one community.

21 June, 2025.

HOME IS LOST ... LOST IS HOME

It's evening, and the cold has seeped through this cheap hotel's window, allowing my skin to reach the same temperature as my soul.

Three years or so ago, I left here in a little truck with a Polish guy named Kret, and I've been traveling ever since. Even though I'm back now, temporarily, like a merchant seaman leaving with the morning tide, I can't shake this feeling of displacement.

A few months ago, Kelli and I were touring the inner outback of Western Australia.

We were asking the Indigenous people we met in the towns what they thought of the Voice, a referendum to include indigenous representation in the Australian Parliament. But instead, we found other stories that left us speechless.

Like the three siblings in Mount Magnet who, as children, had been stolen from their parents and sent to a mission where they hadn't been treated with love. Now they were back here, in a town that the road trains roared through on their way to service the mines, but in their forced time away, their entire tribe's language had been lost.

And even though one of these men was now in his seventies, when he talked about the time when they were taking him away from his mother, before my camera, his weathered eyes began to rain.

Home is lost, Lost is home.

Man, I used to love this town – its grimy buildings and traffic piled up behind its impractical rickety trams. Silent, huge graffitied faces ponderously telling all who looked up that this is an artist's town. Or was, until the fear came. That quiet thief who hid all our mouths behind paper masks, then, as we watched, stole our town's identity, leaving us with nothing but the lie of a familiar view.

A young person told me that her friends said they would never agree to be locked down again. Next time, they'd fight the government.

Would they?

Would they flood the streets like we did in the darker days, when between our signs we beat our drums and called for freedom as our flags unfurled in the winds of change?

There were times then, when I know we felt like we believed we were the only soldiers who could save the world.

But now the marches are empty, and the people are quiet as they continue to chase whatever it was that was so precious to them. They were prepared to burn this town's soul to the ground.

Or perhaps it's just me, trying to find through the mist that's fogging up this window, a warm light that's on, and a door that would open to a room full of people smiling as they welcomed us home.

Maybe it was me who painted these streets with the colours I thought were already there.

Maybe it's always been like this, and it's not a case of anything being lost, but rather a refusal to comply that cleaned my palette. And now I'm here, waiting to leave, and rejoin the others searching for a home.

At the airport, as everyone was on their phones, Dave came up. His eyes were bright like crystals with candles behind them. He'd been to the marches, been pepper-sprayed, and even driven in a convoy to Canberra, where he was present for the birth of whatever it was that called us all there.

Then we met his partner, and the three of us, close and alive, whispered of the battles we'd fought and freedoms we'd defended, and the future.

We were so excited, like babes in the woods who had found each other, and now our combined light was all we needed to survive.

But then my flight was called.

We hugged, exchanged numbers, before I journeyed back into the rushing trees, using my phone like an umbilical cord attached to a truth that, despite all our work, couldn't yet escape the online womb and reclaim its throne.

No, at this moment, I knew that despite believing I was on the right path, my home was lost, and for now, and probably for a while, Lost would continue to be my home.

17 July, 2025.

BRUSSEL SPROUT BLUES

Towards the second half of 2022, our convoy, whose goal was to leave from Melbourne and try to cross the closed Western Australian border unvaccinated, had shrunk to two vehicles, and when we reached Ceduna, the last major town before the border, we owned the biggest stash of marijuana I'd ever seen. Motivated by our chronicling work, and wanting us to keep going, people kept slipping us petrol money, crystals, and little religious trinkets to keep us safe – and bud. Lots and lots of bud.

Before Covid I barely touched the stuff, but back in Epic we'd jokingly called it brussel sprouts, and like a communal in-joke, the name stuck.

With Epic behind us and our new adventure well underway, we were stopping every few days at farms owned by likeminded farmers. We called them Resistance Farms.

Most of them had a shed with a corner dedicated to hanging out: usually they were decorated with a pot-belly stove, a couple of worn but comfy lounges, and from these our country's troubles were turned over and churned through.

One such farm was producing wheat and sheep, but the wheat only grew if the land was carpeted with fertiliser. The farmer showed us a shed half full of the stuff, then went on to tell us that he really needed a whole shed-full, but he didn't have the cash.

I borrowed one of the farm's trailbikes and toured his unsewn paddocks. The earth was beyond dry. The land itself felt spiritually exhausted. There were no insects, no birds, and his herd of sheep, who kept running away from me, left a long trail of dust that hung in the air as though the sky itself was exhausted.

It was hard to see how a herd that size could survive out here without being fed hay, and that too would cost money.

The homestead itself was surrounded by enormous plastic tubs that had once held chemicals. There were so many of them they were piled on each other.

Many of the farms we stayed at were littered with these containers. Was this our world now? When a baby was born, its veins were immediately filled with Big Pharma's chemicals. For in our toxic wasteland of a community, how could this babe possibly survive without it? And out here, when the first shoots of the wheat that would eventually become our bread, pasta, and hamburger buns broke the earth's surface, it too was bathed in a bath of pesticides. They also sprayed this wheat just before harvest. This is called desiccation, and they do this to dry out the crop to make it easier to harvest, and to also kill off the weeds that might interfere with the grain's quality. This wheat had been genetically modified to resist these pesticides.

It appeared like an expensive and unsustainable way to farm a product that ultimately might be proving itself not to be that good for us, but the farmer told me that without these chemicals, the wheat wouldn't survive.

Later we were shown another crop. This was the one that paid the farm's bills.

Fertilised by manure, the marijuana plants were thriving, and the rows between them were thick with spiders, who themselves were harvesting the abundant insects.

Several of these farms were growing the same secret crop. It made me wonder if this gentle, outlawed plant was the only crop supporting our farming communities.

And it wasn't just the farms.

Wherever we pulled up, people discreetly pressed buds into our hands, often from their own secret crops, that bounty of which they were using to pay the rent and other bills.

In Adelaide, one sweet old lady handed me a neatly wrapped present.

"This was my son's," she said, "but you need it more than him." Hidden underneath the cute wrapping paper was something that felt like a couple of hefty buds – no way. The woman looked like she was heading to church.

But it must've been a Rastafarian Church, because my fingers weren't lying.

After I opened it I couldn't stop grinning as I pictured her son coming home:

"You gave my stash to who? And what the hell is a locked out café? Mum! …Mum!"

But now here we were on the Nullarbor, just an hour or so away from finally challenging Western Australia's sealed border. We were all determined to try and cross it, but if we did, we had no idea what would happen to us.

The only story we had to go on was the video of two women who'd been arrested for trying to cross. As far as we knew, they had been thrown into a jail in Kalgoorlie.

So, if I was going to be arrested for crossing the border, I wanted my only charge to be that I was unvaccinated. I did not want to get arrested for drug smuggling as well, therefore the Cheech and Chong stash had to go.

After a long discussion, we decided to bury it, seeing how out here, space wasn't an issue. But if by chance one of us passed this way again, how would we find it?

A road-sign was chosen as our marker. The sprouts, sealed in a plastic container, then went into the earth, safely concealed under the desert.

The way we sold it to the world, via our lives, was as if we were burying a motherlode. We kept joking how, when we did make our way back here, there would be holes everywhere, created by other folk partial to weed, who had gone crazy trying to locate our stash. When they opened the border, a few weeks after we crossed it, Hoodie drove across in his caravan and even a respectable figure like him got into the act.

Claiming that not only did he dig up our sprouts, but when the border guards asked him if he had any fruit and vegetables to declare, he said yes, and showed them our tub.

He claimed they took one look, then after confiscating the lot, smiled at Hoodie and said, "Welcome to Western Australia."

By then, Wendy, Kret, and myself were heading up north, continuing our goal to circumnavigate the country, searching every town we could, to see if there was resistance.

There was. We proved it.

Finally we were home, and our hidden stash was now all but forgotten, surviving only in the company of Freedom People, where it was one of our funny stories.

Then, a year later Maurice called me.

Maurice owned a semi whose trailer was plastered in freedom posters. To me, it was our movement's flagship. Originally a furniture delivery truck, he'd had it at Epic, where he and the truck were stars. Since then, he had scored numerous gigs, delivering furniture up and down the East Coast, and so his truck was a moving billboard that was defiantly selling one product, 'Freedom.'

Now he'd scored a run to Perth and because his wife didn't want to ride along, he'd invited me to come along.

Crossing the country in a semi had always been on my bucket list; but to do it in this truck, I jumped at the chance.

I drove Florence, my new small, second-hand bus, and now my home, to Broken Hill, which itself was a 900-click drive. That was where we rendezvoused.

At Broken Hill I interviewed several people before we drove both vehicles to the tiny town of Laverton, where I left Florence with Stuart, an artist and now a friend. Then we set off to Perth in the truck.

But now things had changed – the border was open and no one was wearing masks. Yet it was clear to see in the people's eyes that the fear of the last few years was still in control.

At Port Augusta we rolled over a bridge that was being upgraded. There were workers in high-vis everywhere.

I saw one young stop-go guy looking up at the truck. When he caught my eye, he gave us a secret thumbs-up, one that he tried to hide from the rest of the crew, and his face was quiet and sad.

What had they done to us, these companies and politicians making plans miles away – in the wake of their actions, an aftershock rippling through, now surfacing as melancholy in this young Australian's eyes?

They peddled protection as panacea, but delivered division: mates turned informers, mums masked from milestone birthdays, and a generation's spark dimmed to embers under the weight of "just comply."

Yet in that young eye's haze, there's a half-hidden glint – the same unyielding ember that lit the EPIC camps, the rallies where black sheep found flock. They've scarred us, sure, but not snuffed us. That melancholy? It's mourning, not surrender.

From the highway, Maurice would try to spark CB radio chatter about these times – but no other truckie took the bait.

It was weird, feeling invisible inside while sitting inside a semi that was screaming Liberty!!! Freedom!!!

Back in Perth I bunked for one night at my parents' and decided to soothe the storms in my soul by sampling some of these Nullarbor-cured brussel sprouts – sadly I discovered upon opening the tub that the buds were a little mouldy.

Guessing that that wasn't healthy, but still willing to risk it, I laid the buds on the blade of one of Dad's shovels and left them to dry in the sun.

Evening slid in over the hills and hauled with it the ghosts from the road – the vaccine injured, the friends lost to us, and the worries about our future.

Needing to escape, I went to roll a joint from this recovered mull, which had been surviving its own odyssey, and I was intending to smoke it, mould or not.

"Dad!"

"Yeah?"

"Where's the shovel that was on the grass near the clothes line?"

"I hung it back in the shed. Why?"

"Oh, well what about the plants that were lying on the blade?"

"What about them?"

"Where'd you put them?"

"Why?" So I told him.

"Oh, I didn't know. I thought they were grass clippings, so I chucked them into the green bin."

To my horror I ripped open the green bin's lid to find it full to the brim with freshly pruned gardenias.

For a while I clawed through the clippings like a dog in a dumpster, but the jewelled, mouldy buds must have bounced down deep into the gaps between the rest of the pruned plants, like coins rattling down one of those fairground games.

Maybe this was their destiny. Maybe, years from now, the letterboxes and the manicured roundabouts of a housing estate, built over a capped landfill, would start sprouting a miniature forest of marijuana.

And no matter how hard the investigators dug, they would never discover the secret to how this was more than mull – this was freedom weed. A rare mull, destined for a grander role than being smoked by a couple of outcasts hunting a country they felt slipping away.

I did think that I had found one bud, but to be honest, I wasn't sure. I rolled a joint regardless, then sat there, in the world's most isolated city, and as the sun set on yet another day, and my phone warned me time and time again about the incoming tide of tyranny, I lit up, alone, and after a long first drag, I knew that what I was trying to soothe myself with was probably a spliff full of gardenia leaves.

31 July, 2025.

CHOICE

It takes a lot to make most men cry.

I didn't know him; he knew us only from our shows, which he hadn't followed for a while.

It was the gloaming – that time when the Lord's greatest brush, the leaving sun, beautifies everything it touches: power poles, dumped and rusting cars, and this man's face as he pretended to study the portraits covering our bus but was really looking through and past them to the moments that had changed him forever – moments now escaping his eyes in fierce tears he kept wiping away.

"I didn't want to take it," he told the bus.

But he had a new business; the business required him to enter council property, and to do that he had to comply.

He'd had reactions – tinnitus he'd never had before, now constant, often threatening to drive him mad.

I'd interviewed a mother who spoke about how mRNA-induced extreme tinnitus had driven her daughter to suicide.

Her daughter had been pro-science, pro-jab, pro-it-all, and had pushed her entire family to comply.

Then her own deafening adverse reaction drove her from doctor to doctor, looking for a cure – or at least acknowledgement.

They ignored her, told her it was only anxiety, until finally the insane ringing sent her voluntarily into a psych ward.

There, after they ignored her too, she decided she had become a burden to everyone she knew, including her country, and so she voluntarily chose to leave us.

To make sure the tragedy of her end didn't cause vaccine hesitancy, her story was all but wiped from history – until her shy, jabbed mother came on Café Locked Out and shared her story.

I met the mother two years later in a café in their town, one of the last living memory-keepers of her daughter's fate.

She didn't want a follow-up interview.

Sitting with jabbed friends, she – blasé – let us know she had released her grip on that secret's burden.

Now the only interview she'd ever given, ours, would become the final gravestone remaining to honour her daughter's truth: a gravestone with no flowers, a memory our government would love to scrub from history.

There were so many stories. And so many of them were utterly gut-wrenching, I could only ponder, some days, why are we the only ones listening?

"I'm going blind," he said.

"I can feel it. I wear glasses now, but it's getting worse."

He was in his early fifties, but that wasn't what was squeezing these tears from his soul.

"Medically raped," I suggested.

"Yes," he replied, and finally he looked at me. "That's it."

It was too late for an interview, so I offered to record in the morning.

"It might be the only justice you'll get," I said, and he nodded. But I sensed he wouldn't return, so I let him empty his soul while God painted a sunset around us, using the pink clouds and jaunty waves as the base of another masterpiece – a staggering, momentary landscape in which, to any observer, our bus, this man, and I would be but small details in the grander view.

Oh, why do we ask so much of God while daily ignoring the miracles presented to us, free of charge?

Do we really think God, or the universe, or whatever is behind all this majestic beauty, went to all this trouble just so this man could weep?

Further down the road another woman noticed our bus and wanted to meet us.

Out of all the stories we have recorded, hers was unique.

She, too, refused to be filmed, so we let her talk.

She told me she had profound regrets.

"In all honesty," she said, "if I had my time again, I'd take it."

"Why didn't you take it?" I asked.

"I was coerced into not taking it," she replied.

One of her sisters – a younger sister – had, in her words, bullied her to remain unvaccinated.

The cost: she'd lost her job of 35 years at the hospital where she'd been a nurse.

Now she was a cleaner, fighting other cleaners for gigs.

A businessman wanted someone to scrub his office toilets, and she was in the fight.

Her income had been slashed, and with the cost-of-living spiralling, life was an endless struggle.

She was fifty-nine.

When I pressed, she confessed she missed the company of her nursing friends, the purpose of her work, the status of saying, "I'm a nurse."

It was morning, freezing, and as she spoke I saw the cleaning gear shoved carelessly into her car.

I suggested she try landing some caring gigs, but her confession went deeper.

"I'm sick of caring for people," she said.

She'd done it her whole life, and now here she was, in a lonely carpark, unable to share this truth with anyone but us. I told her she should buy a van and hit the road. "Who knows? You might end up cooking on a cattle ranch – whatever."

It made her smile but didn't shift her mood.

For her, the economic destitution, the punishment for not complying, was almost complete; such is the hardship of this road. Finally, at a Stand in the Park event in Bendigo – Stand in the Park is like church to me, a place where our community gathers on a Sunday morning to heal our wounds – a teacher told me he was working again, unvaccinated.

He claimed that at one point scores of pupils and teachers were at home, sick, yet some never got sick.

These teachers, he said, had fake vaccine passports.

They'd paid big money for them, and the only thing that threatened to blow their cover was that they never got sick.

So they faked illnesses to stay concealed.

They could never tell anyone – how could they risk it?

Even a divorce might see an angry spouse reveal their deception. All through Covid, and still now, they were the modern-day equivalent of Anne Frank, except the cellar was in their souls.

I'm on the bus now.

Mid-morning, cross-legged on our bed, I can see a puddle left by last night's rain – now a disjointed, mud-framed mirror reflecting the sky and the gums reaching for it.

So much attention to this overlooked beauty; a beauty that – if it was created – was created out of love for beauty, as though beauty itself, in which we are immersed, is the overwhelming evidence of love.

For how could heaven itself transcend such elegance?

Perhaps all this beauty is a gift laid at the feet of our senses, an offering at the altar of us, reminding us constantly that in a culture determined to leave us feeling ashamed and redundant, we are as beautiful – if not more so – than this puddle, this mirror on the floor.

We are an audience for God's impossible art – which includes each other: the current searchers hunting for meaning in the communal frame we call life.

Stop, just for a moment, and know you are meant to be here. Why? That's for you to discover. But I know the discovery is out there.

Nature is thrifty; it doesn't waste so much as a leaf – so why would it plant in you a hunger for meaning if that meaning weren't out here?

We are an audience for God's impossible art – which includes each other: the current searchers hunting for meaning in the communal frame we call life.

Perhaps it's time to saddle the horse of fate and go searching for the Holy Grail – which this ageing man will now suggest is the bravest, noblest version of you.

Greatness is not a destiny; it's a choice.

Even having the courage to strive for greatness is greatness itself.

Currently, our society is under attack, and the meek can't save us.

What we need is an army of greatness.

So choose well, for in the end, in your final days, the harshest judge of you will be you.

10 August, 2025.

MAINSTREAM MEDIA AND THE RETURN OF THE AUSTRALIAN MALE

He was used to slinking. You could see it in his stance. Years of the education system and the state shaming him for being white, for being Australian, for being straight, for being a young man, had sculpted him this way, as they have sculpted numerous young men I have witnessed. But here on the streets of Sydney, following the great march, he smiled as we gave him the thumbs-up. Then, after ripping off his hoodie, he offered the sky that which he valued, that which was helping him break free from all these years of shame: the Australian flag.

Everywhere you looked in the Sydney March, there were men – women too, but lots of men, and most of them, though not all, were white. The majority weren't walking with the rest of the crowd but striding, each either holding their own Australian flag or wearing it like a cape.

Ever since Epic, the tribe I belong to has been trying to attract men to our movement, especially young men. And while we are populated with more mature men than when we started, we have few young men. But this crowd was electric with young males, some looking nervous yet excited as they weaved their way through the older men in an attempt to reach the front.

There was also a sense that these men were ready. If any other group had started trouble, it was easy to see that these men would react. Questionably, this is why nothing really happened. Instead, the entire crowd filled their hope tanks with the size of the crowd and the vista of mainly blue flags unfurling in the clear blue sky.

There were speeches that most of us couldn't hear because the PA system was unprepared for the number of ears it had to reach. But that didn't matter, because the mood of the crowd was nostalgic; we were all feeling something we hadn't felt for years: pride. The organizers had us feeling proud to be Australian, proud to be here, and hungry for positive change that we could feel was possible.

Epic was a spiritual gathering. This was something else. This was an exercise in recruitment, a sea of men having their balls reinvigorated simply by being here. This was the birth of a new patriotic army, whose enemy was the government that for years has been actively emasculating them. This was a return of a character we haven't seen much of in a long time: the larrikin.

I told two skinny, loose-limbed young men, both carrying flags, that their grandfathers would be proud of them. After smiling at this, they turned and vanished into the tsunami of blue Australian flags – warrior banners announcing to this street in Sydney that our men were returning.

And out in front of all this hope, of all this healthy testosterone, was the NSN, the National Socialist Network. The MSM calls them neo-Nazis. So, is this history repeating itself, or just rhyming? Currently, like prewar Germans, our people feel disenfranchised. Our people are confused as to why, with all this mineral wealth, we are broke. Our people know that our government no longer serves us but rules us, while never taking responsibility for any of its mistakes. Many feel that the government's plan for a future, if there is one, has little space for them. The recipe for the rise of some form of nationalist party is here – a recipe being stirred by these young men in black uniforms who marched through the crowd like a brigade.

I am a part of the freedom movement. Ever since Epic, we have been attempting to draw Australians back to the streets, to attract men, and we've failed. Whereas these young men, on their first rodeo, have got the world talking. Instead of the usual black conversations, our blue flag is flying above us like a global symbol of hope, a banner announcing the rise of a people sick of all the agendas – Digital ID, the reworked Voice, net zero, and the like.

I suggest we learn from these young men who, love them or hate them, have the courage to be seen and benefit from that visibility.

Whereas we dress like everyone else – no uniform, no uniting symbol, just reams of shared social media posts that might just map our journey, despite our spiritual connections and all our valid and good intentions, into historical irrelevance.

These last few years have been interesting times, but some have just injected the years to come with a shot of adrenaline. No one, no one anywhere, knows the outcome, but if you were a gambler, be honest, who would you back? The government? The left? Us? Or these boys? In leaving, though, at the Sydney March, an NSN leader got up and spoke, and as he tried to sell the crowd the benefits of – and these were their words – an "Austrian painter," the crowd booed them into silence. A crowd populated mainly by Australian men.

1 September, 2025.

A MAN AND HIS TRUCK: THE TRIAL OF PAUL OFFE

In the trial of Paul Offe, the prosecutor, towards the end, left a freeze frame of the rear of Paul's truck on all the screens of the court.

On the top of Paul's truck you could make out the two bookend Australian flags, and on the rear of his big black truck, in almost luminous green font, someone had written the word Freedom.

This frozen image was from the moments before Paul turned and headed up the ramp towards the top of Canberra Parliament House.

Around the truck, people were everywhere. Some of the police witnesses stated there were thousands of people, then others tens of thousands and finally, later in the same video, one of the officers agreed with the Aussie Cossack that there were a million people there.

The real number will always be debated, but whatever the amount, they are gone, but Paul is still here, fighting for his Freedom.

At first there were only three minor charges, and after waiting three months to contest those, Paul and his devoted brother Michael put in a request to get the truck back, stating that the charges weren't strong enough to warrant confiscating the truck.

This became another point of conjecture, which culminated eight months after the protest with the prosecutor adding two more charges to the list.

Driving recklessly or knowingly at police. And since there were two police, the charge was doubled.

The maximum sentence for this charge is fifteen years in jail.

The weight of this has been hanging around Paul's neck almost three and a half years, all the way to this Supreme Court room, where, after all that time, Paul was finally before a judge.

Over the years, the brothers had raised, with the help of interviews with podcasters like Café Locked Out, $60,000. But by now the lawyers had eaten all that up, then informed the boys that to have legal representation in court, they would need to raise a further $250,000, which they were unable to do.

So now, with a family friend, an old man who wishes to remain anonymous, as an advisor – the court refers to this as a McKenzie friend – Paul is representing himself.

Over the years there had been a series of mishaps, from being king-hit by a stranger that knocked him unconscious, to being officially informed he acquired a head injury during a car accident.

The other problem was his profound dyslexia. Throughout the entire trial, his McKenzie friend has been typing out questions for Paul to ask, in super-large font on a laptop, as Paul attempted to read them out, mouthing the bigger words first before pronouncing them.

This impediment alone is one of the reasons the court case went from being scheduled for two to three days to, at last count, ten.

Yet within those ten days, despite the intense pressure, Paul has never lost his cool, nor has been rude to anyone, even those few witnesses that had a crack at him.

After court, Paul told me that he had placed himself in God's hands so was just doing what had to be done.

But then there was one time when he broke.

Near the end of the trial Paul took the stand to tell his own story. It was here that he began crying. And it wasn't a few shed tears, and it wasn't pathetic sobbing, it was a dam inconsolably breaking, not that anyone in the court was allowed to physically console him.

He was crying not out of fear of going to jail, nor was he crying about these three and a half years, where his life has been spent in limbo. Instead he spoke about the main reason he came to the protest.

Paul had grown up on a farm. His grandmother lived with them, and Paul referred to her as his second mother. During Covid she had been placed in a nursing home, due to declining health.

Initially the staff would bring her to the courtyard so the family could spend time with her. Because they were unvaccinated, the family wasn't allowed in.

Then the nursing home told them they could no longer spare the staff to do this, so all physical contact was cut off.

In an act of mercy, they were granted a half-hour reprieve, where, dressed in full PPE gear, the family was afforded half an hour to communally say their goodbyes.

After that, his grandmother was left to die alone.

As Paul retold this story, through those tears, he managed to communicate his pain so efficiently we in the audience, many of the jurors, and I'd suggest even the judge teared up.

And so Paul had come to Canberra to help all those who joined the Convoy to Canberra, to allow the Government to see that many Australians believed the mandates were going too far.

And while the crowd's numbers will always be under debate, it is now official, thanks to the declaration by the public broadcaster the ABC, that it was the largest protest Canberra had ever seen.

Though this was no ordinary protest. These people had come here, on their own volition, because they had lost family members, or had been kicked out of their families. They had lost their jobs and businesses, some had lost their homes, and so forth.

They should have been furious, which was why, in the basement of Old Parliament House, an army of riot squad officers were waiting in hiding, in case these people began unleashing their wrath.

But the crowd was in such high spirits, based solely on the gift of sharing each other's company, that despite their numbers, the only incident worth talking about was a truck, driven by what the media call a right-winger, who inadvertently went left.

And so the truck became, inadvertently, a symbol of power, of defiance, both for us and the police.

For a few dramatic moments it and Paul became the front line of everything we were protesting against.

But was that intentional?

Originally a country fire truck, Paul had used a small payout from his accident to buy it and restore it.

His goal was to get himself off sickness benefits by creating a business where the truck was used at events and in movies.

He had just acquired his chauffeur's licence a few days before joining the convoy to Canberra.

Where, because of his mechanical skills, he was stopping on the way down to help other members of the convoy whose old cars were struggling with the distance.

Helping people is how Paul has derived worth, seeing how his disabilities have prevented him from acquiring a career of note.

He even carried witches' hats and other gear he'd need to use when working on broken-down vehicles.

And this leaning towards kindness exudes out of his being. Everyone who meets him can discern that he's simply a good, gentle and kind man, who likes to laugh at innocent jokes.

He is not someone who you would expect to have a chance of surviving jail.

Yet that is our view, for whilst he has been on trial, two police officers have been shot, and the Australian Nazi boys have been involved in many of the marches that occurred on the 31st of August, allowing the politicians and the mainstream media to paint all those who came to Canberra three and a half years ago, and anyone else that questions the government, as dangerous sovereign citizens.

Every day the jurors have had to observe Paul, umming and ahhing as he attempts to defend himself against the charges that he drove at police, and every night they've gone home to the news of dead officers. Will they judge Paul based on the evidence and on who they find Paul to be, as a stand-alone man, or will they only see Paul through the prejudice of a sovereign-citizen filter, and a conscience wanting and able to enact revenge?

It seems our chaotic times have conglomerated into a cyclone, and in the eye of this perfect shitstorm is Paul, and next to him his brother.

The jury, all from Compliant Canberra, is now out. And they call it Compliant Canberra because the Australian Capital Territory, unlike every other state and territory, never enforced mandates, yet still nearly everyone living here complied.

From Monday they will start deliberating.

Over the years our community has raised millions of dollars for court cases which have all failed – cases where we tried to point out that the Government was acting illegally.

If only we could have had a fraction of that to afford legal representation for Paul, for by doing so we would actually be defending ourselves.

I was at Epic Park for the entire event. It was not properly organised by people. Anyone who was there would testify, I believe, that it was a spiritual event. A gathering of Australians who just happened to go on a big march.

But at the entrance of the camp I recorded the stories of scores of people arriving, and they all said they had no choice, they had to come. It was a calling.

A calling that I suggest was the birth of a great tribe of Guardians. A birth that came with the gift of these few days, where many felt exalted, but a birth that also came with a responsibility.

The job of spreading our glorious light to ward off the darkness that was besieging our country.

And Paul is the one guardian we left behind. A good man who has been portrayed by the state as an evil one.

So the question is, was Epic more than just a gathering of people who didn't want to take a jab, or is that all we were?

For in my soul's rearview mirror, Epic is a glow of pure hope that is always there, but if Paul is convicted and goes to jail, whilst the majority of us just got on with our lives as though it was nothing to do with us, then I fear that light – our light – will finally go out.

***

Paul was ultimately found guilty, fined $2000 and had his beloved truck confiscated. He was facing up to 15 years in prison.

For many in the Australian community the sheer bastardry of their government's Covid response continues apace, a haunting and destructive episode in the nation's history for which no senior political figure has ever apologised.

Rinse and repeat, that's the fear. A very legitimate fear. That it could all happen again.

21 September, 2025.

ABOUT THE AUTHOR

Michael Gray Griffith, born in Melbourne, Australia, in the mid-1960s, is a playwright, activist, and founder of Café Locked Out, whose work challenges societal control and champions individual freedom. Raised in a middle-class family without artistic lineage, Griffith's passion for storytelling led him to study creative writing and theatre, though specific educational details remain unclear.

At least in public, Michael was never very forthcoming about his educational attainments, or lack thereof. He honed his craft through writing and managing The Wolves Theatre Company, founded to stage bold Australian narratives.

Griffith's theatre productions include The Magnolia Tree (2019), a poignant drama, and Marooned (2020), a suicide prevention play dedicated to his son, Guy May, who died by suicide in 2017.

Marooned toured Australian barracks and resonated deeply with men, earning acclaim at Melbourne's Lawler Theatre (2019).

His 2024 play, My Brother, My Brother, My Brother, staged at Alex Theatre and Red Rock Regional Theatre, explored mateship and mandate resistance, cementing his reputation for bold, socially charged work.

Despite Covid's theatre closures, Griffith persevered, adapting his scripts into novels like The Sandcastles of Quarantine Bay.

In 2021, Griffith launched Café Locked Out, a podcast platform born from lockdown exclusion for refusing vaccine passports.

It amplified stories of nurses, tradies, and others impacted by mandates, growing into a cornerstone of Australia's Freedom Movement, a cornerstone despite onerous censorship by the Australian government in cahoots with international tech platforms.

For example, he faced a 10-year Facebook ban, an outrageous manipulation of the national narrative which the Australian government felt perfectly comfortable with. As revealed under questioning in Senate committee hearings, the government censored more than 4,000 posts on Facebook alone.

The government's involvement in some of the world's most draconian censorship, including of many posts which were later proved to be demonstrably correct, is one of the darkest stains on the history of Australian democracy.

Facing health challenges in 2025, Griffith's resilience mirrors his art's defiant spirit. His works, from plays to essays to multiple podcasts, weave a tapestry of resistance, urging Australians to reclaim their freedoms the country was once famous for.

Given all that has happened, Michael should have the last word: "All my life I have yearned for purpose. Now I have it. I believe our world is heading somewhere not conducive to the human soul, but can I change this, alone? No.

"What I do every day is try to create ripples. Most vanish, but some become little waves.

"And what I know is that the monoliths we call the Twelve Apostles – those towering limestone pillars, stark and sculptural, rising like jagged ghosts from the churning Southern Ocean, etched by relentless salt and wind – are being eroded. Many have gone, but they weren't toppled by a tsunami or an earthquake – just lots of little waves, wearing away at their base.

"Waves that began their life, far out at sea, as a ripple.

"I am, though a choice I make every day, just a small part of this rising tide calling for change. Waves that will continue to strive for freedom long after I'm gone."

www.ingramcontent.com/pod-product-compliance
Lightning Source LLC
Chambersburg PA
CBHW061725070526
44583CB00024B/3011